MW01388253

Feminist Advocacy

Feminist Advocacy

Gendered Organizations in Community-Based Responses to Domestic Violence

Andrea J. Nichols

LEXINGTON BOOKS
Lanham • Boulder • New York • Toronto • Plymouth, UK

Published by Lexington Books
A wholly owned subsidiary of Rowman & Littlefield
4501 Forbes Boulevard, Suite 200, Lanham, Maryland 20706
www.rowman.com

10 Thornbury Road, Plymouth PL6 7PP, United Kingdom

Copyright © 2014 by Lexington Books

All rights reserved. No part of this book may be reproduced in any form or by any
electronic or mechanical means, including information storage and retrieval systems,
without written permission from the publisher, except by a reviewer who may quote
passages in a review.

British Library Cataloguing in Publication Information Available

Library of Congress Cataloging-in-Publication Data

Nichols, Andrea J.
  Feminist advocacy : gendered organizations in community-based responses to domestic
violence / Andrea J. Nichols.
     pages cm
  Includes bibliographical references and index.
  ISBN 978-0-7391-8034-1 (cloth : alk. paper) -- ISBN 978-0-7391-8035-8 (electronic)
  1. Abused women--Services for--United States. 2. Abused children--Services for--
United States. 3. Community organization--United States. 4. Family violence--Law and
legislation--United States. 5. Feminism--United States. I. Title.
  HV1445.N53 2014
  362.82'92570973--dc23
                                        2013030950

♾™ The paper used in this publication meets the minimum requirements of American
National Standard for Information Sciences—Permanence of Paper for Printed Library
Materials, ANSI/NISO Z39.48-1992.

Printed in the United States of America

Table of Contents

Acknowledgments

I would first like to acknowledge the advocates who interviewed for this project for their time, helpfulness, insights, and generosity. In particular, I would like to thank "Jean" for providing important feedback and insights throughout the research and writing process. My mother, and feminist advocate, Gail Nichols' stories and experiences preceded and developed my interest in this project. "Gillian's" willingness to participate in the first rather lengthy interview was invaluable; her insights guided the interview questions and structure for subsequent interviews. "Teresa" and "Summer" were also extremely helpful in spreading the word and encouraging other advocates to participate in this project. Friends, teachers, mentors, and advisors Kristin Carbone-Lopez and Jody Miller encouraged me throughout this project and challenged my thinking in important ways. Thanks to my Forest Park colleagues for providing entertainment and distractions throughout this process. Thanks to the advocates at the Washington Coalition Against Domestic Violence, and the other authors I cite throughout this book, most of whom I have never met, but whose work inspired me: Amy Lehrner, Nicole Allen, Lisa Goodman, Ellen Pence, Melanie Shepard, Susan Schechter, Lauren Bennett Cattaneo, Deborah Epstein, Gretchen Arnold, Laura Logan, and Rebecca Macy. Last, but most important, I want to thank my family—my Brian, Neo, Ethan, my mom and dad Gail and Chuck Nichols, my brother Chad and Jefre and Dane, Jean and Ralph Faulds, Tom and Peggy Nichols, and all my friends and extended family.

Chapter 1

Introduction

Domestic violence victim advocacy in the United States began large-ly with the battered women's movement of the late 1960s. The move-ment occurred in a time of great social change, paralleling the feminist movement of the same time period. The battered women's movement was a significant part of the second wave feminist movement, and em-phasized that equality in society could not occur alongside inequality and violence against women in the home. The battered women's movement began with grassroots shelters and victim advocacy, and largely main-tained this form throughout the 1970s (Goodman & Epstein, 2008). Early shelters were operated in the homes of feminists who recognized that women's unequal earning power, as well as unequal power dynamics in the home, contributed to difficulty leaving abusive relationships (Schechter, 1982). Early shelters were also run by women who had pre-viously been in abusive relationships and wished to offer emotional sup-port and shelter to other women experiencing abuse (Schechter, 1982; Rodriguez, 1988; Srinivasan & Davis, 1991; Saathoff & Stoffel, 1999). These women were among the first domestic violence[1] victim advocates, who provided battered women with an alternative to staying in abusive homes through access to shelter and resources (Schechter, 1982; Nichols, 2013b). As feminism was a cornerstone of the battered women's move-ment, early feminist advocates developed practices that were based upon feminist ideologies of collaboration and empowerment. Feminist advo-cates included such ideologies in developing practices of advocacy—social change activism, survivor-defined practices, and collaborative shelter structures.

Early feminist domestic violence victim advocates developed collab-orative shelter structures because they saw bureaucratic models as patri-archal and oppressive to women (Ferguson, 1984; Rodriguez, 1988; Srinivasan & Davis, 1991; Saathoff & Stoffel, 1999). Grassroots femi-nists suggested that hierarchy and specialization were intrinsic character-istics of bureaucracies. Feminists noted that hierarchy in organizations was highly gendered and male dominated, and both reflected and repro-duced women's roles in subordinate positions (Ferguson, 1984). Feminist advocates maintained that shelters would not be immune to hierarchy and oppression of women unless they worked to build alternative structures. More specifically, grassroots feminist advocates held that bureaucratic

1

structures were a means of implementing subordination of battered women though hierarchal client-professional relationships. If advocates took on roles that dictated abused women's course of action by serving as their "leaders," then that would lead to differential power between advocates and abused women. Feminist advocates initially maintained that such hierarchal interactions oppressed battered women by facilitating the same power and control dynamics that are conducive to intimate partner violence (Rodriguez, 1988; Srinivasan & Davis, 1991; Saathoff and Stoffel, 1999). Advocates pointed out that battered women were leaving abusive relationships in which their actions were largely dictated by their abusive husbands. Such women held a subordinate status in their own homes, and were disempowered in the decision making of the household. If advocates dictated the actions of the women that came to them for shelter and emotional support, then they would similarly oppress women's choices and stifle their decision making and consequent empowerment. Empowerment was a key component of early grassroots feminist advocacy. Advocates noted that empowerment of abused women emerged as such women began to take control of their own lives and their decision making. Consequently, advocates acknowledged that putting decision making in the hands of battered women was an important way to facilitate empowerment. Grassroots feminist advocates believed that without empowerment, entry into abusive relationships in the future would be more likely (Schechter, 1982; Herman, 1997). Consequently, many early shelters resisted any form of hierarchal structure, and developed collaborative shelter structures as well as collaborative practices with the aim of empowerment (Rodriguez, 1988; Gelb & Hart, 1999). Collaborative practices involved shelter residents in the decision making of the shelters, as abused women were perceived as the key stakeholders (Rodriguez, 1988). The rules, roles, and goals of such shelters were developed through group consensus, based upon mutual respect and ideologies of equal power (Rodriguez, 1988; Nichols, 2011). Moreover, collaborative practices in shelters included survivor-defined practices (also referred to as women-centered, woman-defined, or feminist advocacy).

Survivor-defined practices allowed and encouraged women to make their own decisions based upon their own individual goals, situations, and needs with the help and support of advocates, rather than dictating women's choices through bureaucratic structures that forced their decision making (Lehrner & Allen, 2009; Nichols, 2011, 2013a). Advocates combined their knowledge of domestic violence and resources with victims' knowledge of their abusers and needs to form survivor-defined advocacy. Essentially, survivor-defined practices tailored advocacy to each individual woman's needs, choices, and situations. Like collaborative shelter structures, women's empowerment was a primary goal, working to support the decision making of survivors[2] who were taking control of their lives.

Early feminist advocates also maintained that both disempowerment and domestic violence were intimately tied to conditions of patriarchal societies—the unequal distribution of household and social power, education, workplace, and wage opportunities (Tong, 1998; hooks, 2000). Survivor-defined advocacy consequently focused on the empowerment of women through access to employment, economic resources, and economic and social independence as well (Rodriguez, 1988; Srinivasan & Davis, 1991; Herman, 1997; Saathoff & Stoffel, 1999). Such ideologies reflected and paralleled the activities of the larger feminist movement, as one of the goals of the second wave feminist movement of the 1970s was gaining economic equality for women in terms of hiring, promotion, and wages in the workforce. Another parallel to the feminist movement of the same time period was fragmentation within the battered women's movement. Some scholars indicate that the early grassroots battered women's movement has been idealized, romanticized, and homogenized (see Schecter, 1982; Arnold & Ake, 2013). Such scholars note that feminist approaches were not practiced universally, and there was some discord within the movement (Schecter, 1982). In particular, black and lesbian feminists noted that the battered women's movement, like the larger feminist movement, was not meeting the needs of all women equally (Hill-Collins, 2000).

The feminist movement of the 1970s was criticized for marginalizing women of color, lesbian women, and lower class women. Paralleling such criticisms, black and lesbian feminists in the battered women's movement called for advocacy that worked to identify and address challenges women experienced related to their race, class, and sexual orientation (Arnold & Ake, 2013; Nichols, 2013b). Such feminists maintained that gendered oppression is heightened by these identities. Black and lesbian feminists worked to bring attention to the fact that women's experiences with abuse, and the social systems that addressed them, varied according to individual women's unique identities (Schechter, 1982; Smith, Richie, Sudbury, & White, 2006; Richie, 2000, 2005; Potter, 2008; Arnold & Ake, 2013). Such identities may intersect and result in experienc-

3

es with systemic bias and barriers to help-seeking (Sokoloff, 2005; Potter, 2008). Women who were marginalized in the battered women's movement developed intersectional practices[3] to address women's needs based upon intersecting identities, thereby evolving both advocacy and the movement (Arnold & Ake, 2013; Schechter, 1982). Though not practiced universally, some advocates adopted intersectional practices of advocacy to expand accessibility, outreach, and improve services (Arnold & Ake, 2013; Crenshaw, 1994; Nichols, 2013b). Intersectional approaches worked to recognize and advocate toward women's various identities and related needs; such as race, class, sexual orientation, limited English-speaking abilities, and ethnic identities.

In addition to the development and practice of collaborative, intersectional, and survivor-defined practices, grassroots feminist advocates worked to change structural conditions with the goal of reducing violence against women. Prior to the battered women's movement of the 1970s, public awareness of and attention to domestic violence was limited. According to the social mores of the times, abused women were expected to keep their abuse private. Abuse was to be handled within the family. This was problematic for battered women because their male partners controlled the family. Thus, "handling" it within the family produced continued abuse and battering. Consequently, advocates brought the problem of domestic violence to public and political attention to change the conceptualization of domestic violence as a private issue or "family" problem to a public issue and societal problem. Advocates pointed out that privatization of domestic violence, lack of recourse in the justice system, and normalization of male dominance supported violence against women.

Once advocates were able to gain public attention through their grassroots efforts in the battered women's movement, political interest and funding agendas were also accomplished. Public and political interest, as well as funding, was uncommon prior to the movement (Gelles & Straus, 1988; Saathoff & Stoffel, 1999; Dugan, Nagin, & Rosenfeld, 2003). Through grassroots feminist advocates' activism, along with other anti-domestic violence partners (participants in the anti-domestic violence movement also included anti-child abuse and anti-rape activists, as well as nuns, legal, academic, and political partners), domestic violence became an object of political interest, and the funding for support services to abused women expanded greatly as a result (Goodman & Epstein, 2008). Such social change ideology and activism gave rise to the

Introduction

development of the first hotline in 1972 and the first government funded domestic violence shelter in 1974, both in St. Paul, Minnesota. The second government funded shelter in the nation developed in Pasadena, California in 1976. Moreover, in 1978, the National Coalition Against Domestic Violence (NCADV) was formed. The first national hotline was implemented by the NCADV in 1982. Domestic violence organizations greatly expanded their service provision and became better known publicly throughout the 1980s. Advocates gained political ground, and the National Task Force on Family Violence was established in 1984. Further, by the late 1980s, the number of shelters and domestic violence services had expanded from a handful to more than 800 (Gelles & Straus, 1988; Dugan, Nagin, & Rosenfeld, 2003; Goodman & Epstein, 2008).

Professionalization and Funding

With these structural changes came further changes to grassroots advocacy. The resistance to hierarchal practices and shelter structures was largely altered. Gradually grassroots shelters and coalitions became professionalized, bureaucratized, and institutionalized organizations (Rodriguez, 1988; Schechter, 1982). The means for professionalization was mostly through external (government) funding, and domestic violence organizations were then, at least in part, shaped by funders' requirements. Funding was largely influenced by the first passage of the Violence Against Women Act (VAWA) in 1994, which provided $1.6 billion in grants to various stakeholders in the domestic violence movement. The goals of VAWA simultaneously held a victim-centric and justice system focus: preventing violence against women, prosecuting offenders, and protecting victims. Two main streams of funding were initially created by the VAWA. The first stream was provided through the U.S. Department of Justice for criminal justice purposes, such as grants for law enforcement, the implementation of pro-arrest policies, and the prosecution of domestic violence and child abuse. The second stream of funding was provided through the U.S. Department of Health and Human Services for social service support programs, such as domestic violence hotlines and shelters, rape crisis centers, and related education programs (Boba & Lilley, 2009). Thus, the VAWA allowed for increased and more stable funding for domestic violence shelters, services, and justice system efforts to combat domestic violence (Boba & Lilley,

5

2009; Macy, Giattina, Parish, & Crosby, 2010). VAWA was reauthorized in 2000, 2005, and again in 2013.

Most domestic violence shelters rely on a mix of federal, state, and local or foundation funding. While state funding for domestic violence shelters has not considerably changed over the last three decades, most agencies get funding from state agencies that distribute federal funding, such as through VAWA. Organizations typically depend on this federal funding, and have to meet expectations of professionalism to receive it (Macy et al., 2010). When domestic violence organizations receive money from other organizations, such as from the government or United Way, they immediately become accountable for that money in a language the funders understand. This often means an organizational style those funders understand (hierarchy), paperwork they understand (bureaucracy), and professionals doing or at least supervising the work, as this indicates competency, or at least credentials. When grassroots shelters became professionalized and funded organizations, and became dependent on such funding, they had to conform to the expectations and requirements of their funders. Tierney (1982) maintained that the goals and policies of social service organizations become mainstreamed when they are dependent on public funding. Similarly, grassroots shelters largely became mainstreamed when they became dependent on federal and other public funding. They became bureaucratized and professionalized. Hierarchal leadership resulted, as well as credentialed advocates. Grassroots advocacy evolved into agencies, organizations, and service provision (Tierney, 1982; Rodriguez, 1988; Miller, 2008). Advocates began referring to the women they worked with as clients. The trade-off was greatly expanded service provision and widespread access to resources, as well as support from other anti-domestic violence stakeholders.

Community-Based Responses to Domestic Violence

Many domestic violence victim service providers have further evolved to include more organizations with whom they work collaboratively. Collaboration between advocates, social services, and the justice system is generally referred to as community-based responses (CBR), or coordinated community responses. CBR began in the early 1980s, in part due to advocates' social change activism and demand for greater justice system responses to domestic violence. Justice system involvement was based upon the ideology that domestic violence should not be relegated to the private sphere, and women should have recourse for their victimization through the justice system. Advocates believed that if batterers were held accountable for their abuse, it would bring domestic violence into the public realm. On a societal level, this would send a message that domestic violence was not tolerated in society, and domestic violence would consequently decline (Daly, 1994; Goodman & Epstein, 2008). Prior to that time, domestic violence was largely seen by the justice system as a private family issue rather than a public issue, and members of the justice system were generally uninvolved in cases of domestic violence (Goodman & Epstein, 2008). Advocates worked to change the justice system response to domestic violence by lobbying for increased prosecution of batterers and protection of battered women. Policy development included protective orders, mandatory or pro-arrest policies, no-drop prosecution, and importantly, collaboration between justice officials and advocates (Hart, 1995; Shepard & Pence, 1999; Zweig & Burt, 2006, 2007; Goodman & Epstein, 2008; Nichols, 2011, 2013a, 2013b).

One of the first and most well-known efforts toward community-based responses to domestic violence included the justice system working collaboratively with victim advocates in the 1980 Duluth Minnesota Domestic Abuse Intervention Project (Shepard & Pence, 1999). The project involved coordinating and cross-training domestic violence victim advocates, police, prosecutors, judges, and social service providers. The result was victim-advocate informed legislation, police policies and protocols that held offenders accountable and did not blame victims (Shepard & Pence, 1999). For example, court ordered advocate-run batterer intervention programs are part of the Duluth Model. The Duluth program efforts facilitated the collaboration of various stakeholders in combating domestic violence, and allowed advocates to disseminate their expertise to other anti-domestic violence stakeholders (Shepard & Pence, 1999). In the late 1980s, because of the success of the Duluth program, other states began adopting community-based approaches to domestic violence.

In addition to the Duluth Model, the Greenbook Demonstration Initiative is another well-known CBR initiative. Organizations that handled cases of child abuse and neglect, such Child Protective Services (CPS), the Children's Division or Family Courts, or the Department of Children's and Family Services (DCFS), were another grouping of organizations that joined in community-based responses to domestic violence, largely due to the passage of the Violence Against Women Act and the receipt of federal grants in which collaboration with CPS was required (Saathoff & Stoffel, 1999; Findlater & Kelly, 1999; Banks, Landsverk, & Wang, 2008; Banks, Dutch, & Wang, 2008). The National Council of Juvenile and Family Court Judges produced a set of guidelines and model program initiatives toward collaboration of victim advocates with child protective services in 1999 (Banks et al., 2008). This later became known as the Greenbook (because it was literally published as a green book). The Greenbook Demonstration Initiative developed from the 1999 model program initiative. The federally funded project involved collaboration between CPS and domestic violence shelters in six communities. The project findings indicated that collaboration between advocates and CPS workers had positive outcomes for abused women and their children, because of women's increased ability to access resources to ensure safety for themselves and their children (Banks et al., 2008). The likelihood of further abuse to both abused women and their children decreased when CPS referrals to domestic violence victim advocates were made (Berk, 1986; Zweig and Burt, 1997; Banks et al., 2008). In contrast, when CPS did not make such referrals, and did not identify domestic violence, it presented challenges to battered women. Thus, the Greenbook Initiative indicated collaboration between advocates and CPS was important.

Community-based responses expanded on a larger scale throughout the 1990s and 2000s, in part due to the availability of federal funding for collaborative models like Greenbook and the Duluth Model (Boba & Lilley, 2009). A primary focus of VAWA grant funding, particularly through reauthorization of the VAWA in 2000, was to strengthen victim services through coordinated responses involving multiple agencies (Shepard & Pence, 1999; Zweig & Burt, 2007; Miller, 2008; Boba & Lilley, 2009). These legislative, funding, and research agendas still primarily came from the Department of Health and Human Services, through the Centers for Disease Control and Prevention, and the Department of Justice's National Institute of Justice (Miller, 2008). The reauthorization of VAWA involved new grant programs, including the STOP Program (Services, Training, Officers, and Prosecutors) and the Arrest Program (Grants to Encourage Arrest Policies and Enforcement of Protection Orders) (Boba & Lilley, 2009). Consequently, community-based responses generally included advocates working hand in hand with police, judges, hospitals, social workers, and federal government workers

(Boba & Lilley, 2009). Moreover, victim advocates were increasingly employed in police departments and the courts.

In their current iteration, community-based responses generally include domestic violence victim advocates working cooperatively with police, judges, and social services (Boba & Lilley, 2009). Community-based responses vary in their forms and members in different sites, but generally, their responses can be defined as "comprehensive or at least [including] multiple options in the justice and human services systems" (Hart, 1995, p. 6; Muftic & Bouffard, 2007). Members of these groups coordinate and integrate services with a shared goal of reducing domestic violence.

Effectiveness of Community-Based Responses

As community-based responses have become more common, a growing body of research focuses on their effectiveness (Wathen & MacMillan, 2003). Several studies find positive outcomes for abused women working with multiple organizations. Zweig & Burt (2007) found that battered women using domestic violence services reported higher levels of helpfulness when their advocates worked with other agencies and provided multiple services. Importantly, there is evidence that CBR may be significant in terms of helping women to escape from violent relationships. Allen, Bybee, & Sullivan (2004) found that women who used multiple domestic violence services as part of an experimental group were much less likely to experience re-abuse than women in a control group that did not use multiple services. Significantly, women in the experimental group were also less likely to experience re-abuse after two years (Sullivan & Bybee, 1999) and women who reported more social supports and better access to community resources experienced a lower likelihood of abuse over time (Bybee & Sullivan, 2002). Similarly, Websdale & Johnson (1997) evaluated a program in Kentucky that provided advocacy, education, careers, child care, health care, and criminal justice interventions. They found that 82 percent of women using these services did not experience revictimization by their abuser. Hart (1995) found that the availability of more resources increased women's safety, protection, and likelihood of leaving abusive relationships.

9

Chapter 1

Challenges of Professionalized and Community-Based Responses

Grassroots feminist advocacy has evolved into professionalized, specialized, and collaborative organizations. Advocates now specialize beyond the shelter setting, working in police departments, the courts, hospitals, shelters, outreach, counseling, and transitional housing. As noted, there is some evidence that the overlap in services is effective. Yet it is unclear how the shift to CBR models has impacted feminist advocacy and advocates specifically. In fact, a growing body of work by both researchers and practitioners articulates the challenges of bureaucratization, professionalization, and collaboration with other anti-domestic violence stakeholders (Rodriguez, 1988; Lehrner & Allen, 2008; Goodman & Epstein, 2008; Arnold, 1995, 2011; Macy et al., 2010). One challenge is the co-optation of the ideologies, policies, and practices of feminist organizations. In other words, when feminist organizations collaborate with other organizations, their feminist ideologies, survivor-defined practices, and social change agendas may shift to gender-neutral service provision (Schechter, 1982; Arnold, 1995; Shepard & Pence, 1999; Moe, 2000; Lehrner & Allen, 2009; Macy et al., 2010).

More specifically, some researchers have found the ideologies of structural and gendered sources of domestic violence and the social change activism that attempts to change them, so strong in early advocacy days, are abandoned in favor of standardized service provision and the development of rigid rules and mandatory classes women must attend as a condition of receiving shelter or other services (Srinivasan & Davis, 1991; Haaken & Yragui, 2003; Moe, 2007). For example, Haaken & Yragui (2003) noted that strict confidentiality policies shelters prevent women from accessing social support resources. This barrier to social support networks outside of the shelter prevented women from gaining additional social supports to help them leave abusive relationships. Tautfest (2008) noted that women may be expelled from shelters for violating confidentiality or curfew policies. Such rigid policies are antithetical to the survivor-defined practices of the grassroots era.

In fact, Lehrner and Allen (2009) found many contemporary advocates did not know there was a battered women's movement. They found such advocates were not focused on structural or political changes, and believed domestic violence was an individual problem rather than a societal problem rooted in inequality. Yet, imagine what anti-domestic violence structures, organizations, and services would look like today if early advocates had not had a social change agenda: it is likely that community-based responses and widespread availability of shelters, hotlines, and other resources would not exist in their current form.

Failure to recognize the impact of structural gender inequality on domestic violence also potentially alters advocacy and opens the door to victim-blaming and decline in survivor-centered practices (Moe, 2000, 2007; Macy et al., 2010). Researchers find that when advocates view domestic violence as an individual problem, they may believe victims are at fault and blame victims for their own abuse (Macy et al., 2010). Further, such circumstances lead to the hierarchal relationships between advocates and victims that grassroots feminists worked hard to avoid. Hierarchal advocacy involves "telling women what to do" instead of providing information and listening to battered women to assist them in making their own decisions. Furthermore, advocates are writing about their negative experiences with rigid policies that are not flexible and survivor-defined and calling for change. For example, advocates from the Washington State Coalition Against Domestic Violence and the Minnesota Coalition For Battered Women are currently addressing these shifts in the field. This call for change suggests going back to the roots of feminist advocacy, including flexible survivor-centered collaborative policies and practices. This call for change is based upon their negative experiences adhering to rigid policies that can be problematic for the battered women they work with (Hobart, 2006; Olsen, 2007, 2008; Adams & Bennet, 2008; Avalon, 2008; Curran, 2008; Lindquist, 2008; Tautfest, 2008).

Effectiveness of Feminist Advocacy

Survivor-defined advocacy and social change activism have both historically been major components of feminist advocacy. Survivor-defined approaches assume that victims are capable of making their own decisions, and their individual needs should be considered when providing advocacy. In practice, advocates work to explain different options and choices, and supply information so victims can make their own informed decisions (Goodman & Epstein, 2008; Lehrner & Allen, 2009). Women report better outcomes and higher satisfaction with services involving survivor-defined advocacy (Zweig & Burt, 2007; Goodman & Epstein,

2005, 2008; Nurius et al., 2011). Women's agency is central to the practice of feminist advocacy, and research finds it is key to shaping outcomes (Weisz, 1999; Zweig & Burt, 2007; Goodman & Epstein, 2008). For example, Weisz (1999) found that women working with advocates practicing survivor-defined advocacy were more likely to bring further legal action toward their abusers. In her qualitative study of 19 women in domestic violence shelters, Moe (2007) also found that women in control of the services they received were less likely to return to their abusers. In contrast, victims who were denied agency through non-survivor-defined practices, such as when judges told victims to get along with their abusers instead of prosecuting, were more likely to return to their batterers (Moe, 2000). Zweig and Burt (2007) found in their quantitative study of 890 women in shelters that abused women reported service provision as more helpful when they had a higher level of control over their services. If women felt they were not involved in the process, or their input was not regarded, they reported that their willingness to use services declined (Zweig & Burt, 2007). Abrahams and Bruns (1998) compared a feminist CBR coalition to a gender "neutral" CBR coalition and found the gender "neutral" coalition took part in victim-blaming practices, focused on individual rather than socio-structural sources of violence, and did not work to support women in making their own choices. These practices resulted in deterring women from using services in the future, and returning to abusive relationships. Women who have control over their role in prosecution have lower rates of future re-abuse than those who do not (Ford & Regoli, 1993). Moreover, Goodman & Epstein (2005) found women were more likely to cooperate with prosecution if they felt they were listened to. Kulkarni and colleagues (2012) found that survivor-centered practices were associated with a higher sense of self efficacy among abused women, and such women reported that it was important to them that service providers respect their needs and choices. Such approaches in the courts may also be associated with lower rates of depression and higher quality of life among survivors of abuse (Bennett Cattaneo & Goodman, 2010). Similarly, Bell and colleagues (2011) found survivor-centered practices are what women want, as women reported valuing such approaches and devaluing approaches that marginalized their input. In sum, the research suggests the significance of advocacy maintaining feminist practices, as it produces better outcomes for women, both in its survivor-defined approach and in the social change activism that resulted in availability of social services and justice system responses (Abrahams & Bruns, 1998; Weisz, 1999; Zweig & Burt, 2006, 2007; Goodman & Epstein, 2008).

Yet, aside from the handful of studies cited in this discussion, it remains unclear how shifts in professionalization, funding—and specifically CBR models—have impacted feminist advocacy. Given the bureaucratization of their work environment, increasing government control over funding, and collaboration with nonfeminist organizations, to what extent do advocates today hold feminist identities, ideologies, and practices that are similar to those of their grassroots predecessors? What does feminism mean to contemporary advocates? How does feminism inform their practices? Have advocates retained their practice of survivor-defined advocacy, or have they become "neutral," or even controlling in their practices? To what extent do they maintain gendered ideologies of domestic violence and social change perspectives and practices? To what extent do they maintain intersectional feminist perspectives and practices? Are advocates in the justice system less feminist than their peers in traditionally feminist organizations? How is advocacy practiced in community-based responses—in traditionally feminist organizations, child protective services, and in accessing criminal justice system interventions? How do advocates' practices with survivors and in the social change arena interact with their feminist identity, meanings of feminism, and meanings of domestic violence? These questions remain to be answered. Because such questions involve gendered identity, ideology, and practice, they can be addressed with simultaneous attention to the organizational frameworks in which they operate.

A Gendered Organizations Framework

Decades of feminist research indicates that organizations are gendered (Daly & Chesney-Lind, 1988; Acker, 1990; Britton, 1997, 2000, 2003; Risman, 2004; Miller, 2008; Britton & Logan, 2008). Yet, the literature focusing on gendered domestic violence organizations remains limited (Nichols, 2011). The theory of gendered organizations is especially applicable to domestic violence organizations because they have evolved from gendered (feminist) structures and continue to be shaped by collaboration with the justice system and social services.

The concepts "gender based" and "gender neutral" illustrate how organizations' processes can be gendered. *Gender "neutral"* models purportedly ignore gender under the ideological assumption of "sameness," that men and women are the same and should be treated as such (MacKinnon, 1987). The policies and practices of organizations are uniformly applied and consequently do not take gender dynamics into consideration. Yet, many researchers note that gender "neutrality" is biased for the very reason that it does not take gender dynamics into consideration. Neutrality was described by Chesney-Lind and Pollock (1995) as "equality with a vengeance" in their study of women's prisons. Men and women ostensibly followed the same policies under a "neutral" framework, but because the policies were based on a male standard, the specific backgrounds, social positions, and needs of women were not taken into consideration, and the policies were consequently biased (see also Kruttschnitt & Gartner, 2004).

A common *gender based* model is that which reflects the ideological assumption of "difference" between women and men (MacKinnon, 1987). Gender based models can be categorized as either patriarchal or feminist. *Patriarchal gender-based* models assume women are passive, dependent, in need of protection, and lacking in agency. In addition, such models often reproduce traditional gender inequality by recreating power structures that take away women's choices or relegate women to less powerful positions (Chesney-Lind & Pollock, 1995). For example, Allen's (1987) content analysis of court reports in London in the 1980s found that women convicted of violent crimes were required to resume the roles of mothering and housewifery in an attempt to rehabilitate them. Similarly, women in U.S. prisons were historically taught to be good mothers and housekeepers, and received domestic training (Chesney-Lind & Pollock, 1995). Although policy in women's prisons has changed to be largely punitive (see Britton, 2003); women's prisons still offer gender stereotyped vocational training and programming (Chesney-Lind & Pollock, 1995; Britton, 2011). *Feminist gender-based* models also recognize differences between men and women, but assume women's agency as rational, independent, capable decision makers. Feminist models may also label any "differences" as socially constructed, and as such, they are able to be deconstructed (Britton, 2011). In addition, feminist models do not perpetuate traditional gender inequality. For example, grassroots feminist shelters are categorized under a feminist gender based model, because feminist advocates recognized gender differences in abuse, access to resources, and the societal inequalities that impacted women's experiences with abuse. These "differences" informed their shelter structures involving empowerment through survivor-centered advocacy, collaboration, and assistance accessing resources.

Acker's (1990) theory of gendered organizations maintains that organizations are institutional sites of gendered processes. The claim of this book is that gendered processes in domestic violence organizations can be neutral, feminist, or patriarchal. Specifically, Acker's framework indicates that the following interrelated processes can be gendered aspects of organizations: the structure of work organizations, identities within organizations, ideological assumptions, and the actions and interactions of workers. Each of these processes can be seen in the work of domestic violence advocates. First, Acker describes identity as the "internal processes in which individuals engage as they construct personas that are appropriately gendered for the institutional setting" (Acker, 1992, p. 568). Many early domestic violence advocates had a feminist identity, which was perfectly appropriate for the setting, as both shelters and advocacy were born from the broader second wave feminist movement. A "feminist" is labeled as a gendered identity, because both the internal persona and the outward representation of a feminist center on recognizing gendered inequalities. Thus, the internal processes of feminist identity and their manifestation are clearly gendered. In turn, in the context of advocacy, "neutral" identities are also gendered because such identities *don't* incorporate the recognition of gendered inequalities or phenomena into their identities. This "neutrality" can lend itself to gender bias.

Second, cultural and ideological assumptions about gender include images, symbols, and ideologies present in and influencing organizations. Acker maintains that such ideological assumptions come from multiple sources, such as language, popular culture, the media, and other symbolic representations (1990, p. 146). In the case of advocacy, feminism was a symbol of the early battered women's movement, and the ideology of feminism shaped advocacy. The ideological assumptions of the feminist battered women's movement included recognizing gendered inequalities and the domestic violence resulting from such inequalities. Such ideological assumptions "explain, express, reinforce, or sometimes oppose" gendered phenomena (Acker, 1990, p. 146). For example, feminist ideology in the battered women's movement opposed gendered assumptions leading to inequality and abuse. In contrast, gender "neutral" ideological assumptions do not recognize the gender dynamics of intimate partner violence or the gendered structural sources of inequality that may impact dynamics of abuse and leaving an abusive partner (Abrahams & Bruns, 1998; Goodman & Epstein, 2008; Lehrner & Allen, 2009; Macy et al., 2010). Further, patriarchal gender-based advocacy lies on the ideological assumption that battered women cannot make their own decisions, and need to be taken care of. This "for your own good" mentality may lead to hierarchal policies and practices.

Third, the theory of gendered organizations maintains that an organization's structure can be comprised of policies and practices that perpetuate gender inequality—or alternately promote gender equity. For instance, some shelters have policies that ban teen boys from staying there. This policy results in gender inequality—for the boy whose masculinity is feared or perceived as threatening, and for his mother who is consequently denied shelter due to her mothering role. The policy is both neutral and gendered. It is gendered in the assumption of violent masculinity, and it is neutral in ignoring that most primary caregivers of children are women, and women may not want to leave their mothering roles to go into shelter. Policies often guide practices—the practice in this case would be denying the mother and son shelter because of the entrance requirement. Acker maintained gendered processes involve "overt decisions and procedures that control, segregate, exclude, and construct hierarchies based on gender, and often race" (1992, p. 567–568). Certainly a policy denying shelter to boys with their abused mothers excludes, segregates, and to some degree controls their outcomes based on gender. Further, patriarchal gender-based practice denies women's agency based upon the assumption that battered women cannot make their own decisions—such as requiring women to get a protective order, regardless of their circumstances.

In turn, gendered practices can also be feminist, and work to promote equality in organizations, such as the feminist and collaborative practices of early domestic violence shelters that were intended to empower women (Rodriguez, 1988). In addition, survivor-defined advocacy is labeled as a feminist practice because it is centered on the individual needs of women, facilitates women's agency surrounding those needs, and acknowledges the gender dynamics of intimate partner violence. Moreover, intersectional practices that expand outreach and accessibility of resources to women of color, lesbian women, or women with other identities who may experience systemic bias directed toward such identities are feminist practices, as they work to expand equality and resources to meet the needs of all women. Further, social change activism in advocacy is a feminist practice, as it works to improve battered women's access to resources, recourse, and the social environment.

Moreover, Acker argued that gendered processes are interrelated. For example, Acker included practices as a part of structure, but also included practices as a form of action/ interaction (Acker, 1990, 1992). In addition to the interconnectedness of practices, interactions, and structure, other gendered processes can also be interrelated. This is clearly the case with feminist identity and corresponding feminist ideologies. Holding feminist ideologies themselves are what make an individual more likely to identify as a feminist. The interrelated nature of ideology, policies, and practices is apparent—social change ideologies of early victim advocates were related in obvious ways to social change activism. In addition, feminist ideologies of socio-structural sources of domestic violence were associated with the social change activism that worked to change them, as well as collaborative shelter structures and survivor-defined practices. In contrast, gender "neutral" and patriarchal gender based ideologies are related to victim-blaming practices because advocates who use such practices understand domestic violence as an individual problem rather than stemming from broader gender inequities of power and resources (Macy et al., 2010).

In addition to the interrelated nature of identities, ideologies, and practices, Haney (1996) suggests that the gendered nature of organizations is complex and may have competing ideologies, policies, and practices working simultaneously. In her research, she found complexities reflected in organizations in the juvenile justice system. One of the organizations she researched, Alliance, a group home for juvenile females, maintained feminist practices and worked to cultivate "the determination and strength the girls already had" (Haney, 1996, p. 764). Within this same organization, however, she found patriarchal gender-based practices as well. For example, she noted that probation officers would threaten to send girls to juvenile hall if they refused to break up with "unfit" boyfriends. She also found inconsistencies in gendered policies and practices both within juvenile programs and between different programs.

In turn, organizations that serve battered women may be gendered in complex, competing ways as well. Some shelters may maintain gender "neutral" or even patriarchal policies, like eligibility requirements, while they may simultaneously apply feminist gender-based ideologies and practices within various domestic violence organizations. Yet, it remains to be seen whether the gendered processes of advocates—such as their identities, ideologies, and practices—have implications for advocacy in contemporary contexts.

Though criminologists have explored gendered organizations in the context of prisons, courts, policing, and juvenile facilities (Martin, 1980; Jurik, 1985, 1986; Chesney-Lind & Pollock, 1995; Haney, 1996; Britton, 2000, 2003), research examining the gendered processes of domestic violence stakeholders and the impact on advocacy remains limited. Community-based responses (CBR) to domestic violence benefit women through multiple coordinated service provision. Yet, some challenges remain for advocates who assist abused women in CBR. Specifically, a small but growing body of research finds that the use of feminist advocacy is diminishing. This is problematic because such advocacy has been found to increase abused women's agency and thus improve their outcomes, and has also produced widespread social change (Weisz, 1999; Zweig & Burt, 2006, 2007; Goodman & Epstein, 2005, 2008; Nurius et al., 2011). Feminist identity, ideologies and practices of domestic violence victim advocates working in community-based responses to domestic violence are explored throughout this book, drawing from the experiences of twenty-six advocates in two counties in a Midwestern State. The study settings included a metropolitan county and a rural county to reflect the experiences of advocates working in different regions.

Study Settings

Background Information on Glawe County

To deal with an increasing number of domestic violence-related calls to police, rural Glawe County developed a domestic violence victim services program in 1994. The program initially involved the addition of a full-time domestic violence victim services coordinator to the Sheriff's Department staff, and has since evolved to include a community-based response team.

In 2008, the Domestic Violence Response Unit (DVRU) developed in Glawe County, and expanded to a professional staff of three advocates in the Sheriff's Department, all of whom are trained by the State Coalition in domestic violence victim advocacy. Advocates have access to police reports and aim to make contact with all victims who report abuse to police. Advocates provide information to victims about the justice system and assist them in filing for a temporary protective order and safety planning. They also offer information about and referrals to other community resources, such as mental health and substance abuse programs, legal services, and shelter.

The DVRU currently includes the director of a mental health facility that offers counseling, individual and group therapy, and substance abuse counseling. The co-chair from the local Family Violence Council and the director of the county's only women's shelter are also a part of the DVRU. In addition, DVRU includes other justice system stakeholders in addition to the advocates working in the police department. Part of the team includes two detectives who investigate cases of domestic violence. Detectives investigate domestic violence cases involving any domestic violence felony, as well as misdemeanor cases involving recidivism, any degree of potential lethality, and/or cases involving children in the home. There is also an advocate in the prosecuting attorney's office and a prosecutor who are both exclusively assigned to cases involving domestic violence. A probation officer, who deals with the majority of cases involving domestic violence, is also a part of the DVRU team. While all DVRU members are trained in domestic violence through the [State] Coalition Against Domestic Violence, there is no evidence of a present or historical battered women's movement in this rural county, nor is there a local coalition.

Background Information on Faulds County

While the various anti-domestic violence partners are centralized in one distinct community-based response group in rural Glawe County, in Faulds County, which contains a large urban city and surrounding metropolitan area, domestic violence organizations are relatively small separate organizations. While there is some coordination between various groups, each has a distinct independent organizational structure. Most specialize in specific area(s) such as legal services, shelter, transitional housing, outreach, drop-in counseling, or long-term follow up, although they typically provide multiple services. While the organizations are small, and generally have small staff sizes, there is strong recognition of the larger state and local domestic violence community. There are regular "community meetings" among members from various organizations and a collaborative e-mail list-serve in the local feminist anti-domestic violence coalition. They also are highly involved in, and receive education and training from, the [State] Coalition Against Domestic Violence. There are high levels of informal relationships among advocates in both traditionally feminist organizations as well as advocates working in the justice system. Referrals to one another's various specialty organizations are also high. So, while they are generally small specialized organizations with their own distinct organizational structures, they together form a cohesive local coalition.

The battered women's movement in Faulds County dates back to the early 1980s, with strong feminist leadership and mentoring that has continued to date, with some "movement veterans" in directors' positions throughout the domestic violence community in both the justice system and in traditionally feminist settings. Additionally, Faulds City (a large urban city adjoining Faulds County) has two prominent universities that are known for their feminist curriculum that maintain internships in the local domestic violence community (Personal communication with Confidential, 2010).

In 1986, the justice system in Faulds County initiated Domestic Violence Legal Advocates (DVLA) who assist victims with the legal system, the courts, and law enforcement. By 1995, the group became a non-profit domestic violence organization. DVLA also provide advocacy, safety planning, and referrals to social services within Faulds County. Specifically, DVLA has a partnership with the City police department; three advocates have their offices in the department and directly work with officers and the Domestic Violence Detective Unit (DVDU), composed of ten detectives. DVLA also has court advocates present in the Faulds City and Faulds County courthouses.

The Victim Service Division (VSD) in Faulds County works under the umbrella of the prosecuting attorney's office and provides counsel, information on the justice system, and referral to community resources to clients. VSD staff and volunteer advocates assist victims of domestic violence with obtaining protective orders and creating victim impact statements, and also provide support by accompanying victims to court. The Domestic Violence Division is a part of the VSD and includes five prosecutors trained in domestic violence who specifically take both misdemeanor and felony domestic violence cases such as: assault, kidnapping, felonious restraint, false imprisonment, violation of adult abuse orders, unlawful use of a weapon, harassment, and stalking.

Introduction

Regional Similarities and Distinctions

The sites are similar in that they both follow the same state laws related to domestic violence, including but not limited to: no-drop prosecution, pro-arrest, and discretionary permanent and temporary protective orders. The sites are also similar in that they have community-based response teams in place that include collaboration between law enforcement, the courts, advocates, and social services. The differences between the sites include a strong local feminist coalition and history of a battered women's movement in Faulds County compared to Glawe County. Another difference is availability of more services in Faulds County, and local universities in Faulds County that provide education in feminist studies and internships in domestic violence organizations. In addition, Glawe County has a more centralized CBR team compared to Faulds County. These two sites are useful for comparison because they provide an opportunity to examine the experiences of advocates in rural and metropolitan contexts. For example, dynamics of advocacy surrounding pro-arrest and no-drop prosecution might look different in practice/ implementation in regional comparisons, although both sites are required to adhere to the same state laws.

Notably, the majority of organizations from which the advocates came had very small staff sizes with high caseloads; in many cases staff consisted of two or three people. In total, eleven different organizations participated. Because of small staff sizes and the limited number of some types of organizations, in the presentation of the research findings in the following chapters, the organizations were conflated into two distinct groups to preserve confidentiality. "*Justice system advocates*" included those working in or employed by the police department and the courthouse, while "*traditional advocates*" included those working in historically woman-centered contexts, such as shelters, outreach, transitional housing, a drop-in center, and a hospital.[4] These groupings are used throughout this book. The experiences of advocates in different organizational and regional contexts were examined in-depth. In particular, the variations in advocates' identities, ideologies, and practices across these groups were explored.

Chapter 1

Outline of Chapters

This book draws from a gendered organizations framework to examine various facets of advocacy in community-based responses to domestic violence in Glawe and Faulds Counties. All of the chapters examine the relationship between feminism and advocates' practices as well as regional and organizational comparisons. Beginning in chapter 2, the feminist identities and ideologies of victim advocates are examined through advocates' narratives, detailing how feminist identities and ideologies relate to the practice of advocacy. Further, the concept of co-optation is explored by comparing the feminist identities, ideologies, and practices of advocates working in the justice system to those of advocates working in traditionally feminist organizations. Chapter 2 further investigates how advocates describe feminism, detailing the complexities and contradictions of meaning. In addition, the ways advocates' conceptualization of feminist identity relates to their various and multifaceted ideologies are examined, as well as the ways advocates negotiate their feminist identities in community-based responses. Last, the interrelated nature of feminist identity, ideology, and practices are clearly delineated, exposing the ways in which feminism shapes the practice of advocacy and why it is important. Advocates' detailed descriptions of survivor-defined, intersectional, and social change practices in community-based responses to domestic violence are used to illustrate these areas.

Chapter 3 focuses on advocates' experiences with the criminal justice system. Gendered policies and practices in the criminal justice system related to protective orders, pro-arrest, dual arrest, and no-drop prosecution are examined, as well as advocates' strategies to mitigate both batterer-based and systemic revictimization of battered women. While generally supporting criminal justice interventions and using them as tools for advocacy, advocates simultaneously recognized the potential for resulting batterer-based and systemic revictimization. Advocates consequently developed strategies to avoid revictimization resulting from such difficulties, including survivor-defined, intersectional, and social change practices.

Chapter 4 explores policies and issues involving children that affect victim advocacy, including charging battered women with "failure to protect" children from witnessing or experiencing abuse, lost custody, mandatory parenting classes, and abusers' use of children to manipulate both the system and victims. The ways these policies and related practices are gendered and how they challenge victim advocacy are examined, as well as the techniques advocates developed to deal with them. This chapter draws from advocates' descriptions of challenges within the system as well as their survivor-defined and social change practices addressing both batterer-based and systemic revictimization of battered women.

Chapter 5 focuses on advocates' experiences within traditionally feminist organizations: shelters and transitional housing. The gendered complexities of shelter rules are examined. Specifically, the chapter emphasizes advocates' practices related to the shelter rules that have been most contentiously debated in the practitioner-based literature: accepting adolescent boys into shelters, confidentiality, curfew, mandatory classes, entrance requirements, and chores. Chapter 5 highlights how advocates describe such policies as assisting or problematizing their ability to help survivors and how the policies relate to survivor-defined, intersectional, and social change practices. Advocates both resisted and reproduced different forms of gendered practices. They were reproduced when patriarchal or neutral shelter rules facilitated revictimization of battered women. Yet they were simultaneously resisted through survivor-defined, social change, and intersectional feminist approaches.

In chapter 6, implications of the research findings for practices of advocacy and gendered organizations theory are detailed. The findings led to a number of recommendations for advocacy responses in shelters, children's services, and various facets of the justice system. The contextual differences between regions and the importance of such distinctions for gendered organizations theory are offered. In addition, contextual comparisons between advocacy in traditionally feminist organizations and advocacy in masculine (or "gender-neutral") organizations are illustrated. Further, an extension of the gendered organizations framework is offered by exploring "resistance"—essentially, the practices countering gendered processes.

Chapter 2

Feminist Advocacy

Chapter 1 described how early feminist advocacy was grounded in survivor-defined practices and social change activism rooted in feminism. Chapter 2 examines the relationship between feminism and advocacy among contemporary advocates. Specifically, the interaction between feminist identity, ideologies, and practices is explored. First, an overview of advocates' self-identification as feminist by regional and organizational contexts is illustrated. Further, the ways advocates described feminism is explored, detailing the complexities and contradictions of meaning. The relationship between advocates' conceptualization of feminism, and how their feminist identity related to their various and multifaceted ideologies is also examined. In addition, the ways advocates negotiated their feminist identities in community-based responses is described. Last, the interrelated nature of feminist identity, ideology, and practice is discussed, clearly delineating how feminism shapes the practices of advocacy and why it is important. Particular attention is given to survivor-defined, social change, and intersectional practices of advocacy.

Feminist Identity

Of the twenty-six advocates who were interviewed for this book, seventeen identified as feminist and nine did not. There were some differences by regional and organizational contexts in self-identification as feminist. Advocates in metropolitan Faulds County and justice system advocates in both study settings were more likely to self-identify as feminists (see Table 1, p. 52). First, in metro Faulds County, only three of eighteen advocates did not identify as feminist. In contrast, six of the eight advocates interviewed in rural Glawe County did not identify as feminist. Thus, there were some regional distinctions in embracing a feminist identity. In Faulds County, the higher proportion of feminist advocates is likely related to the strong local coalition, the history of a robust battered women's movement, and availability of higher education and internships with feminist curriculum. In addition, all directors in Faulds County identified as feminist, and a majority described feminist programming in their organizations. Such dynamics may be a product of a metro environment compared to a rural environment, and seemed to

25

Chapter 2

facilitate feminist identity. For example, Charlotte, a veteran in the field, discussed the influence of a very strong feminist coalition in Faulds County:

> Well, it's so funny because I never used to [identify as feminist] and then another advocate from another agency, said "but Charlotte, you really are, you just don't recognize it about yourself." Probably I have become more of a feminist than when I first started . . . I'm an old buffalo in the field. I was here when the victim's rights statute was written. There are very few of us left in the field who were around when that statute was written. So I think it's [feminism] being a voice for varying different aspects for our field. In terms of being a voice for women, I'm lucky to be working in a very, very pro-women setting.

In similar discussions, several other advocates in Faulds County also indicated the importance of the strong local feminist domestic violence coalition in perpetuating feminist identity among advocates. In fact, advocates in many of these organizations undergo training prepared by the local coalition. This training is informally called DV 101 and formally called "Violence against Women: An Introduction. Welcome to the Movement." The training includes a history of the feminist battered women's movement, the gender dynamics involved in domestic violence, and the foundations and principles of advocacy. In addition to local coalition training, advocates in metro Faulds County were also trained by the [State] Coalition Against Domestic Violence in best practices of advocacy. The [State] Coalition Against Domestic Violence has links to the early feminist anti-domestic violence movement, and movement veterans in Faulds County are still active in the [State] Coalition Against Domestic Violence.

In comparison, in rural Glawe County, neither of the directors identified as feminist, nor did feminism appear to be a part of the programming in organizations. There was no evidence of a battered women's movement or a strong centralized local feminist coalition. Advocates received training from the [State] Coalition Against Domestic Violence in "best practices" of advocacy, but did not get education and training from a local feminist coalition. The only two advocates in Glawe County identifying as feminists had college degrees in women's studies. Feminist identity was not as common in Glawe County, where feminist directors, programming, and local feminist coalitions did not exist.

Feminist Advocacy

These findings are consistent with prior research indicating that feminist directors and managers with a background in domestic violence provide mentorship in and thus preserve feminist advocacy within their organizations (Arnold, 2011; Lehrner & Allen, 2009; Macy et al., 2010). It is also consistent with research finding that feminism is less likely among rural domestic violence victim advocates, who are not as likely to be exposed to feminist mentorship, programming, education, and social movement philosophy (Lehrner & Allen, 2009; Websdale, 1998).

Second, in addition to regional distinctions in feminist identity, there were differences in feminist identities when comparing those working in the justice system to those working in traditionally feminist organizations. Prior research has expressed concern that when advocates are employed by traditionally masculine organizations their feminist identities, ideologies, and practices may be co-opted and lost (Arnold, 1995, 2011; Avalon, 2008; Macy et al., 2010). Contrary to prior research, in this study advocates in the justice system were *more* likely to identify as feminist than their peers working in traditionally feminist organizations, in both study settings. Therefore, existing concerns over co-optation through employment of advocates by the courts, police departments, and hospitals, and advocates consequently not identifying as feminist or practicing feminist advocacy, were not necessarily supported when examining the experiences of advocates in Glawe and Faulds Counties (Shepard & Pence, 1999; Avalon, 2008; Nichols, 2011). However, it should be noted that in the metro justice system, individuals typically attained their positions because of their background in domestic violence. For example, one of the justice system advocates previously worked in a highly feminist batterer intervention program. Another worked in a shelter before getting her position working in the police department, and yet another had a degree in women's studies. Both directors of victim services in the courts were veterans of the domestic violence movement. In the rural setting, the only advocates identifying as feminists were working in the justice system, but had college degrees in feminist studies. Thus, the institutional setting may be less important in solidifying feminist identity than the background, education, and experience of the individuals in organizations, as well as strong local feminist coalitions. Such dynamics may mitigate co-optation of feminism by masculine organizations.

Chapter 2

Meanings of Feminism

"I'm Not a Feminist, but..."

Whether an advocate identified as feminist or not depended on her definition of feminism. Many advocates who did not identify as feminist had different meanings of feminism from the meaning generally accepted by feminists—that women and men should have equal rights, opportunities, and status. Some advocates did not identify as feminist, yet all advocates believed women and men should be equal. Thus the interviews divulged conflicting and multifaceted meanings of feminism.

When advocates do not label themselves as feminist, it may not mean that they do not support some or all of the components of feminism. Feminism may have a negative connotation to some; not all women or men want to identify with it (hooks, 2000; Rowe-Finkbeiner, 2004). For example, a majority of advocates who did not identify as feminist made seemingly contradictory statements: they expressed belief in equal rights for all, but did not identify as feminist. Shelli, a self-identified feminist, came across the same dynamic in her education and awareness programs: women did not want to associate themselves with feminism, although they supported its premise of equal rights. When Shelli was asked to describe what it meant to be a feminist, her initial reply was flippantly sarcastic. But she went on to note some of the defining characteristics of a feminist identity:

> It means I hate men! (laughs) I have to tell you one of the saddest things, is when I go in and talk to young women and they say they're not a feminist. Older women too, but if you ask them what it means— they don't know! First of all, a feminist can be male or female, number one—get over it everybody! Some of my biggest supporters throughout the years have been male feminists. So anyway, a feminist to me is someone who realizes that there is oppression and inequality of different peoples in the world, and that one of the biggest ones are women— you recognize that there's an inequality in the dynamics of power and control and oppression—you then commit yourself to bringing about the systemic changes that will bring that down, that's a feminist.

Shelli's experience generally reflected my own in this research project. Advocates who did not identify as feminist did not know what one was or had a meaning of the word that was inconsistent with its most basic definition shared by various types of feminists.

First, the misconception of feminism as a desire for "superiority of women" as opposed to "equality for women" led some advocates to not identify as feminist. For example, when Eve was asked, "Would you describe yourself as a feminist?" Her response was, "Okay, I'm not really good at putting people in pigeon holes, I believe in e—qual—i—ty." Eve was then asked what feminism meant to her in order to clarify her response. She said, "I believe in equality for everyone, albeit man, woman or child." Eve's example delineated her reluctance to identify as a feminist, but she supported equal rights for all persons. Further, although Eve did not identify as feminist, she expressed a strong recognition of both the sexed and the gendered nature of domestic violence. Eve described domestic violence as largely male-to-female violence, and a display of masculinity and "gendered privilege." She repeatedly discussed hierarchal arrangements in society, the oppression of women, and the relationship of these to domestic violence. So, while she did not label herself as a feminist, she supported feminist ideologies.

Yet, the meaning of feminism is complex; a feminist must recognize gendered inequalities in the first place to understand what wanting equal rights means. While Eve did recognize gendered inequalities, a majority of nonfeminists did not. Not identifying as a feminist largely coincided with not recognizing gendered inequalities. For example, when Belinda was asked if she would describe herself as a feminist, she replied, "No, a humanist." When asked to explain what that meant to her, she stated:

I care about everybody. We all have our part in this world. We're all part of the fabric of life and the universe, and I don't want to be exclusive. I want to be inclusive. I value men and women, children, the whole nine yards.

Belinda's response, representative of other nonfeminist advocates, indicated that her meaning of feminism was the desire for women to be superior to men. For clarification, she was asked, "So feminism to you would mean putting a higher value on women, or at least more of a focus?" and she replied in the affirmative. When asked how her perspective related to victim advocacy, Belinda explained that domestic violence services should not focus more on women than men. In this example, one might initially think Belinda is a feminist and just does not know it because of her incorrect definition of feminism—she clearly supported equality. Yet, she did not recognize the gender dynamics of domestic violence (that the vast majority of victims are women, and the majority of perpetrators are men) and the disproportionate need for services and resources for women. As feminism largely centers on recognizing gender inequalities and changing them to create an equal society, "neutral" ideologies presented in advocates' descriptions of domestic violence do not represent feminism. Except for Eve, nonfeminist advocates generally did not have gendered ideologies of domestic violence and the sociostructural gender inequalities that impact domestic violence.

Another contradiction of meaning occurred when an advocate conflated lesbian identity with feminism. When Vicki was asked if she would describe herself as a feminist, she raised her eyebrows, and gave a short "No." She was then asked, "What does that word, feminism, mean to you?" Vicki stated:

> You know I guess I look at a feminist as someone who has extreme women's rights. I guess I see someone who marches in gay pride and doing things like that. I guess—I just—I'm all about women's rights, but (shrugs).

Vicki's example indicates her association of feminism with lesbian identity. While she supported women's rights, she did not support all women's rights, such as lesbians, or gay rights which in turn shaped her identity as a nonfeminist. One other rural advocate expressed this same definition—that one had to be a lesbian to be feminist.

Then What Is a Feminist? Feminist Ideologies

Among advocates that did identify as feminist, their meanings of feminism were also complex. All advocates identifying as feminist described a feminist as someone who wants women to have the same rights and opportunities as men. For example, when asked if she would call herself a feminist, Kari stated, "Absolutely!" And when further asked, "What does that word feminism mean to you?" she replied: "I've always gone with the more broad term which is simply—you desire a higher quality of life and equal rights for women, that's it." Advocates identifying as feminist unanimously stated recognition of gendered inequalities as a part of feminist identity as well. In addition, all but one feminist advocate believed a feminist must be an activist to be a feminist, and a majority of feminist advocates clearly stated that a feminist must recognize how other inequalities such as race and class factor into gendered inequalities. Thus, for those advocates who did identify as feminists, their meanings of feminism were intimately related to their feminist ideologies, such as gendered, social change, and intersectional ideologies.

Gendered and Social Change Ideologies

Feminist identity was related to acknowledgment of the gendered nature of domestic violence and social change perspectives. First, since feminists are generally aware of and actively seek to change gendered inequalities, it is not surprising that feminist advocates held gendered ideologies of domestic violence. For example, when asked if she thought feminism applied to domestic violence, Amy indicated the importance of recognizing the gender dynamics of domestic violence:

> I'm going to use men as the offender and female as the victim, I think through society we need to make changes on how we view gender roles and women are supposed to do this, and men are supposed to do that, and I think that . . . contributes to, "I can, she's mine, I can control her, I can hit her, or I can assault her or take advantage of her." So it goes hand in hand with domestic violence and these men learning and seeing and thinking that it's okay to do that.

Like most feminist advocates, Amy integrated social change perspectives with her recognition of the gendered inequalities involved in domestic violence. She believed that societal changes in gender dynamics would diminish domestic violence. In another example, when asked if she would describe herself as a feminist, Jean said, "Oh absolutely!" Jean then elaborated on the meaning of feminist identity:

> To me being a feminist is, first of all, understanding that the society that we live in is—not only patriarchal but hierarchal. I think, it's too, as a feminist I feel that there is a commitment to educating as much as possible. Many people don't understand that sexism still exists to such a large degree in our society—I think it's a part [of feminism] to educate people about that.

Like Amy and Jean, a majority of other feminist advocates expressed a feminist identity and perspective very similar to those of the early feminist advocates described in chapter 1. In the above example, Jean recognized societal gender dynamics and held a social change ideology. Similarly, Liz stated:

> Specifically, how can I work to empower women specifically in a culture that doesn't necessarily make that a priority? So for me that's what being a feminist is about—looking for ways that women can be empowered to identify ways in which a hierarchy is in place that works against women and to call that out and to say that this isn't okay. I think that like a lot of people don't necessarily look to see how much privilege we give men in our culture—because we are just so inundated with it everywhere. Again, it gets back to that whole cultural thing about how we socialize men in this country, how we socialize women in this country. So we're talking about cultural shifts and cultural changes. My feminist perspective has a lot to do with my social change perspective, they are totally linked together.

Like Amy, Liz, and Jean, in Faulds County such gendered and social change ideology was expressed by all advocates identifying as feminist. In contrast, gendered and social change ideologies were not articulated by nonfeminist advocates. In rural Glawe County, feminist ideology was expressed by both of the advocates who identified as feminist, and was only conveyed by one of the six advocates who did not identify as feminist. None of the nonfeminist advocates expressed social change ideologies, and one rural feminist did express social change ideology (see Table 1, p. 52. Among the advocates interviewed, feminist identity was related to the conceptualization of domestic violence as gendered, as well as social change ideologies.

Intersectional Ideologies

Feminism was related to intersectionality as well; some advocates in this study stressed the importance of recognizing intersecting identities. Aileen described what it meant to her to be a feminist:

> It means that it's the theoretical framework through which we try to understand unequal distributions of power and access to resources and

that we look at it as a gendered issue. How does gender play out in that? And how do intersections of race and class influence how we "do gender" and how that limits access to resources?

Like Aileen, most advocates with feminist ideologies also expressed intersectional feminist ideologies and integrated intersectional feminist perspectives in their advocacy. For example, like Aileen, Ingrid stated:

> Feminism is all about seeing how women experience inequality and how women experience their inequality based on their race, class and other backgrounds. Disability is a big one. Working with very over-weight women, I see biases there too. And that has everything to do with gender and how women are supposed to be to get privilege.

Advocates explained how intersecting identities related to gender, victimization, and advocacy. Such identities included race, class, ethnicity, sexual orientation, limited-English speaking abilities, disability, and obesity. Advocates with intersectional ideologies were exclusively self-identified feminists, thus feminist identity was related to intersectional perspectives. Most feminist advocates described intersectional ideologies of their own accord, without specifically being asked about them. When advocates who did not describe intersectional ideologies were prompted; the responses of nonfeminist advocates included, "there are no biases," "I don't know," and "I can't say I know about that."

In metro Faulds County, nonfeminists did not express intersectional ideologies, but most feminist advocates did. Advocates with intersectional ideologies were more prevalent in Faulds County, where there were a larger number of feminists. In rural Glawe County, rural advocates who did not identify as feminist (six in all) did not express intersectional perspectives while the two feminist advocates did. In Faulds County, advocates in the justice system were slightly more likely to than those in traditionally feminist organizations to maintain intersectional ideologies. In Glawe County, the advocates with intersectional ideologies were both in the justice system, and none of the advocates in traditionally feminist organizations had intersectional viewpoints. In sum, intersectional ideologies were related to feminist identity and region. Again, this suggests that the organizational setting is less important than other dynamics, including a feminist identity and metropolitan setting.

Chapter 2

Toning Down Feminist Identity

Advocates who self-identified as feminist described the ways in which they publicly negotiated this identity in their role as advocates. Advocates who were feminist reported toning down their outward representations of feminism in collaborating with other organizations, interacting with community-based response (CBR) members, and in the general community. They used neutral language in community education programs, training programs, and organizational materials. Advocates described pressure from board members and others involved in community education programs to not use feminist or gendered language when talking about domestic violence in education and training programs in the community. For example, Ingrid described use of neutral language in training programs:

> Oh good lord. Don't get me started. Like we have to pretend that men are abused like women are to be accepted and to get anyone to listen to what we have to say. So, we have to say perpetrator/ victim" or "abuser/victim." You show me the demand for our services from men and then I'll change the language! But it's ridiculous to do training using this neutral language when what we get 99.9% of the time is women and their abusers are men. Period.

Shelli stated a similar experience; she was asked by a board member of a batterer intervention program to tone down feminist language in educational trainings:

> Pronouns! "Don't say he, make sure you say only abuser or perpetrator, or this, or her husband—use the relationship term for it." [If] one of the guys from SUCCESS [a batterer intervention program] is going with us to talk, "let him start out the show. Let him set the scenario because it's more believable coming from him."

Shelli, Ingrid, and other feminist advocates described using neutral language in training programs. This is consistent with prior research finding advocates may tone down feminist identity in the presence of funders, board presidents, the courts, and their communities (Arnold, 2011; Macy et al., 2010).

In addition to use of gendered and gender-neutral language in trainings, advocates also reported concealing feminist identity in their interactions with other community-based response (CBR) stakeholders. Advocates in Glawe County described hiding their feminist identity both with other nonfeminist advocates and with CBR members. For example, in rural Glawe County, Kari described hiding her feminist identity at work with other nonfeminist advocates and police officers:

> So I tend to keep my education and my feminism under wraps, nobody knows that and I don't know if they would get it, if I did tell them. If they did, it would probably marginalize me. So I just to try and keep a better working relationship for victims, I tend to try and fit in, and not be too feministy . . . not identify that my [college] degrees are in feminism.

Kari's outward representations of identity took different forms depending on the group, organization, or individuals she interacted with. While she had a strong feminist identity, she negotiated this identity within her environment to represent it in more acceptable terms and hid her accomplishments in feminist studies.

In the following statement, Summer, who worked with Kari, depicted the mentality of the nonfeminist advocates that Kari worked with. When Summer was asked if she'd describe herself as a feminist, she said, "No. I can't wait for you to ask the next person this question because I would love to hear her answer, because we have one here [a feminist] ..." Her response was stated in an excited jesting manner, and indicated the novelty of feminist identity within her organization and community. Thus, it is not surprising that Kari would tone down her feminist identity in such circumstances. Summer then insightfully described the local context and its impact on feminist identity, suggesting why feminist identity was rare in rural Glawe County:

> I think that the fact that I work in a law enforcement agency with 99% men, you have to kind of keep in check in a small town. This is rural small town, and so if you're going to fit in and have the respect of the people that are around you, you can't come across as being someone who thinks that all victims deserve the benefit of the doubt . . . To me that is a little bit of a feminist attitude—I guess to describe a feminist, I'm not ultimately for the female.

Her words describe her interpretation of how feminism is received in her rural community and within a male-dominated justice system, further suggesting that successful navigation of feminist identities in such a context largely requires hiding them from others.

Like Kari in the rural justice system, two advocates in the metropolitan justice system stated that they had to hide or negotiate their feminist identity, and if they did not, they would "get flak" from officers and attorneys. Teresa, who worked in the urban justice system, described having a good relationship overall with officers, her chief, lieutenant, and the detectives she worked with. However, Teresa maintained, "If I were to walk out in the police department and say 'I'm a feminist,' they [officers] would say 'no you're not!' because they have a very different idea of what a feminist should be." Teresa then described her perception of officers' definition of feminism: "There are still some that think that they [feminists] just hate men." She illustrated officers' behavior in such circumstances by drawing an analogy to a time when she told a few officers she was a Democrat and one of them called her a communist. "Like with the police officers if I tell them that I'm a Democrat—I got called a Communist this last year, I was like 'a Communist really?!? I'm a communist?!?' they have definitely serious opinions about that." Teresa indicated that such officers generalized to extremes; the officers who saw Democrats as communists also saw feminists as man-haters. Teresa also recalled experiencing harassment from attorneys, who associated lesbianism with feminism as well: "The other thing that occasionally comes up is that we must all be lesbians because we're a group of women who work in the same office—attorneys like at the Order of Protection Court will say things like that."

Moreover, justice system advocates in Faulds County described that some feminist advocates working in traditional settings did not see them as "real" feminists because of their work in criminal justice organizations. They described feeling somewhat marginalized in the larger domestic violence community because of their organizational setting. For example, Teresa described not only navigating her identity with the officers and the courts, but with other advocates who did not work in the justice system:

> They [other advocates] think that is where you find distinctions—about whether or not you work with the government. Or advocates define you also and your feminist idea by that [working in the justice system] as well, so I think that is why we're seen a little bit less like a true advocate.

Feminist Advocacy

Emily expressed similar sentiments:

> Not a lot of advocates want to work with police at all, so they [other advocates] see us as very different than them, maybe not as feminist as them, maybe that's a good way to put it, I don't know. I think that there are some, I would say it's a few, but there are some who see us [advocates working in the justice system] *as* them [police].

Advocates working in the justice system thus walk a thin line in their feminist representations—other advocates not working in the justice system may not accept the justice system advocates' feminist identity because they work in largely masculine institutions. But at the same time, they have to negotiate their feminist identities within the justice system as well. This dual approach to identity—hiding and simultaneously revealing—was present in both Faulds and Glawe Counties.

Outside of the justice system, when asked how feminism was received in collaborative responses, Shelli, who did not hide her feminist identity, said, "Humor, people use a lot, jokingly [others say] 'watch out for them [feminists].' [laughs] That's a euphemism for 'they're bitches!'" Her statement indicates that such individuals feel uncomfortable, threatened by, or even feel that it is acceptable to make fun of feminist identity. They choose to mitigate this perceived threat under the veil of humor. Shelli's interpretation, that feminists are perceived in a negative light, was supported by other advocates who described that they had to hide their identities or experience harassment.

In a slightly different focus, the websites, brochures, mission statements, and pamphlets of the organizations in both study settings were examined to provide additional context for the environments advocates worked in and how they may relate to advocacy. In both rural and in metro contexts, there was no mention in these material items of feminism or the battered women's movement. All material representations of the organizations in Glawe County were otherwise neutral, while there was a mix of neutral and feminist language in material representations of organizations in Faulds County in both the justice system and in traditionally feminist organizations. The language was neutral for some organizations, and clearly indicated services were available to women and men, or used non-identifying generic language. For example, one mission statement of an outreach program used gender neutral terminology: "to provide counseling, emergency sanctuary, and other critical services to adults and children who have been impacted by domestic abuse, as well as to increase awareness in order to create a supportive community. The vision is to end domestic abuse, restoring safety and peace one family at a time." Neutral mission statements and brochures also largely framed domestic violence as "family violence" as opposed to "violence against women." In Glawe County, the gender neutral patterns in titles, mission statements, and material items largely matched the nonfeminist ideologies of the advocates working in the organizations.

Yet, other websites and brochures stated the gender dynamics involved in domestic violence, framing domestic violence as violence against women, largely male-perpetrated, and related to masculinity or oppression of women. Further, some mission statements clearly indicated the organization provided services specifically for women. For example, one mission statement of a shelter program in Faulds County was gendered in a very feminist way, reminiscent of early feminist models: "to provide safe shelter and support services to battered women and their dependent children and to empower women to make informed choices about their futures." In Faulds County, organizations that had feminist mission statements had a majority of advocates that were feminist working there. Yet, advocates working in organizations with neutral materials were majority-feminist also. However, all advocates in the sample participated in the local feminist coalition as well, which has "violence against women" in its title.

In sum, outward representations of feminism are somewhat mitigated in collaborative responses—through use of neutral language in trainings and in material representations of organizations, as well as hiding feminist identity to avoid negative interactions with officers, attorneys, and other advocates.

The Practice of Advocacy

While feminist identity generally guided social change and intersectional perspectives, as well as ideologies of domestic violence as gendered or neutral, the relationship to practice was more complex. This section details the practice of feminist advocacy, how it relates to feminist identity/ideologies, and why it is important. As described in chapter 1, historically, feminist advocacy was largely composed of two parts: social change activism and survivor-defined practices, and to a lesser extent intersectional practices. A survivor-defined approach works to empower abused women through providing information, resources, and support so women can make their own informed decisions. The survivor-defined approach of feminist advocacy assumes women's agency, considers individual cases and needs, and provides resources and support to empower victims (Goodman & Epstein, 2008; Lehrner & Allen, 2009; Jordan, 2004; Jordan et al., 2010). Intersectional approaches are a part of survivor-defined approaches, and work to specifically advocate to the individual needs based upon the race, class, sexual orientation, ethnic, and other unique identities that women hold in addition to their identities as women. Social change activism involves recognition of the gendered nature of domestic violence, and works to change the sociostructural inequalities that support it. Because of the historical link of these approaches to feminism, the expectation was that feminist advocates would be more likely to have survivor-defined, intersectional, and social change practices in their advocacy compared to their nonfeminist counterparts.

Survivor-defined Practices

Contrary to such expectations, a majority of advocates, whether they held feminist identities/ideologies or not, practiced survivor-defined advocacy. In this section, feminist advocates' approaches to survivor-defined advocacy are detailed, and how they stem from their feminist ideologies. Then catalysts to survivor-defined approaches among nonfeminists are illustrated.

Feminist Survivor-defined Advocacy

A typical response of feminist advocates to the question, "What is your approach to advocacy?" is represented in Gillian's description:

> The situations that women find themselves in, and what may help to remedy things for them, is varied. To do this from other than a woman-centered approach, you're just not going to connect with a woman and really provide something that is meaningful, without finding out what's meaningful to her. To do that you have to be woman-centered. When they [survivors] are in a relationship with somebody who is sucking up all of the control, and to engage in a relationship with that person [the

survivor] in which you also assume a role of control and authority, it's not what she wants or needs. Now, it's not that the advocate has this role of you just kind of roll over and play dead, it's more of a partnership, where I know a ton about domestic violence, I know a ton about resources in the community, and this woman knows a ton about her life, what matters to her, what has worked before, she knows the ins and outs of the person who's making problems, and so it is really a partnership of putting those things together. Then coming up with a plan. It's an active role but you don't get sort of dominant, so it's respectful and it's built on her knowledge and expertise and really it's about her making the choices and decisions—but that all comes about from this bigger conversation with the advocate.

In this example, Gillian compared a controlling style of advocacy to abusive relationships and suggested that women-centered (survivor-defined) forms of advocacy were more effective and "respectful." Similarly, Glenda discussed why feminist advocacy is important in psychological terms:

Because I think the women that come here haven't had it [empowerment]. I think once they begin to do that it gives them the courage and it builds up their self-esteem, their image of themselves that they can do it and it's empowering.

Glenda too illustrated the parallels between controlling advocacy and an abusive relationship, arguing that empowerment is key and cannot emerge within the constraints of controlling practices. Such beliefs remained central to advocates with feminist ideologies in both Glawe County and in Faulds County.

Jean also noted the importance of feminist advocacy to women who chose to stay with their abusive partners. She indicated that women may have plans to leave, but might be waiting for practical reasons, such as getting a job or finishing college, and that advocacy is essential to women's safety in the meantime:

I think that we need to work with women where they are at. If they are at home with an abuser we need to provide her support in the home. Whether that's by the telephone or meeting with her, we need to discuss with her what is a safe way for us to provide support for her, where can we meet how can we talk, how can we continue to assist her with her goals. Many of the women that I've worked with, they want to leave, eventually, but first maybe they want to finish their education, or they want to get a job, and he's putting obstacles in the path of their doing this. We may be able to work together to help her get over those obstacles and meet her goals; because, she wants to be able to leave.

Jean indicated that individual goals were central to survivor-defined advocacy. Ingrid also exemplified the threat to women's safety if advocacy were not survivor-defined, in the context of women who stayed with their abusers:

> If they are not ready to leave they are not ready to leave, and if we don't work with them, that is a threat to their safety. If we try to force them, they won't come back or call in the future and it puts them in additional danger because we can't help.

When asked about why feminist advocacy was important to victims, and what would happen if the advocacy was not woman-defined, Aileen stated:

> That makes us no different than her abuser. What's the advantage? There is *no* advantage and we have to be able to hear her when she says, I can't leave right now, or I have absolutely no intention of ever leaving. I just need to know how to be safe within my living situation.

Her example indicates that controlling models parallel abusive relationships. In addition, in a conversation about survivor-defined approaches, when asked, "What's the problem with doing it the other way, trying to convince her to leave her abuser if she doesn't want to or isn't able to?" Jean delineated the importance of safety:

> It's just not safe, first of all, if she's not ready to leave him she's not going to leave him. So, she's still in an unsafe situation but without the help that we can provide in terms of helping her with a safety plan at home with that abusive partner. We're also denying her our support while she's in that abusive relationship . . . we have to trust her [the survivor]. I think that's the crux of the problem and I think that's a sexist problem in our society that we still have a patriarchal attitude toward women. They need to be taken care of, they need to be told what they need to do, we're smarter than they are, and we have to help them learn how to be smart, and live better, and be better parents, and all of that.

Jean clearly illustrated the importance of collaborative and empowering advocacy to women's safety, and related it to feminist ideologies. She described how each individual woman she worked with had specific needs that were important to safety. Listening to women and noting what their needs were played a significant role in her advocacy. If individual cases and needs were not considered in patriarchal or "neutral" advocacy, then women's safety could be compromised because they would have no support or recourse. So advocates associated survivor-defined practices not only with feminist ideology, but with the reality of improved outcomes and safety through feminist survivor-defined approaches. Feminist advocates consistently described what individual women wanted and needed as the cornerstone of their advocacy. They highlighted listening to victims in order to best work for their safety, even when victims chose to remain with their abusers, as safety depended on victims' willingness to use and access services. Feminist advocates regularly related survivor-defined models to feminist ideologies of empowerment and agency of victims. This represents feminist gender-based practice.

So Why Do Nonfeminists Practice Survivor-defined Advocacy?

Feminists practiced survivor-defined advocacy, clearly indicating it was because the approach was consistent with their feminist ideologies as well as the realities of women's safety. However, the findings indicate that all nonfeminist advocates also described their approach to advocacy as survivor-defined. Personal experience as survivors, experience with safety issues as an advocate, training from the [state] coalition, and feminist programming in organizations were sources leading to survivor-defined approaches among nonfeminists.

For example, Belinda, who did not identify as a feminist, offered her approach to advocacy as woman-centered advocacy. Although she did not identify as a feminist, she eloquently described how utterly damaging controlling practices can be to women who are already suffering from abuse. Drawing from her own experiences of abuse and eventually leaving her abusive relationship, she related it to her advocacy:

> We practice woman centered advocacy, yes, absolutely! Because the opposite of being abused and oppressed most people think it's love, no! The opposite of being abused and oppressed is having your own per-

sonal power. Being part of that process when a woman empowers herself to be her own person, to reclaim her life, to reclaim her spirit, it requires that we respect her decisions, requires that we respect her opinions and her experience, and we honor and we reverence it, and we don't judge it, we don't put it down, we don't minimize her. So it's very, very important here. So while some of the decisions that women make that we're working with may not be what we think are appropriate, she knows the best thing for her. She knows her abuser better than we do, and her timing is her timing and I respect that. It took me a long time to get out of my abusive relationship. Well-meaning people lost interest in me a long time before I ever made my way to safety. So having patience, having respect and regard and watching her personal power grow is so motivational, and so satisfying to us.

When asked why she thought her approach was beneficial to victims, Belinda began to discuss hierarchal approaches:

I don't like that because that takes her personal power away from her, that says your way is not good enough, you have to make it our way, and she has been told she's not good enough for so darn long . . .

While Belinda was not a feminist, she did recognize hierarchy and its impact in individual advocacy. She chose to forgo such controlling advocacy in favor of the survivor-defined model similar to that of feminist advocates. Such ideologies and related practices came from being in an abusive relationship herself and consequently understanding victims' needs.

Feminist programming in organizations also facilitated survivor-defined practices among nonfeminists. Aileen, a feminist director of an organization, delineated the role of feminist programming at Safe Harbor:

. . . Whether individual advocates identify themselves as feminist or not, we have an extremely feminist design in the programming . . . So we design our services to help her take control of her life. It's all about helping her put together the resources she needs to have control of her life, the way that she defines it. So, it's very woman-led advocacy. She defines it. She sets her goals. We help her get the resources she needs and help her understand how to put those together to live a life she wants as she defines it, not how we tell her she needs to live.

43

Aileen's example indicates the significance of programmatic design, which may explain why advocates working at Safe Harbor (a transitional housing program) who did not identify as feminist practiced advocacy reflecting feminist survivor-defined models. For example, when asked if feminism was part of her advocacy, Heidi, who worked with Aileen, maintained that she was not a feminist nor was feminism a part of her advocacy. However, she also went on to describe her practice of survivor-defined advocacy:

> I think it's important to empower them [abused women] to make their own decisions, I think a lot of what we do in advocacy is to provide them with a lot of different resources and suggestions and ideas, but what's really important is to respect their decisions, and respect this is what they've chosen regardless of what we think is best for them, but providing them with the resources to make the best decision . . . that they can stand and be economically independent and empowered to make choices for themselves and their children.

Thus, feminist programming at the organizational level may facilitate survivor-defined models in advocacy organizations.

In addition, training from the [State] Coalition Against Domestic Violence worked to educate advocates on survivor-defined approaches. Nonfeminist advocates described training as very important to developing and maintaining survivor-defined approaches. For example, Eve stated:

> The coalition has come up with a wonderful power and control training for us and we will refer to that. You get job burnout. You get cynical. You become judgmental. And as an advocate you can't! So I don't care if you have heard one story or you have heard fifty stories today, she demands the respect, time and attention. But working in a shelter where you're working 24/7, it gets hard. And you do get tired. But you have to remember why you are here. The [State Coalition] meetings give you kind of a re-set.

In addition to personal experience as a survivor, [State] Coalition trainings and feminist programming in organizations, a majority of nonfeminist advocates found survivor-defined approaches were most effective and adapted to them over time. For example, while Vicki did not identify as a feminist and was not a part of a feminist organization with feminist programming, she described survivor-defined advocacy and how she eventually changed to this form based on her experiences as an advocate:

> You know I think that until they're [victims] ready to make their own decision regardless, like it doesn't matter what you tell them. . . "I'm not here to tell you to get a divorce, to stay, to leave, I just want to make sure that you have all of the options that are available to you, so that you can make the best decision for you." I guess when I was younger I probably had a different philosophy, "you need to do this, this and this type thing" and it doesn't get you anywhere. You find out they are less likely to call back [an advocate] in that case . . .

Vicki was asked, "Is that why you changed your model?" and she said:

> Mmmm hmmm, and that's when I worked at Family Services, "you need to do this, this and this," and then I guess with age, time and I guess just, experience, you realize it doesn't work. So it's up to them to figure out what works best for them and then go from that point.

Vicki, while not a feminist, concluded that hierarchal or controlling advocacy did not work, and gave victims lack of recourse if they felt their choices were dictated. While arrived at through experience rather than through feminist ideologies, Vicki's viewpoint was otherwise identical to feminist advocates in regard to safety. Nonfeminists practiced survivor-defined advocacy, a feminist practice, albeit without the feminist label.

Social Change Practices

While all advocates practiced survivor-defined advocacy, the social change activism component of feminist advocacy was conspicuously absent from all the advocates who were not feminists. In contrast, of feminist advocates, all but one described that social change activism was a part of their practices. Feminist advocates spoke freely about social change activism without being specifically asked about it. For example, Anais delineated the difference between feminist advocacy and social service provision. Her example indicated that to her, advocacy also included social change activism:

45

I think that certainly some advocates look at it as just like a social service job that we are providing and that's not as interesting to me, because we are not really changing anything or making things better... when in reality if we are not only getting women to safety but also getting them resources or support to make their life better, they are less likely to go back to their abuser and are more empowered not to get into abusive relationships in the future. But we are also [not only] sending the message that domestic violence is wrong, and you don't deserve to be treated that way to the women, but to the general community so [if] we are creating a community where DV [domestic violence], and then also the oppression of women, is not tolerated or accepted, then it is making the community a safer place for all women that live there, so that's interesting and exciting to me.

Anais described her advocacy as including societal changes in perceptions of both gender and intimate partner violence. Like Anais, Shelli suggested that feminists are those who recognize gender inequality and actively seek to change it. Her social change ideology and activism was interrelated with her feminist identity. Shelli elaborated on the interconnectedness of social change and feminist identity, describing how she liked asking other women if they were feminists:

I love asking people those questions. So you'd rather not have a checking account in your name? Don't want to vote, huh? Don't want to own property, do ya? Don't want to keep your birth name? Ohhh okay. [The women I ask say] "Yeah I want to do all of those things," [I say] Then you're a feminist! Do you realize that there is inequality and oppression? That's all, and then the next step is that you have to commit to actively do what you have to do, to bring that system down, because I don't believe that you can be a feminist just by recognizing it. You have to do it. You have to commit to do something, and I don't care if it's a small little thing, but you have to commit to do something. You are not a bystander.

Shelli further described how social change was a part of her approach to advocacy largely through community activism, education and awareness programs, and activism through the local feminist coalition. Similarly, Glenda stated:

Well, I think it [social change] means to have a level playing ground, to have a model of self-empowerment, a participative model; to do everything you can to change the patriarchal system in which we live in, and to really do everything that I can to change the 'isms' in our culture.

In contrast with Shelli, Anais, Glenda, and other feminist advocates, Heidi, who did not identify as feminist, emphatically stated:

I don't describe myself as the reason I do this work is because of being feminist. I think it's that, so feminism is basically empowering women and I am that but I hesitate to say I'm feminist as to why I do this work. I do this work because I care about women and children. It's not because of a greater cause of women's rights.

Heidi indicated that to her, feminism and women's rights were unrelated to victim advocacy. She believed feminism included social change activism and, unlike the feminist advocates, she did not support that in her own advocacy. At the same time, she supported her co-workers' right and desire to engage in social change activism.

Shelli, Anais, and the other advocates with social change perspectives largely highlighted community education as a part of their social change practices. In other words, they worked in schools, colleges, universities, hospitals, and police departments to provide education about the dynamics involved in domestic violence. They also emphasized being active in changing social systems in the community through their activism and in the justice system, with child protective services and in shelters. This activism was almost exclusively present in largely feminist Faulds County, although one feminist advocate in Glawe County, Kari, described writing an article for publication that she saw as activism within academia, and she tried to change a shelter rule without success. Feminist identity generally predicted social change practices, and also predicted intersectional practices as well.

Intersectional Practices

Of those identifying as feminist, the majority had perspectives emphasizing women's varied experiences with abuse and with social systems based on their sexual orientation, ethnicity, disability, racial, and class distinctions. Advocates with intersectional practices recognized such distinctions and actively sought to mitigate potential bias in the system in their practices. Thus, current feminist practices in both Glawe and

Faulds County generally combined survivor-defined practices, intersectional approaches, and social change activism. For example, when asked if feminism played a part in her advocacy, Jean described an intersectional approach:

> Well, feminism plays a huge role in advocacy, partly because when you are working with a woman as an advocate you have to see how she fits in this societal stratification, not only she is a woman but . . . she may be a black woman, she may be a lesbian woman, she may be a disabled woman . . . there's all of these layers of oppression and you have to really understand those to be able to advocate for a woman, that's true with the police, with the courts, with our agencies, with our own domestic violence agencies, who don't often see the sexism in their own organization, how it may be operating.

Jean believed feminist advocacy included not just recognition of gender inequality, but how other identities women hold affect their experiences with domestic violence, victim services, and the justice system. Like Jean, advocates with intersectional approaches stated this perspective was imperative in order to know how to advocate for women's individual needs, and to counter the various biases such women experience because of sexual orientation, ethnicity, race, or other social identities.

For example, Kari described how some officers did not take cases of domestic violence seriously when it occurred in the context of a gay or lesbian relationship. She recognized some biases among a few officers and she recalled talking to them to get better results for the victims she worked with in rural Glawe County. The following example illustrates Kari's intersectional feminist practices in her advocacy:

> I think a lot of times there are a lot of assumptions about gender roles from all over the place from officers and what not—so things like that as a feminist like I do bring that in, I'm like, "Really? Why is that relevant?" Or if they are a gay couple. "Since when do GLBTQ folks not have the same rights under the law? It doesn't matter that they are gay!" I do bring it [intersectional practices] in a lot.

Kari went on to describe educating some officers about the gender dynamics of domestic violence, and how these dynamics play out with gay and lesbian couples in the same way. Aileen expressed similar sentiments:

> Male victims are overwhelming abused by other males so it's still male violence and certainly there are women who are abused by other women, but it always goes back to, it's the power and privilege dynamics and power and pressure dynamics, and whether they fall strictly on gender lines. What we find is there is still gendering of a certain nature within those relationships that a feminist framework really helps us understand; and that, in same sex relationships where there is an abusive partner somebody is taking control of the resources or preventing somebody else from taking control of resources, and how they "do" gender can often have a lot to do with where they are in sort of 'access to resource' stratifications.

Feminist frameworks were applied to understand gender dynamics in gay/lesbian relationships involving domestic violence as well. Thus, the majority of feminist advocates suggested intersectional practices could be used to address potential systemic bias.

In contrast, nonfeminist advocates did not recognize the inequalities that their feminist counterparts both recognized and addressed. For example, Vicki, who worked with Kari, was prompted about intersectional practices. When asked, "Does the race, class, or sexual orientation of the women you work with factor into your advocacy?" Vicki replied, "No, I don't think so." She was then asked, "Do you notice a difference in the responses of officers or judges?" Vicki stated, "No. I would say no." In the current study, feminist identity was associated with intersectional practices; advocates who did not have an intersectional frame of reference did not recognize intersecting identities and the potential for inequalities that their feminist counterparts did recognize and specifically advocated towards.

Conclusion

In sum, feminist identity largely predicted social change and intersectional practices. However, both feminists and nonfeminists practiced survivor-defined advocacy. While nonfeminist advocates were practicing survivor-defined advocacy, social change and intersectional approaches were absent from their practices. As rural advocates were less likely to identify as feminist, they were less likely to have social change and intersectional approaches. However, both advocates that did identify as feminist in rural Glawe County expressed intersectional feminist advocacy, and one feminist advocate incorporated social change practices into her advocacy. Because justice system advocates in both counties were more likely to identify as feminist, they were also more likely to hold social change activist perspectives and intersectional approaches compared to their counterparts in traditionally feminist organizations. However, the majority of advocates in Faulds County in the traditionally feminist organizations did identify as feminist and had such perspectives and approaches as well, whereas none of the traditional advocates in Glawe County did (see Table 1, p. 52).

Why does it matter if advocates have feminist identities and corresponding ideologies? Simply put, because identity guides their practices. The majority of advocates in this study did identify as feminist. They had feminist ideologies and survivor-defined, intersectional, and social change practices. While the survivor-defined model reigned within practice, nonfeminists did not recognize gender dynamics of domestic violence and socio-structural gender inequalities. They also did not have social change perspectives. Advocates may run up against system obstacles in the courts, with police, and with social services—and removing those obstacles requires system change. Advocates who are not feminist may not recognize those obstacles, or think they are acceptable. Failure to recognize systemic gendered inequality and processes leading to revictimization does not work to change those gendered processes or even to address them.

In addition, most advocates identifying as feminist expressed intersectional feminist perspectives and thus recognized barriers based on intersecting identities. Nonfeminists who are unable to see such barriers relating to societal unequal distributions of resources by gender, race, class, sexuality, disability, and immigrant status are unlikely to work to change such barriers, and may not be able to advocate specifically to explicit needs. An intersectional approach to advocacy works toward recognizing individual identities and backgrounds and how they relate to domestic violence, and can also work to avoid potential biases within the system.

Why does it matter if advocates maintain feminist identity and representation? It is important to recognize domestic violence as gendered or the context for why violence occurs is lost. It is predominately male-to-female violence as a display of power and control, not neutral "family violence" (Dobash et al., 1992; Ferarro, 2001; Osthoff, 2001; Goodman & Epstein, 2008; Britton, 2011). Violence against women is primarily the context in which domestic violence occurs and early feminist social change targeted that explanation by developing coalitions, hotlines, shelters, and collaborative responses. If the perception of domestic violence becomes neutral and it is not recognized as largely male-to-female violence, social change efforts will not be targeted accurately—or exist at all. Similarly, resource allocation may also be targeted inaccurately. Certainly male victims are important, but because their victimization occurs in much smaller numbers, resource allocation should parallel this dynamic accordingly. For example, "hot spot policing" targets geographic areas that have higher rates of crime. Increased presence of officers and patrols are provided in these high-crime areas because of the greater need. Similarly, resources directed toward women experiencing abuse should be greater, because of the greater need for them. However, if intimate partner violence is perceived as gender "neutral," this context is absent. At the same time, intersectional practices should also emphasize the unique experiences of male victims, and their specific needs within various systems addressing domestic violence.

Research suggests that survivor-defined, intersectional, and social change practices produce better outcomes for victims of abuse. Survivor-defined approaches are associated with lower levels of future abuse, higher rates of leaving an abusive partner, further legal action toward an abuser, use of multiple services, and higher satisfaction with services (Allen et al., 2004; Goodman & Epstein, 2008; Weisz, 1999; Zweig & Burt, 2006, 2007). Social change activism has produced all of the social services and justice system resources currently available to domestic violence victims (Goodman & Epstein, 2008). Intersectional approaches work to increase access to services, address individual and systemic bias, and better meet the needs of survivors from various backgrounds and identities (Arnold & Ake, 2013; Bent-Goodley, 2004; Donnelly et al., 1999, 2005; Richie, 2005; Sokoloff, 2005). Consequently, it is important to facilitate such practices in advocacy, as their absence would be detrimental to survivors of abuse. The following chapters explore how advocates used their survivor-defined, intersectional, and social change practices in community-based responses, further clarifying the importance of such practices.

Table 1

Participants	Self-Identified Feminist	Feminist Ideologies	Survivor-Defined Practice	Social Change Practice	Intersectional Practice
Rural Justice System					
Summer	No	No	Yes	No	No
Kari	Yes	Yes	Yes	Yes	Yes
Vicki	No	No	Yes	No	No
Jasmine	Yes	Yes	Yes	No	Yes
Rural Traditional					
Eve	No	Yes	Yes	No	No
Deb	No	No	Yes	No	No
Gwen	No	No	N/A	No	No
Beth	No	No	N/A	No	No
Metro Justice System					
Teresa	Yes	Yes	Yes	Yes	Yes
Emily	Yes	Yes	Yes	Yes	Yes
Liz	Yes	Yes	Yes	Yes	N/A
Amy	Yes	Yes	Yes	Yes	Yes
Charlotte	Yes	Yes	Yes/No	Yes	N/A
Annie	Yes	Yes	Yes	Yes	Yes
Metro Traditional					
Aileen	Yes	Yes	Yes	Yes	Yes
Anais	Yes	Yes	Yes	Yes	Yes
Heidi	No	No	Yes	No	No
Sheila	No	No	Yes	No	N/A
Belinda	No	No	Yes	No	No
Glenda	Yes	Yes	Yes	Yes	Yes
Jean	Yes	Yes	Yes	Yes	Yes
Gillian	Yes	Yes	Yes	Yes	Yes
Cheryl	Yes	Yes	Yes	Yes	N/A
Shelli	Yes	Yes	Yes/No	Yes	Yes
Delia	Yes	Yes	Yes	Yes	Yes
Ingrid	Yes	Yes	Yes	Yes	Yes

Chapter 3

Advocacy in the Justice System

The justice system is labeled as a masculine organization; as its actors, leadership, hierarchy, and structure are largely male dominated. Further, the policies and practices in the justice system related to domestic violence are at times gender "neutral" or patriarchal gender-based in nature. Chapter 3 illustrates how survivor-defined, social change, and intersectional practices work to mitigate revictimization of battered women in the justice system focusing on areas where advocates collaborated with the justice system the most: protective orders, pro-arrest, and no-drop prosecution. While generally supporting these criminal justice interventions and using them as tools for advocacy, advocates simultaneously recognized the potential for resulting batterer-based and systemic revictimization directed toward the women they advocated for. Advocates consequently developed strategies to avoid revictimization resulting from such difficulties. Generally, nonfeminist advocates used survivor-defined approaches to respond to these challenges, and feminist advocates used survivor-defined, intersectional, and social change approaches. Chapter 3 delineates how policies and practices within the justice system can be gendered in multiple ways, and how advocates responded through their own gendered practices—sometimes in contradictory ways.

Protective Orders

Efficacy of Protective Orders

Gaining recourse for battered women through the justice system was a primary goal of the battered women's movement. The availability of protective orders is regarded as a milestone in the battered women's movement because it was one of the first steps the justice system took in becoming actively involved in addressing domestic violence (Shepard & Pence, 1999; Goodman & Epstein, 2008). Protective orders gained widespread availability throughout the 1980s, largely due to feminist social change activism (Schecter, 1982). Currently, all 50 states provide some form of order of protection for victims, although the terminology and

53

meaning may vary from state to state and even from jurisdiction to jurisdiction; such as "protective order," "restraining order," and "order of protection" (DeJong & Burgess-Proctor, 2006; Goodman & Epstein, 2008; Jordan et al., 2010). Protective orders legally bar or place limitations on abusers' contact with victims (Logan et al., 2005; Goodman & Epstein, 2008). Protective orders generally include a "stay away" provision, which aims to limit abusers' contact with victims by preventing them from going to the home, workplace, or school of the victim. Protective orders may also include "no contact" provisions, which aim to prevent other forms of intimidating or harassing contact such as e-mails, phone calls, or delivering items to the home. Orders of protection can also be somewhat tailored to the situation—such as arranging child custody and visitation, mortgage and support payments, use of any shared vehicles, or requiring abusers to relinquish firearms (Sorenson & Shen, 2005; Goodman & Epstein, 2008). Generally, a victim of abuse will first gain a temporary order, and then file for a permanent order if it is desired. Protective orders are not strictly mandatory in cases of domestic violence reported to police, but they may be required in specific instances, or encouraged by various anti-domestic violence stakeholders. For example, some shelters may require women to obtain an order of protection to gain entry to the shelter; or if child protective services are involved, generally a protective order is necessary to retain custody. Police may also encourage obtaining an order of protection, particularly in cases involving repeated calls over a period of time.

Survivor-defined Practices

All advocates practiced survivor-defined advocacy in addressing the use of protective orders, and based their advice to victims on each woman's individual case. Advocates primarily focused on collaborating with and facilitating the choices of battered women. Survivor-defined practices were imperative in the protective order process, as advocates found a "one size fits all" approach to be injurious to some battered women. While advocates unanimously supported the availability of protective orders as an option, they consistently stressed the importance of survivor-defined advocacy to victims' safety. In some cases an order of protection stopped the abuse, but in other cases, it could increase the abuse. Thus, whether advocates recommended protective orders or not was determined by collaborating with survivors and listening to their assessments of their batterers. Using women's knowledge of their batterers and situations is a cornerstone of survivor-defined advocacy.

First, all advocates described protective orders as a potential tool to help victims avoid revictimization from their abusers. For example, Jasmine said, "Sometimes it will stop somebody. Sometimes when someone else knows about the abuse, they [the abuser] will back off." Advocates unanimously agreed that in some cases, a protective order was enough to deter future abuse of the women they worked with. Advocates unanimously stated that protective orders could sometimes deter abusers from continuing their abuse. This finding is consistent with a wide body of literature examining the effectiveness of protective orders, which finds that victims with permanent orders of protection are less likely to experience re-abuse (Keilitz et al., 1997; Epstein et al., 2009; Goodman & Epstein, 2008). Like Jasmine, other advocates also noted that an order of protection stopped the abuse in some cases, and provided other benefits as well. For example, Shelli stated:

> Well, you know for that abuser who in all other senses is law abiding, it will keep him away from her, and it shows her abuser that she's beginning to break away and that she is willing to take the steps necessary to do that. She is going to bring the community behind her to do it! That's the biggie; see when you get an Order of Protection what she's feeling is "the community is now supporting me in these efforts." She feels that and that's really, really important.

In this example, Shelli noted that protective orders could deter some abusers, resulting in safety. In addition to safety, protective orders could provide empowerment to survivors; another cornerstone of survivor-defined advocacy is empowerment. Shelli continued to describe orders of protection as providing empowerment to survivors:

> It gives her the opportunity to publicly declare that this person has done something to her. It's a big step in her taking back some of that power from him. So there's a lot to be said for what it does psychologically.

Like Shelli, other advocates also indicated that when survivors made the decision to file for a protective order, it represented a shift in power, where they aimed to prevent their abusers from controlling or harming them.

Further, a majority of advocates explained that orders of protection also offered some women further assistance that went beyond protection from abuse. For example, Gillian indicated that protective orders provided benefits because they gave victims credibility in the eyes of people they may need help from:

> The benefit may be that the police are going to take you more seriously, and you need the police to take you more seriously. That may end up being a benefit, it may protect her because the police are going to be more responsive. It may not change the abuser's behavior, but it may change the people's behavior that she needs to help her. It may help her with her employer, it may help her with her landlord. People that she needs to be on her side in some way, may be more inclined to be on her side if she has this sort of protection.

Similarly, Eve explained that the justice system took victims more seriously when they had a protective order:

> It is the legal protection that she needs for police officers to respond. It sets up visitation, it sets child support, and without that legal document there is nothing that the courts or the police officers can do to protect her if the abuser keeps coming back, and coming back, and coming back.

Moreover, depending on the situation, having a protective order could provide additional benefits to battered women with children. Gillian indicated that the use of survivor-defined practices was helpful in addressing concerns of the women she worked with in terms of the children:

> I think for women who have decided to get an Order of Protection, it's sorting out, "is this going to be helpful or not? Is this going to make matters worse?" And sometimes she may think that it would make matters worse, like it's going to aggravate him and he's like to escalate, but there maybe things about it that are still real important to her. So one of the things that an Order of Protection can do is gives her a document as to who has custody of minor children that they have in common, so if she is someone who's worried that when she splits from him he's going to try to snatch the kids then she may find that an Order of Protection could be helpful to her in that regard even if it might light a fire under him in another way. Because if he takes the kids there's just nothing to say who the kids belong with. So he could take the kids, take them to

his mom's. She could call the police and say, "He took my kids, he took my kids!!" The police can't tell by looking at the kids, "do they belong here or do they belong there?" And they will often say, "there's nothing we can do, you have to work this out in court." If she has the Order of Protection already worked out, she can say, "please no, the kids go with me." So again, woman defined advocacy, finding out what worries her around separation, what are her concerns and bringing up things, like "so what about the kids? Any worries about the kids? Has he ever said anything to make you concerned that if you split up from him, he was going to snatch the kids?" So to find out, are there benefits as well as risks, then take it from there.

Her example clearly delineates survivor-defined practice; Gillian worked with her clients to see if a protective order was a good choice in each individual circumstance. By collaborating with survivors, advocates could uncover concerns that protective orders could potentially address. In some cases, protective orders deterred abuse and provided empowerment and recourse through the justice system.

Yet, advocates suggested that the efficacy of a protective order varied widely. While recognizing that orders of protection provided significant benefits for some, advocates consistently delineated that orders were not effective for others. While advocates cited benefits of protective orders as including psychological empowerment, usefulness with others in the community, and protection from further abuse, advocates clearly recognized that different women had different needs, a central tenet of survivor-defined advocacy. For example, when asked what the benefits and challenges to protective orders were, Cheryl replied:

Well in theory, the benefit is that it will keep the perpetrator away from the victim and will keep her safer, in theory. In practice, it can have an opposite effect. So I mean we have a lot of women that don't want Orders of Protection and rightfully so, that oftentimes it just makes the perpetrator angrier. So it can harm the woman more than not having the Order of Protection. The perpetrator just sees it as a piece of paper and it's not really anything that can truly defend her or protect her that okay, so if he kills her or hurts her, then you can say "there was an Order of Protection there that he broke the Order of Protection," but is it actually going to protect her? No! So I don't know, I think for some men it stops them, so it's a good thing in certain circumstances, because some men will see it as "okay I need to abide by the law and I'm not supposed to talk to her and so I won't," but in some circumstances it doesn't.

Like Cheryl, a majority of advocates in both regions and those working in both justice system and traditionally feminist settings noted that protective orders were enough to stop otherwise law-abiding abusers, but high-risk abusers did not abide by them. Advocates regularly described high-risk abusers as those who had criminal records and a criminal history of abuse. In such cases, a protective order was not necessarily the best option. Liz provided a typical response of advocates:

> I think that they [orders of protection] have been a blessing and a curse. Some days I think that they are the most useless piece of paper that was ever printed, because they don't really do any good, but, they do for a certain type of population. So if I'm the kind of batterer that, I've been in and out of prison, and I'm not at all intimidated by the police, an order of protection is useless against me . . . So they are not a silver bullet, but I do think that for probably 85 percent of cases they are important.

Summer conveyed the benefits and challenges of protective orders in such case-by-case variation, and the sometimes extreme end-result of domestic violence:

> Temporary orders and orders of protection are wonderful for law abiding citizens—that being said we have had a couple of domestic murders here in the last year—they both had orders. It's great for people who say "ohh my gosh, I would never break the law and I'm going to abide by it."

These findings coincide with prior research; in a meta-analysis of thirty-two studies, Spitzberg (2002) found on average 43 percent of protective orders were violated, and violence increased in 21 percent of cases. Further, a large body of research finds that abusers with a criminal history are more likely to violate orders and perpetrate further abuse, putting victims at increased risk of revictimization (Keilitz et al 1997., 1998; Klein & Tobin, 2008; Jordan et al., 2010). For example, Jean described a case in which an abuser was a regular law-breaker, and did not take the justice system seriously:

... and that's where an order of protection doesn't do much good at all. For those women, an order of protection is likely to put them in danger, that's why I think so many of the women that I've worked with do not want an order of protection is simply because they know that it's going to make things worse in their situation. It's going to make him mad, he's not going to care. For one thing he doesn't think he's ever going to really go to jail over an order of protection. He feels that he can violate it with impunity. I've seen this happen where women have gotten an order of protection, he keeps violating it, but he runs away before the police get there. So, she feels very helpless. So the order of protection that she felt was really going to help her stay safe does not help at all. Of course, we all know of incidences where women have an order of protection and they still end up being killed by their abusive partner. Thank goodness it's rare, but it does happen.

Similarly, Shelli stated:

The bad thing about it is that everybody thinks it's an automatic fix and it's not. You know, some guys it just ticks them off even more. So she has to really know how he's going to respond to this Order of Protection. Is it now going to make him so angry that he's going to become more physically violent, or is it going to push him to where he starts stalking, which is sometimes more psychologically damaging. So those are the bad things. The other bad thing it is that in so many jurisdictions he can violate that Order of Protection so many times and nothing happens to him. There are no repercussions.

Thus, in particularly high-risk cases where abusers had a criminal history and had no regard for the law, advocates noted that protective orders could be ineffective. Because victims' individual situations varied, advocates used survivor-defined approaches to determine whether a protective order was the best course of action. This involved collaborating with victims to uncover predictions of abusers' behaviors. Summer described her survivor-defined approach to advocacy in the protective order process:

An order of protection is such a touchy thing, and being an advocate I think most people think that is probably the first thing that we want our victims to do and it isn't. Normally what we tell victims is, "You know him better than anyone. Is this going to help you, or is this going to hurt you?" So we leave it up to them to use their best judgment.

Chapter 3

Like Summer, advocates used survivor-defined approaches to determine whether a protective order was the best course of action, and to assess whether or not they were dealing with a high-risk abuser. Gillian described how survivor-defined advocacy worked to provide safety to women in such situations:

> The person who said "I'll kill ya, you serve me with any papers I'll kill ya." Who's made a lot of threats about that, I'll be telling them [victims] a little bit about what it [order of protection] is and then saying, "So tell me how you think he'll react when he gets served with those papers?" So the woman that says something to the effect, "He will be over here in a heartbeat, pouring gasoline around the house and lighting a match,"—not a good thing—so I find that an order of protection is a really good way to talk about woman defined advocacy and how it can play out, because, what makes it good or bad, you learn about by talking with the woman.

Her example indicates how important recognizing individual cases and needs are to women's ultimate safety. Similarly, Kari described her survivor-defined approach to advocacy in determining whether a protective order would benefit or harm the women she worked with:

> Well, I think some of the challenges are sometimes it can make the guy more mad, and I think a lot of times it works for the suspects who are somewhat afraid of the system, but for those who aren't afraid of the system and think they can always subvert everybody, I can see an order of protection might make things worse. So I always tell victims, "You know best, do you think he would actually abide by this order? Do you think it would scare him enough to stay away or do you think it would make things worse?" And they know the best answer. Sometimes they will tell you, "Yeah once he gets served with this thing he is just going to ignore it and then start calling me all of the time and maybe come to my house." Or some might be like, "Yeah I think it might scare him enough to stay away from me." It really varies on a case-by-case basis. I always leave it up to the victim, "You know him best. Do you think this would be something that would be useful for you?"

All advocates used such survivor-defined practices to determine their recommendations to victims. They unanimously described approaches similar to Kari and Gillian. They consequently avoided controlling practices; they worked collaboratively with victims and put control over the decision to get a protective order in the hands of the women they worked with, all central tenets of survivor-defined advocacy. This approach is comparable to that of the early grassroots feminists. They used survivors' input and knowledge of their abusers to predict the outcome of gaining a protective order, and planned accordingly. In the case of high-risk abusers, advocates emphasized that it was imperative to use survivor-defined practices to avoid further victimization. This was a feminist-gendered practice, whether individual advocates labeled it as such or not, because it highlighted women's control, agency, and assumed they were capable decision makers. As indicated in chapter 2, both feminist and nonfeminist advocates engaged in survivor-defined practices. Using survivor-defined approaches to determine whether or not to recommend an order is also supported by the research literature, which finds that collaboration between victims and advocates produces the best outcomes (Jordan, 2004; Goodman, Dutton, & Bennett, 2000; Weisz, Tolman & Saunders, 2000; Heckert & Gondolf, 2004; Campbell, 2004). As the benefit of an order of protection varied according to the response of the abuser, the known limitations to orders and specifics of individual cases were imperative to safety planning.

Safety planning was a big part of survivor-defined advocacy. While survivor-defined advocacy assumes women's agency as a feminist model, it also enables agency by providing information and resources so women can make their own informed choices. For example, in addition to asking women about whether a protective order would be a good choice in their situation, Summer described the importance of talking with victims about the limitations of an order of protection in individual cases as a strategy to best plan for safety:

> We try to make sure that the victims that we deal with are very educated about what that piece of paper is and how it works and that you don't have a false sense of security because you got this, because it doesn't mean that he isn't going to come and find you.

A large volume of research finds that the support of an advocate focusing on developing a safety plan is crucial in avoiding further violence (Goodman, Dutton, & Bennett, 2000; Weisz, Tolman & Saunders, 2000; Heckert & Gondolf, 2004; Campbell, 2004). In fact, many women may underestimate their risk (Campbell, 2004). However, when women collaborate with advocates and develop safety plans, their understandings of risk and their likelihood of revictimization is reduced (Nichols, 2013a).

61

Advocates in this study were acutely aware of the importance of such a safety plan. Importantly, development of such a plan relies on collaborative practices between advocates and victims, another component of feminist advocacy. When women are involved in their safety plan, their outcomes are improved (Goodman & Epstein, 2008). Such survivor-defined practices are feminist gender-based because they facilitate the agency of battered women. Thus, safety planning was tailored to the predicted efficacy of protective orders uncovered through survivor-defined approaches, largely following the gendered ideologies of collaboration and empowerment similar to that of early feminist advocacy.

Intersectional Practices

Advocates were also able to make use of protective orders in their intersectional approaches to advocacy. Advocates reported protective orders were more or less likely to be effective depending on their client's social backgrounds. For example, Jean found protective orders were potentially more beneficial in cases involving immigrants:

> It is so individualized to the situation, because for some women getting an order of protection is going to really help. An immigrant woman in particular, where her abusive partner may fear deportation, especially. Even though that's not likely to occur, they [abusers] still worry about it, and so an order of protection can be very helpful in keeping an abusive partner away from a woman who is being abused, or help to deescalate or stop some of the violence that he is perpetrating.

Jean illustrated both survivor-defined and intersectional approaches to advocacy in this example. It is survivor-defined because she was looking at women's individual cases, and offered support that was tailored to the situation. It is intersectional because Jean recognized how immigrant identities may shape the outcome of getting a protective order. Thus, intersectional approaches take survivor-defined practices a step further by looking specifically at social identities.

Several other advocates noted social class as important in choosing whether a protective order was a good option for victims. Recognizing class identities and their association to protective order outcomes is an example of intersectional advocacy, Jean said:

Also if he's an important businessman or something and he doesn't want to be served at his office with a summons related to an order of protection, or they just don't want to be in trouble with the law [it would be useful]; but a lot of abusive men do not care about that at all, and that's where an order of protection doesn't do much good at all . . .

This is another example of how intersectional approaches can relate to survivor-defined advocacy. Social class may be related to the effectiveness of a protective order, but advocates must look at individual cases and the survivor's assessment of her abuser before making a recommendation. A majority of feminist advocates used intersectional approaches in determining whether to recommend getting an order of protection or not.

In contrast, nonfeminist advocates did not describe using intersectional approaches in their survivor-defined practices. In fact, they did not recognize a difference or see the importance of women's social backgrounds. Feminist identity facilitated intersectional practices in the protective order process. This is notable because agency and empowerment, as well as outcomes, derived from survivor-defined approaches may look different depending on victims' social identities and backgrounds. Nonfeminists may did not see how women's intersecting identities might impact their experiences in the protective order process. Some advocates noted that social identities could be important in interacting with the justice system. Ingrid illustrated a typical response of intersectional feminist advocates:

So, I had this woman in my office, whose abuser poured acid on her car, and broke in the house and took the gun collection and left a nasty note. The neighbors also told her they saw him driving by and sitting on the curb across from the house. So, she was scared. This guy is armed, and was displaying threatening behaviors. So, this is before she found us, she goes in to file for an order, and she's Phillipina. Her English is ok, but you really have to listen. And, I think they just couldn't understand what she was saying, didn't want to bother with her, and they told her she didn't have reasonable fear. I mean, come on!! So, thank goodness she sought help, and she found us here. I had her write it all out, what happened, so we'd get everything, and to prove reasonable fear. And I went with her to the courthouse. I think it helped them having it all laid out on paper, to address the language barrier, but it shouldn't have come to that. They have interpreters, but someone was lazy and didn't bother.

In this example, Ingrid noted that she recognized her client's limited English-speaking abilities likely had a negative impact on her experience trying to get an order of protection. She tailored her advocacy to the situation to get a better outcome for this woman. Without such perspectives and practices, women may experience inequality in the protective order process. Thus, it is important that advocates address systemic bias through survivor-defined and intersectional practices. Nonfeminist advocates were lacking in such intersectional perspectives and practices. In addition to the efficacy of protective orders, advocates indicated that system imposed protective orders were sometimes challenging to their advocacy.

System Imposed Protective Orders

Survivor-Defined Practices

Survivor-defined advocacy was imperative in cases where a mandated protective order could be a safety-risk for a survivor. Most advocates experienced challenges when community agencies required victims to get an order of protection. At times, this was not in the best interests of victims. In such cases, advocates responded by engaging others in various systems in a conversation about individual women's needs, and consequently working toward survivor-defined approaches to meet women's goals. For example, Delia stated:

> There was a push from the Children's Division that they would actually force people to actually get an Order of Protection, and/or in addition to kicking him out of the home, otherwise they were going to take their children, and so, I think there are still a lot of people that are still afraid that that would happen as well.

Delia further described how some women felt getting an order would make the abuse even worse, or put their children at further risk. Delia advocated for women in such cases by calling the director of Children's Division:

So, when that happens, I can make a call to Karen. I know her from a community project we worked on together. I can tell her the case, how the protective order could be harmful, provide documentation that this woman and her child are in a shelter and that she doesn't want the order because she fears it will set him off. She just wants to get out of it as quietly as possible.

Thus, some advocates educated others about victims' cases using information derived from survivor-defined approaches to get better outcomes for the women they worked with. More specifically, advocates solicited responses of others that worked for the individual interests of survivors.

Social Change Practices

In addition to system-imposed protective orders from the Children's Division, advocates also indicated that they experienced challenges with police officers who did not understand safety risks for some women in getting protective orders. Advocates described collaborative responses that facilitated system change as important in helping women negotiate complexities within the justice system. Teresa indicated that she experienced challenges with officers who did not understand safety risks for some women in getting protective orders. She described how officers would try to push women into getting orders, even in high-risk cases. Teresa, and a majority of advocates working in the justice system in both rural and metro contexts, indicated that while some officers were wonderful, other officers were not using survivor-defined approaches. They did not listen to battered women, did not collaborate with them, or consider their individual cases and needs. In such instances, officers' approaches were patriarchal gender-based, because they assumed that abused women were not capable of making decisions about the effectiveness of an order of protection and its consequences for their safety. Instead, officers at times opted for hierarchal practices, which resulted in disempowering battered women. Other advocates made similar statements when asked about challenges to their advocacy in collaborative models: that patriarchal practices by some officers interfered with empowering advocacy. Teresa described how officers would tell women to get protective orders, even in high-risk cases:

65

What's difficult is that they [officers] want to tell her what to do. So they see it as "it's my job to keep her safe by telling her what to do and she should follow what I say." They don't really look at maybe what you think would be harmful. So, like with the orders of protection, sometimes it makes it more harmful for the victim to have that order. It's very hard to get police to understand that—that this could actually get her killed, not help her.

Teresa and other advocates described officers' assumption that abused women were not capable of making decisions about the utility of an order of protection and its implications for their safety. When asked if she could give a specific example where officers might not understand safety risks related to orders of protection and how she responded, Teresa illustrated an incident revolving around the Nuisance Property Law:

There is a nuisance property law that is in effect in [City]. So if some-body calls the police two times in a year for the same reason, they can get a cease and desist letter. And then they [the City] can start charging them for 9-1-1 calls, which ends up domestic violence a lot of the time, are the ones that you are going to get a lot of repeat calls for. You're supposed to do something to change the nuisance. So in most police of-ficers' minds, for domestic violence, that means you get an order of protection. Because then you're telling him to stay away, you want him to stay away. So they [officers] just kind of do that as "you need to go get this otherwise we're going to start charging you."

Teresa met with the Lieutenant, whom advocates noted as having a victim-centric approach, and with the officers to advocate for victims' safety in response to the practices of some officers:

They came up and I was actually talking to the Lieutenant about it. I have a really big problem with them going in and saying that "you have to do this," so we're talking about it and the problem property officers came up. So, we got to the point where we're like it could be more harmful, let her make the choice and [officers said] "Ohh okay, if she can make the choice— maybe it is a little harmful or could be."

Teresa educated officers about survivor-defined practices, and met with the Lieutenant on behalf of victims to promote system change toward survivor-defined practices through hierarchal channels. Similarly, other advocates dealt with this challenge by working toward system change or educating individual officers in the dynamics of domestic violence and safety risks for women. They would seek changes in officers' practices by communicating with their police lieutenant.

Enforcing Protective Orders

Survivor-defined Practices to Address Loopholes

Advocates described loopholes in the system as one of the most common problems with enforcing protective orders. For example, some advocates noted that frequent phone calls, driving up and down the victim's street, continuous harassing e-mails, or other contact on social media were not included in the protective order provisions in their jurisdiction. Rather, they were considered as falling under stalking charges. Thus, in some cases, officers could not legally stop these behaviors through enforcing a protective order. For example, Liz delineated such a loophole: "I think the problem is too, that you call the police and you say, 'he's been driving up and down my street.' Okay, well it's a public street. They can't stop him from driving up and down your street . . ." Emily explained why survivor-defined advocacy is important in addressing loopholes:

> It goes back to that Empowerment Model. If we can explain all of that [loopholes] and help kind of get her or empower her to help gather some of that evidence. If he is calling 12 times a day and she understands that she can save the messages, or keep the log, so that when she does report it to the police, it is so much easier for the police, and it is so much of a better outcome for her because of what she was able to do.

In this example, Emily highlighted the use of survivor-defined approaches in community-based response models. She worked with individual women to assess their needs, and shaped her advocacy to meet those needs. Advocates responded to limitations to protective order enforcement by telling victims the limitations of the law, and developing a strategy revolving around stalking charges. In this way, victims were not as frustrated with police, who they would otherwise perceive as not enforcing the protective order. Victims were encouraged to make a log or journal of intimidating behaviors, which legally did not qualify as violating an order, but could potentially be brought up as stalking charges.

In addition, survivor-defined approaches are intended to be empowering. Thus, not only was advocacy oriented to individual needs in such cases, it also put some level of control in the hands of victims. Such control is associated with positive outcomes, empowerment, and is certainly consistent with the survivor-defined component of feminist advocacy (Zweig & Burt, 2006, 2007; Moe, 2007).

Social Change Practices to Address Loopholes

In August, 2011, a year following the interviews for this book, a senate bill was signed into law which incorporated stalking behaviors as criteria for getting an order of protection and for enforcing it. Thus, the loopholes and challenges described above, such as phone calls, e-mails, driving up and down public streets near victims' homes or workplaces, were addressed by this important bill. Some advocates in Faulds County, and the local and [State] coalition were active in getting this bill signed. Such social change activism resulted in legislation that benefitted battered women, and will benefit battered women for years to come. The bill, as well as advocates' social change activism, would be considered feminist gender-based, because the bill disproportionately impacts women in a positive way by facilitating agency and choices with the end-goal of safety and freedom from harassment. None of the advocates in Glawe County were actively involved in getting the bill signed. This suggests that rural environments may be less conducive to activism. Further, in Faulds County, participation in the local feminist coalition largely drove activism involving the bill. Glawe County advocates did not have access to such a coalition, which likely impacted their noninvolvement as well. In sum, interrelated dynamics of feminism and region were related to social change activism in this context.

Survivor-defined Practices and Community Collaboration

In addition to getting the bill passed and encouraging survivors to log stalking behaviors, advocates noted that they could get assistance with enforcing orders by contacting community partners. Cheryl illustrated how she sought assistance on behalf of her clients, and the importance of a strong local coalition as well as collaboration with police lieutenants or sergeants:

> Most of the collaboration that we do with the police is through our community collaborative meetings, like Family Violence Council and our local [coalition] meetings. So that's on a broader basis, our connection to the Faulds City police. When we have a specific issue with a client we will call either James Hopper or Matt Jones, who are friends on the police force, and talk to them specifically. Where one of our women is in need of some sort of help . . . we feel like we have a contact person that we can advocate on behalf of our clients by calling that contact person, saying "hey this is what's going on with our client."

Similarly, advocates in rural Glawe County worked with the detectives try to get offenders who violated protective orders into the justice system. For example, Summer reported:

> . . . when suspects violate orders . . . those are also cases that we can refer out to DVRU [Domestic Violence Response Unit]. Usually we have ones [abusers] that we see time and time again. Those are ones that we start or have red flagged that this person has violated the order three, four, five times in the past two weeks and our DVRU detective will . . . try to help stop that.

This collaborative strategy worked to reduce further batterer-based revictimization. Thus they used collaborative practices with officers and detectives, and used survivor-defined approaches by getting victims the help they needed and wanted in their individual cases in enforcing protective orders. All advocates, regardless of feminist identity or region, used survivor-defined approaches by first collaborating with victims to understand their needs and goals, and then contacting community members to facilitate those goals. In this way, when survivors had difficulties with abusers who were violating orders, they could get better responses through the justice system.

Survivor-defined Practices involving Problematic Officers

Yet, at times, officers themselves were problematic in enforcing protective orders. Advocates stated that when some officers were called to enforce an order, they took part in victim-blaming behaviors, or behaviors that were revictimizing. Anais described a situation in which she had such a problem with an officer:

> One challenge I've seen is not necessarily giving the correct information to the victim. I never want to bash the officers, they do a great job, but sometimes they will say incorrect things about Orders of Protection. They will say, "don't violate your own order, or we'll arrest you." Well, that's not possible, you can't violate your own order.

Emily indicated officers sometimes said such things as "tough love," with the good intention of keeping victims away from their abusers. Yet, such patriarchal gender-based practices deny women's agency, and prevent women from contacting the justice system in the future according to advocates in this study, because "they no longer trust him [police]." Such police practices may be disempowering, and feminist advocacy in collaborative responses works to change that. Amy indicated that it was important to contact individual officers and educate them, whether it was to inhibit "for your own good" practices, or to address challenges like peace disturbance charges:

> Then at the same time we can talk to them [officers] and say, "Hey, this is how things work, please enforce the order of protection this way and please don't write them up for peace disturbance when he hit her," which sometimes happens.

If women called the police to address enforcement of a protective order, and ended up getting charged for peace disturbance, this inhibited their likelihood of using the justice system in the future, and consequently denied them recourse. Similarly, Emily indicated other problems revolving around enforcing protective orders and officers' practices, with some officers telling victims things that were not accurate:

> I believe that they are well intentioned, but officers will tell her "if I get a call back tonight you're both getting locked up!" Or something like that. Or "if we come over and he's here, you're going to get in trouble for violating your own order of protection." Things like that that aren't true, they can't do that, but I get the feeling that it's a little bit of a tough love kind of thing. That they feel they can be tough with her and say "you need to do this or this is what could happen!"

Emily elaborated when I asked her for an example:

> There was a district officer and he said everything that I would want
> him to say as an advocate. Safety planning, all of this stuff, but he ru-
> ined it in thirty seconds. The last thirty seconds he [said] "and if that's
> not enough to convince you, I'm actually going to take my time to
> come to you next time when you call for help!" I'm like "ohhhhhh."
> Then it's just done, because the victim no longer trusts them. She's not
> going to call the police. She doesn't feel like she's going to get help.
> But he did so good up until that point.

A majority of other advocates, particularly in Faulds County, made
similar statements when asked about challenges to their advocacy in
working with the justice system: that the approaches of some officers
posed safety risks to women. Most advocates, both feminists and nonfeminists in both regions and primarily in the justice system, dealt with
this challenge by attempting to educate individual officers.

System Change and Problematic Officers

However, feminist advocates in Faulds County also dealt with this
challenge by working toward system change. They would educate individual officers, but would also "go to the top" to seek changes in officers' practices by communicating with their police lieutenant. Thus, advocates worked toward system change to promote survivor-defined
advocacy in systems that sometimes challenged it.

Like Amy, justice system advocates in Faulds County were consistently working toward system change by communicating with CBR
members and further incorporating appropriate responses into police
training. Emily said, "In the police academy, they get like 40 hours or
something for domestic violence." She continued, "We just did a six-
hour training for the entire police department last year. I think it was like
37 trainings and it was like 1,000 police officers." Similarly, Teresa mentioned:

> We do the advocate part when we do the training with the police offic-
> ers, and they did it as continuing education training. We've tried to do
> all advocates in one room and the police having a panel so they can

71

explain what they should do [in enforcing orders], and kind of talking back and forth.

Further, Glenda stated how her local coalition supported advocate-informed training of officers:

> I have to give kudos to the Faulds City Metropolitan Police Department. They are very invested in training, or retraining, or refreshing new and established police officers. And the Commander of the Domestic Violence Unit that's Lieutenant Hopper, he is so invested in not only his staff being trained, but himself. You know there is no separation of well I'm the boss now, so . . . it just makes a world of difference he is just fantastic to work with, yes they do their police work. Their charges are different than our charges, but, we could not feel more respected.

In sum, there were regional distinctions in the ways advocates addressed enforcement challenges, and distinctions by feminist identity as well. First, justice system advocates in Faulds County, who were exclusively feminist, regularly incorporated social change practices in their collaboration with police. Advocates in the Faulds County justice system consistently described working with officers to get better outcomes for victims as well as providing education and training to address the challenges in the police departments, and working towards system change through hierarchal channels. System change approaches to advocacy were almost exclusively practiced by feminist advocates in Faulds County. However, justice system advocates in rural Glawe County, of whom only two were feminist, largely did not work toward system change in similar situations. Only one of the feminist advocates interviewed described doing so, and unsuccessfully. Feminist advocates in Glawe County did not have the organizational or community support to advance system change in rural Glawe County. Nonfeminist advocates generally did not take part in system change approaches, although they did work on an interactional level with the domestic violence detectives and officers to get help with enforcing orders. This indicates that feminist identity and corresponding ideologies may result in social change practices in community-based responses to domestic violence, while the absence of feminism leads to the deficiency of such practices. Importantly, organizational and community support for social change also impact system change.

Protective Order Challenges in the Courts

While collaboration with detectives, most police officers, probation officers, and most prosecutors was described in a generally positive light, collaboration with particular judges was labeled as problematic in all regional and organizational contexts. This section highlights how advocates responded to judges' gendered practices in the protective order process through social change and intersectional practices.

Social Change Practices

Some regional differences appeared between the study settings related to social change practices in the courts. In Faulds County, advocates responded to challenges in the courts through social change activism, whereas advocates in rural Glawe County did not incorporate social change activism. This was the same pattern found in responses to problems with officers, explained above. First, advocates in rural Glawe County indicated there was a judge who did not grant orders of protection to battered women who needed them, even with police records indicating evidence of abuse of the victim and prior abuse of the abuser's previous girlfriends. He was described by one advocate as an "asshole" another indicated that he "hates victims" and "absolutely will not work with women who have returned to their abuser, it's a 'you got what you asked for mentality' even though it is against the law." Another advocate, also in rural Glawe County, indicated that their CBR process was coordinated well between various stakeholders, but subverted at the discretion of this same judge in their system. One judge's practices could be described as patriarchal, as the judge was consistently described as victim-blaming towards abused women. Eve stated that it could be difficult to get an order of protection, as the success in obtaining an order largely depended on the presiding judge:

> Especially if the judge in your county is not in favor of giving temporary orders or feels that the temporary order is not necessary. So a woman that truly needs it might be stopped right there at the order part of it and not even receive the legal representation that she needs.

73

Chapter 3

This particular judge refused to give orders of protection, even in the presence of well-documented evidence of reasonable fear. For example, Vicki stated:

> Probably our biggest barrier with orders of protection is the judge that they are heard in front of. I don't know that he quite understands domestic violence. So I've had victims who legitimately should get orders of protection who finally have enough courage to go through, get the application, get the temporary order and then go to court and are denied. So that it just really pushes everybody back two steps in order for them to get to recover and get services.

When asked, "What is the reason that judges give for denying an order of protection?" Vicki replied:

> Like he said to one of my ladies who her husband threatened to slit her throat and he said "has he acted on it?" and she said "well, no!" He replied "you can talk—it's freedom of speech, and basically unless he has acted on it you're not getting it [order of protection]." Now this is somebody who grew up in foster care and has been involved with system after system. So for her it was a big step, to go and apply for an order, but then to have a judge humiliate her in front of her abuser, and she said "I will never go and get an order of protection again! It's just not worth it!"

The judge was assuming that the victim did not understand the threat her abuser posed, and despite her proof of reasonable fear, he determined the abuser was not a threat. This opposes the survivor-defined practices described by advocates. This patriarchal practice denied the victim her agency by not allowing her to use a protective order as a tool for safety.

While nonfeminist advocates recognized a problem with this judge in Glawe County, they did not actively work to change it. A majority of advocates in the rural system were not feminist, and did not have the social change perspective typical among feminists. The advocates who did identify as feminist described hiding their feminist identities, and did not express any social change practices involving the courts. Social change activism was generally not an active part of advocacy in Glawe County, with a few exceptions by one feminist advocate discussed in chapter 5. Thus, the issue with judges remained a significant challenge. This indicates that feminist identity and ideology inclusive of social change activism is important; such systems do not change unless they are actively critiqued and targeted for organizational change. A feminist community is empowering to individual advocates: social change perspectives did not translate into practiced activism without community, coalition, or organizational support.

In contrast, while advocates in Faulds County indicated similar challenges, their strategies also included social change activism. Anais stated that victims had different outcomes depending on the judges in Faulds County. At times, certain judges served as barriers to accessing orders of protection. Anais said:

> They [Faulds County] now have a family law court. There are three judges doing all the orders of protection, but before it was a toss-up who you got. And some judges were great and some weren't. But, overall I've had good experiences with judges. There are a couple who are really bad. They are victim blaming—victim blaming, impatient.

In Faulds County, a majority of advocates said that some judges would not grant orders if a woman had no hospital record, or a partner could not be served, or if a judge was simply victim-blaming. Glenda discussed how some judges provided challenges in which social change activism was warranted: "I think some judges feel like you have to be all beaten up before its domestic violence, you know, how do you prove it?" Jean further described different experiences depending on the judge, some of whom may require strong evidentiary requirements before granting an order:

> Well in my role, I worked mostly with women coming through the emergency room. In what I've seen in court is sometimes the judge really understands domestic violence and understands that women are primarily the targets of domestic violence. So, he sees pretty clearly what's going on. If the abuser is present, and sometimes the abuser will be present, and says that the victim is actually the perpetrator—and these kinds of things happen. Some judges they see through that kind of thing. Other judges I've noticed that they may ask for a lot of particular information and real evidence from the woman who wants an order of protection. They'll want her to bring anything that she may have— photos, testimonials—but mostly they are looking for things like emergency room reports. Those are the things that will weigh more with some judges. Which is unfortunate about that, you know, it means that the abuse often has to go on until somebody needs to make an emergency room visit.

Belinda noted that in metro Faulds County through the local coalition, advocates developed a social change approach to address the problems they were having with judges—a Court Watch Program. The Court Watch Program involved advocates' presence in the court in cases of domestic violence, in which advocates would document unfair decisions by judges, victim-blaming statements, and negative attitudes towards victims. In such circumstances, judges received a written notice from the local coalition of their documented behaviors and in some cases a meeting with advocates was requested. Shelli said, "We do have Court Watch. I think that helps for sometimes judges to know that they are being monitored." Belinda, Shelli, and other advocates described getting better results for women when Court Watch was established. Belinda was not feminist, but she did participate in Court Watch as part of the local feminist coalition. Cheryl, a Faulds County feminist described Court Watch:

> I think that it depends upon the judge and through the years the court watch program that's kind of looked in on how the judges treat the women, how the Orders of Protections are provided and different judges are different. The clients that we've had some are treated more fairly than others. It depends upon the judge, it depends upon the municipality and the county. I think that probably the worst feedback that we get is from Glawe County. It's kind of the feeling that we've gotten from Glawe County is that old boys network out there.

In contrast with Glawe County, this suggests strong local coalitions in Faulds County offered organizational support for social change activism. Court Watch also worked to avoid problematic judges, as it worked to notify advocates of "bad judges." For example, Shelli accompanied women in her shelter to court. When she noted that a "bad judge" was going to be in court to hear the case of the woman she was working with, she did the following:

> What you could do is dismiss a judge without cause—you have to do it as soon as you get the notice of a full hearing. You have to write them and say, "I dismiss Judge X, without cause." I don't ever have to tell you why I did that. You can't do it a second time; you can only do it once [per client]. So sometimes you would do that to get a different judge, or we would call the County and we would find out who's hearing it that week, or that day, and if it was a judge that we knew who was just horrible, we would just tell them [victim] to stay inside the

shelter until tomorrow, and we will go with you tomorrow. You don't want to risk this, getting this today.

Her example delineates that advocates can mitigate the negative responses of judges by avoiding them as part of a Court Watch program. In contrast with Glawe County, social change activism was prevalent in Faulds County, where a majority of advocates described themselves as feminist and indicated social change activism was an integral part of their advocacy. Importantly, even advocates who did not identify as feminist, or express social change ideologies, ended up participating in some form of activism by being part of the local feminist domestic violence community. This suggests the importance of group dynamics: feminist coalitions support social change. Without them, the present research suggests that social change perspectives are less likely to result in activism and consequential system change. At the same time, and important regional distinction was present, in that there was only one judge in rural Glawe County that heard the order of protection cases. This left advocates with few options. Any social change would have involved eradicating this judge in a tightly knit small rural community.

In sum, advocates' narrative accounts are consistent with prior research, in that orders of protection are not always granted when requested based on subjective interpretations of judges or strong evidentiary requirements (Moe, 2007; Römkens, 2006). In addition to subjective judgments, Moe (2000) found "condescending" judges exemplified a patriarchal ideology by supporting the abuser, being firm, victim blaming, and patronizing. Such judges in Moe's study also made inappropriate jokes about abuse and victims' treatment of the abusers. Victims reported feeling degraded and humiliated, illustrating systemic revictimization through judges' practices (Moe, 2000).

While the research in Faulds and Glawe Counties finds similar challenges, it also indicates how advocates respond to such challenges. Advocates in Faulds County, who were predominantly feminist, incorporated social change activism through their local feminist coalition to address the challenges with judges through development of the Court Watch Program. Through this program, advocates in Faulds County also avoided judges who had a record of victim-blaming practices, requiring hospital records, or who had a low rate of granting orders. Advocates in Glawe County expressed that they did not have organizational or community support for change.

Intersectional Practices

A number of advocates described women facing barriers to obtaining an order of protection based on race, limited English-speaking abilities, and sexual orientation. Advocates used their intersectional approaches to understand and better advocate for women experiencing specific barriers to accessing an order of protection. This approach was exclusively described by feminist advocates. For example, Anais declared that there were problems specific to immigrant women in the courts, including barriers to accessing orders:

> I've had a lot of problems in the county with women speaking limited English, not allowing them to use interpreters and asking them to talk directly to the judge when they can't answer the questions because they don't have the language—she can't say what she needs to say directly to the judges. Judges seem to be impatient with using interpreters because it takes twice as long. So I've had judges get really impatient and frustrated and hurry it along without getting the full information for the domestic violence cases. It is challenging for me and the women who are trying to tell their story and maybe not understanding everything. Even if you are proficient in conversational English, when they start throwing around legal terminology, it's even more important that they have an interpreter. It's her future, her life.

In these cases, Anais described working to get interpreters for victims through a local agency and attempting to work with judges in getting translation in the courts. She also described using Court Watch to avoid judges who did not work well with women who had limited English-speaking abilities.

Like Anais, Jean also used intersectional advocacy to identify and advocate for immigrant women. She described particular problems that immigrant women experienced, including how their abusers could manipulate the justice system because of their partners' lack of English-speaking ability:

> With immigrants it's a real problem because when she gets the court Summons, one woman I worked with that couldn't read English—he [abuser] told her that it was just something that says that it's okay for me [him] to stay here, or something like that. Anyway, he didn't tell her what it really said and it was a court summons to appear for this order of protection that he [the abuser] had gotten against her [the

victim]. Well, even if she had gone with him she wouldn't have known what it was for [because she didn't speak English]. And especially I found with men who have been in an abusive relationship prior to this one, where this is not their first abusive relationship, they know all about orders of protection, they have had them taken out against them in the past, and now they are using the court system to get the upper hand with their current partner that they are abusing . . . I have seen that happen quite a bit, and it's a little bit alarming.

She described calling a local non-profit agency that provided interpreters to ensure that women could read the court documents they received. Like Anais and Jean, a majority of feminist advocates also incorporated intersectional approaches in Court Watch, and worked to get interpreters through a local institute. Advocates in Faulds and Glawe Counties support prior research indicating the process of obtaining an order can be difficult for some women, particularly immigrant women whose English-speaking abilities are not conducive to understanding the language of court documents and processes (West, Kantor, & Jasinski, 1998; Moe, 2000). However, advocates' narratives also show how they responded to such challenges.

In addition to limited English-speaking ability, sexual orientation was described as another barrier to getting an order. Two advocates indicated that this had been an issue with accessing an order of protection. Ingrid described an experience with a lesbian woman she worked with:

One woman I worked with who was a lesbian petitioned for an O.P. [order of protection] and she had a lot of documentation, medical and emergency room reports and she had records of really pretty severe physical abuse but the judge denied her O.P.

Jean illustrated how advocates used social change activism along with an intersectional approach to respond to such challenges:

I had a case where I worked with a lesbian woman, and she had been to the emergency room, she had broken bones, and there was strong, strong evidence of domestic violence. But the judge didn't grant her the order. I brought it up at a community meeting and this is something we are going to address because it is unacceptable.

The strong local domestic violence community has a record of taking up an issue and working toward social change, primarily as an extension of Court Watch.

Some advocates in Faulds County indicated that race could be a factor in getting an order of protection as well. Three advocates described a negative perception of African American women in the community as being loud and violent. They suggested that it is important for African American women in particular to maintain a calm demeanor in the presence of police and also in the courts because of this perception. When asked, "Do you think there is a race difference in how judges perceive victims?" Emily stated:

> I will say, you know, racially there is. In my experience in Faulds City, African American women can be—and everyone is going to be different individually—but culturally they are more outspoken . . . like they feel the safety to be angry now [in the courts] and to express that anger and I think that maybe comes off different than it does for someone who is white.

In a conversation about African American women in the protective order process, Teresa said:

> A lot of times people expect the victims to be scared and shy, crying instead of the person who now feels safe—because there is a sheriff standing between them—to yell at the offender. So we try and talk with victims about people's perception of domestic violence as to how they can help themselves get the order of protection. "Don't yell at the offender, even though you are mad at him and you have every right to be." So I think that becomes the difference.

So, keeping in mind the potential for racial biases in CBR, some advocates described using their intersectional approaches and survivor-defined advocacy to help victims understand the importance of demeanor. Interestingly, some advocates themselves appeared to have these biases while simultaneously using them in advocacy. In addition, maintaining an acceptable "victim demeanor" is to some extent patriarchal in addressing or influencing traditional femininity. Yet, if victims do not maintain this demeanor, they may not get their protective order. Prior research notes that outcomes will be different for "good victims," who appear passive, do not fight back, and are white. For example Osthoff

(2001, p. 237) stated, "One of the stereotyped images of a "real battered woman" is that of a timid, literally beaten-down (white) woman who cowers in the corner ... and has done nothing "wrong" (i.e., has never fought back, is very passive ... never yells ..." The biases that advocates reported to be aware of in the justice system are consistent with prior research finding perceptions of Black women victims as angry, violent, or resilient to the extent that they are perceived of as not in need of help, by service providers and by law enforcement (Hill-Collins, 2000; Donnelly et al., 2005; Potter, 2008). Yet the findings additionally suggest that advocates recognized and used their awareness of such biases to mitigate them.

There were significant distinctions in intersectional practices related to feminism. As advocates worked with women consistently in getting orders of protection, they were familiar with the orders and when they can and cannot be legally granted. In considering advocates' expertise and experience in this area, the expectation was that advocates would likely be able to recognize discriminatory practices when they occurred. Yet, all the advocates who described barriers based on individual identities were feminist. There were *no* nonfeminists with such perspectives, and they consequently failed to recognize such biases.

In fact, in Glawe County, when asked about differences in the protective order process by race, class, or immigrant status, nonfeminists indicated that there was no problem and no difference. In contrast, the feminist advocates in Glawe County did recognize differences by individual identities and were able to describe specific examples. For example, Kari said:

> Here's kind of the example, [Glawe] County is extremely low income. Most of our people are kind of the very stereotypical ideal of what you would think of as like trailer park hood. But when we get somebody who isn't like that, people are really excited. People are like "she even has a job!" And she is employed, and really well spoken. So, I think people definitely take notice when people [victims] are educated, better dressed. So I definitely think they get better treatment by police or by judges, or by the prosecutor.

Kari and Jasmine, the feminist advocates in rural Glawe County, delineated class as a barrier. In other contexts, while Glawe County is 97 percent white, and advocates have less opportunity to interact with women of color or immigrant women, feminist advocates in Glawe County indicated limited English-speaking abilities and race as a barrier as well, despite their lower numbers in rural Glawe County. Kari and Jasmine also recognized sexual orientation as a barrier, whereas their nonfeminist counterparts did not.

Survivor-defined Practices

Advocates noted that it was important for judges to be educated in dynamics of domestic violence. At times, an abuser would threaten or manipulate their partner to drop an order of protection, and advocates noted that it was important for judges to be able to sort out whether the victim truly wanted to drop the order, or if her request to drop the order was a consequence of the abuse:

> She may be coming back in because he's got her child and if she doesn't dismiss the Order of Protection she is going to get beaten up as soon as she gets home, but we don't know, and she's not probably going to say that to the judge otherwise the judge is going to be like "I'm not letting this drop!" and it's not about . . . offenders do it. We have had offenders that are here. They will bring her here and sit with the child and you need to go and tell them that you are recanting your statement. You know that it's a bad situation, because they're using the child to get her. Yeah, and she is not doing it of her own free will. I think that's a part of why the judge does it [refuses to drop an order] is because she doesn't know if they are doing it by their free will or if it's somebody else forcing them but then it can still cause a dangerous situations. You can't tell which ones are going to be that way.

Amy noted that "good judges" will work to "sort it out," and both "good judges" and victims benefitted from having an advocate present in the courts to assist both victims and judges in this determination. Amy noted, "you can't ask the victim that in front of the abuser," and further indicated that both judges and advocates had to be savvy to remove responsibility from the victim if she chose not to drop the order. Amy, Anais, and several other advocates maintained that collaboration with judges was particularly important in such cases, to get the best outcomes for victims. Anais provided an example of a "good judge" listening to battered women, and soliciting what they wanted and needed in a drop-order request:

Sometimes the judge, I haven't seen this but after meeting with the judge actually yesterday, she told a story about how a woman came to say I want to drop my order, and she asked her, "Is he here? Is he with you? Is he encouraging you to do this?" "Well, yeah he's outside with my kid. I want to see my kid." They will use the child to either get her to drop the charges or drop the order of protection.

Anais noted that in such instances, judges would collaborate with women and their victim advocates to determine the best course of action. Judges who did not understand aspects of domestic violence, and would not drop an order under any circumstance, represent patriarchal gender-based practices, as this likely represents the "for your own good" mentality that ignores individual cases and needs, as well as women's agency and decision making capabilities. Sometimes women are not coerced into dropping an order of protection; they may want to do so for other reasons. Further, judges who simply dropped orders without listening to victims or their advocates were described as problematic as well. Their gender "neutral" practices ignored dynamics of domestic violence, and the possibility that dropping an order was an extension of the abuse. In contrast, the feminist gender based model included survivor-defined practices involving collaboration and listening to battered women's situations and needs, which facilitated women's agency.

Pro-Arrest

Mandatory or pro-arrest policies were implemented in many states beginning in the early 1990s, in part due to the social change efforts of advocates, who lobbied for greater justice system responses to domestic violence (Goodman & Epstein, 2008). Along with the availability of protective orders, pro-arrest is regarded as another milestone in the battered women's movement. Pro-arrest is also linked to the Duluth Model, described in chapter 1. A field-based controlled experiment by Sherman and Berk (1983) had a large impact on the implementation of mandatory arrest as well. The experiment found that mandatory arrest of batterers was more effective than mediation or separation. Twenty-six states and the District of Columbia implemented mandatory arrest policies or proactive arrest policies by the end of 2005. Mandatory arrest requires an arrest in any call of domestic violence where physical violence is apparent. Pro-arrest does not require an arrest, but arrest is encouraged, a police report must be made, and the choice not to arrest must be rationalized in the report. Such policies meant that batterers were more often arrested. For example, in 1990 in the District of Columbia, only 5 percent of accused batterers were arrested when victims called 911. However, after the implementation of mandatory arrest policy, by 1996, arrests were made in 41 percent of such cases (Goodman & Epstein, 2008).

Research is mixed in the area of mandatory arrest. Sherman and Berk's experiment, described above, is regarded as the first and most well-known. In fact, the study gained so much attention that without further analysis of the findings or replication studies, and without the recommendation of Sherman and Berk, forty-seven urban police departments implemented mandatory arrest policies following the study (Ferraro, 2001). Further research has found different results from Sherman and Berk (1983), including the original researcher (Schmidt & Sherman, 1996), and some research even finds increased reoffending (Sherman & Smith, 1992). Some scholars even find that victims are being arrested along with their abusive partners for self-defensive or retaliatory battering, which is a negative latent consequence of the policy (Ferraro, 2001; Nichols, 2011).

In 1989, [State that Glawe and Faulds Counties are in] enacted pro-arrest. Pro-arrest is similar to mandatory arrest in its focus on holding batterers accountable, but an arrest is not mandatory. Rather, arrest is strongly encouraged and pro-arrest requirements are put in place. Under pro-arrest, if an arrest is not made, an officer is required to write a report stating why an arrest did not occur on a call for domestic violence. Basically, they have to provide a justification for *not* making an arrest. Arrest is the norm, and not making an arrest is supposed to be a qualified exception. In addition, if an officer does not make an arrest and another call from the same address occurs within twelve hours, then an arrest *is* mandatory.

Pro-arrest differs from jurisdiction to jurisdiction in its implementation. Both Glawe County and Faulds County practice pro-arrest under the [State] law. However, in Glawe County, pro-arrest was largely framed *as* mandatory arrest by advocates—they even used the language "mandatory arrest" as opposed to "pro-arrest." Whereas in Faulds County, advocates indicated that the law was in fact "pro-arrest." Advocates in Glawe County specified that in any call to police, the person that used the highest degree of lethality would be arrested, and an arrest was made in all cases if there was any sign of physical violence. Thus, in this rural context, pro-arrest policy took the form of mandatory arrest. In Faulds County, police used more discretion. In fact, in some cases advocates indicated that some officers would not even make a report, or even follow the pro-arrest policy. Yet, in most cases, they noted officers would make an arrest regardless, which advocates generally preferred. In this section, advocates' descriptions of the benefits and challenges to pro-arrest/mandatory arrest, as well as advocates' responses to the challenges of pro-arrest/ mandatory arrest policy are examined.

Social Change Practices

In this research, all advocates unanimously supported the availability of pro-arrest while simultaneously recognizing some of the challenges it posed. Feminist advocates referenced the social change efforts of advocates in the movement that resulted in improved justice system responses. In the experience of two movement veteran advocates, they both detailed how arrests were infrequently made prior to implementation of the policy. The policy caused systemic change, in which domestic violence cases were taken more seriously in the justice system. For example, Emily described how pro-arrest was a positive social change in the battered women's movement. She further stated how this improved the responses of officers:

> I think one of the big benefits of the pro-arrest laws are setting guidelines and standards for the officers. That's not to say that it [not taking dv calls seriously] still doesn't happen, but to some extent it gets away from the situation where officers are coming out like over and over and saying "take a walk around the block," that kind of a thing. They are required by law to proceed with a police report and all of that, if they see that a crime has been committed. I think that it really improves the response.

Other feminist advocates made statements almost identical to Emily's. However, such accounts of system change were exclusively made by Faulds County advocates, as the battered women's movement did not exist in Glawe County and there was no local coalition. In Glawe County, pro-arrest was implemented because of the [State] law, distanced from the efforts of feminist social change advocacy. There was one movement veteran in Faulds County who was involved in getting the policy on a state level more than twenty years ago. In addition to viewing the policy as a result of advocates' feminist social change efforts, advocates related the policy to survivor-defined approaches in complex and competing ways.

Survivor-defined Practices . . . (Kind of) . . .

The most common reasons both feminist and nonfeminist advocates gave in both regions and in both organizational contexts for finding the policy beneficial was that it empowered victims by providing an opportunity to get out of the house without the abusers' interference and gave advocates a chance to offer advocacy. Summer said, "We have time to try to find her a place to go if she so chooses, [or she] certainly has time to deescalate the situation." Basically, arrest resulted in a window of opportunity for advocates to provide survivor-defined advocacy. For example, Vicki's statement was similar to all the justice system advocates in both regions:

> I think with the mandatory arrest, it at least gives us a window to try to make contact with victims while he is not there. Hopefully, then we can talk to them about what has been going on and then encourage them to follow through with prosecution or at least seek services.

Summer further indicated another layer of complexity—that at times victims would act like they did not want an arrest in the presence of their abusers, but would later disclose to advocates that that they did in fact want their abusers to be arrested either to deescalate or to potentially deter the abuse. Summer stated that fear of the abuser resulted in this behavior:

> It's not unusual for us to see victims turn on our deputies when the deputies are trying to arrest the suspects. I think that's something that is really difficult, no matter how much we talk about it, for deputies to understand that the victim maybe really, really wants for him to be arrested but she can't show that she wants for that to happen. We're only going to keep her safe for twelve hours while he is locked up. Twelve hours from now, who keeps her safe? Nobody!

Advocacy in the Justice System

In this particular context, advocates related pro-arrest to survivor-defined practices. Because a victim does not want to be retaliated against after the short period of reprieve—generally twelve hours—she cannot visibly support the arrest in front of the abuser. Consequently, a majority of advocates believed the policy worked in favor of women's choices in these circumstances.

Advocates' responses were consistent across regions and organizational types. Both feminist and nonfeminist advocates unanimously supported pro-arrest. They described the benefits in the following ways: it meant the justice system took domestic violence more seriously than it had in the past, it gave victims some recourse for their victimization, it placed responsibility for arrest on the State not on the victim, and it provided an opportunity to deescalate the situation or gave advocates an opportunity to provide survivor-defined advocacy.

Yet, even with such benefits, advocates simultaneously delineated challenges with pro-arrest because it was a standardized response with little discretion. Advocates, in a direct contradiction, suggested that it resulted in approaches that were not survivor-defined because the victim did not always get to choose whether an arrest was made or not. In some cases, advocates described how victims did not want their partners arrested because they feared retaliation once their abuser was released, regardless of "displacing" blame onto the state. For example, Cheryl stated:

Again, in some situations it can put the woman at more risk, because the perpetrator can get angrier and take it out on her that he was arrested. Often times she doesn't want him arrested. She doesn't want to see any harm being done to him. She just wants him to stop hurting her. So if that's not what she wants, it might make her less willing to call the police if she knows that if she calls the police her husband or partner is going to get arrested. And it depends what happens after the arrest. So if they arrest him and then he is let go right away, what is that actually doing except making him more angry?

Similarly, Amy delineated the benefits and challenges of pro-arrest:

Sometimes it makes the offenders madder, and so as the advocate we think not always . . . it's not always safe to leave, sometimes we say if you feel safe staying, stay. So a lot of times, or sometimes, we will see the offender get locked up and then the victim is mad because when he gets out he or she is going to be so pissed and come back. Although I

87

still think the mandatory arrest policy is good, it sometimes can put the victim in more danger.

Such findings are consistent with prior research. For example Dugan, Nagin, and Rosenfeld (2003) found that some victims in cases of mandatory arrest for protection order violations were at an increased risk of homicide, including white unmarried women and Black unmarried women. Additionally, research suggests that 20–30 percent of batterers who experience mandatory arrest will commit further acts of violence before and after the court process (Goodman & Epstein, 2008).

In a related dynamic, Belinda stated the importance of removing the victim from the arrest situation:

> If the arrest is done by police officers and they don't make any overt connection to the victim, that's one thing. Sometimes they visibly involve the victim in that process and that endangers her. So it's a very scary thing for her to, first of all, call the police, or have maybe neighbors call the police. She feels that only more retribution will be reaped upon her because the police were involved. It's so funny—it's not funny, it's really tragic—how these abusers look at anything and twist it into it's her fault [that he got arrested for abuse], she's constantly being blamed. So if there is any way she can be blamed for it, they will latch on it and then she will pay a price at some point. So if he perceives that she is encouraging arrest, and she may not be at all, but you cannot apply logic to these abusers, you just can't apply the rational thinking that you and I or even the victim would, but they irrationally want to twist it so that it's her fault, they don't want to be accountable. So yes, I think it's a good thing if the victim can be somehow out of the loop, nonvisible or something, and I don't know how easily that can be done, or how difficult that is sometimes, but for her safety.

In the present research, if the victim did not want to leave her abuser and feared retaliation, advocates mitigated the negative side of pro-arrest by calling the abuser after his release to explain the law. They explained that it was not their partner that had them arrested, and their partner tried very hard not to get the perpetrator arrested. For example, Kari stated:

> So then, I'll tell them that, "if he's hassling you, it's not up to you, you didn't do anything, we're doing it [the police department]. I'll talk to him if you need me to. If he needs to call me I would be happy to tell him, 'not up to you.'"

Advocates did not directly resist pro-arrest policy, even though in some cases it was not survivor-defined, such as when women did not want their partners arrested. Advocates' rationale for supporting the policy reproduced both feminist and patriarchal elements of the policy. Support was feminist in its social change agenda to create a society that was not tolerant of violence against women. Yet, while pro-arrest gave women a window to get out of the house safely, or provided a temporary reprieve from the abuse, it was patriarchal because the arrest occurred without the victim's input or consent. For example, Jean described a typical case:

> I certainly have had that happen a number of times and it's not only because they're afraid that the violence will be worse but it is often because they generally don't want him to get into trouble, they just want to get away, or get safe but they don't necessarily want to get into trouble, and with immigrants, especially, they are worried about deportation and things like that.

Further, Cheryl illustrated victims' lack of choices in pro-arrest in the context of control and future use of services in the justice system:

> Well, I think that if she knew that if she would call the police that she would no longer have a choice of whether to press charges, or to leave, or whatever, that the decisions were just by that first phone call the ball was going to be rolling and everything was out of my hand, then, personally I would think twice about making that first phone call, because then you lose the control from that point on.

Thus, depending on individual cases and needs, pro-arrest could limit women's agency because it is not survivor-defined, or it could facilitate agency by providing justice system recourse for their victimization. The problem is confounded when women retaliate against their abusers in self-defense and are arrested themselves, or are arrested for outstanding warrants when they called police for help.

Dual Arrest

One latent consequence of pro-arrest policy that has been documented in the research literature is arrest of both an abuser and a self-defensive or retaliating victim (Ferarro, 2001; Osthoff, 2001; Nichols, 2011). Advocates in both regions said that this was a rare occurrence. In Glawe County Kari said, "We rarely . . . we don't see it too often, so that's good." In Faulds County, Teresa said, "We don't get a lot of dual arrests." When dual arrest did occur, advocates stated that it often happened under the following circumstances: self-defense, self-defensive battering in which the victim "escalated the violence," or when the victim engaged in a "preemptive strike."

Summer described the typical scenario in cases of dual arrest in which the victim was also arrested for self-defensive battering:

> Normally, the deputies' wording in the report is that they absolutely cannot determine who the primary physical aggressor is because they both have done injury, left marks on one another. Because we don't go by who started anything it's the degree of lethality that is used. So if it becomes that they are both punching each other and the deputy absolutely cannot sort it out then he will arrest both people. Often times when we get those reports I look at all of the past reports that we've had. If we have a lot of reports where she has been the victim and now we have one and she has been arrested, we're still going to work with her, because we get that she is the victim and she's defending herself.

Summer indicated that she used survivor-defined approaches, and looked at the specific background details of each case. She collaborated with both the male and female partners, to gain both perspectives of the abuse. In such cases, when one partner had a string of charges in abusive relationships, and the other partner had none, and upon listening to their accounts of abuse, Summer indicated that it was clear when a victim arrested under dual arrest was really a victim acting in self-defense. In such cases, charges would not be filed, and the victim would be offered advocacy and legal assistance.

Further, Jean indicated that victims were often smaller than their abusers and less physically capable of defending themselves, and sometimes used objects to defend themselves. In such cases, victims were labeled as the primary aggressor since they "escalated the violence" by using an object. Jean provided an example to illustrate:

> For instance one example is the couple are having the police there . . . sometimes the child has called the police, or a neighbor, but in any case, the police will say that they can't tell who's being the aggressor, apparently. So, they say that they have to arrest both of them, but I

90

know that is against the law. It's a police officer's job to determine who is the aggressor and to deal with it accordingly, and instead and often it's threats, they just threaten to arrest them both; but that makes a woman shut up real fast and I've had women say that they don't plan to call the police because they don't get any help from them. Certainly, there are instances of self-defense, and, the way that [State] law is if you, or whoever, ups the ante in terms of a weapon, gets arrested. So, a man might be beating a woman and she may be pretty defenseless, in terms of being able to defend herself against somebody who is beating her; but if she grabs like a pan that's on the stove and hits him with it, now, she's become the aggressor and I've had situations like that where a woman was then arrested and charged with domestic violence.

When asked, "How does something like that affect your advocacy?" Jean replied:

Well, it's very difficult for two reasons. One is, now you're trying to deal with somebody who's in jail until she gets her first hearing [use of a weapon involves a criminal felony charge], arraignment, and some-times that can be days, sometimes a week or more, and so you're trying to work with them on the telephone and you don't have very good ac-cess to them and to be able to help them; but I think it really affects ad-vocacy in that I can tell people "if your husband is beating you, try to get out of the house, call 9-1-1, to do all of those things;" but if they call 9-1-1, and the police come and instead they get a threat to go to jail or they are told that if this guy is beating them then they should just leave. [Police] not understanding the complexity of the problems, that it may not be possible to leave, or what we find is that leaving does not end the violence. So, they are faced with things like that. So they are hoping to get help, and instead often their concerns are minimized, and, or they are threatened, and they are not helped. Sometimes they are put in jail, and for doing what—defending themselves. And if they don't defend themselves they're put down for being a door-mat, or wanting this man to beat them. If they do fight back, now they are the criminal and they are in jail. The women that I have worked with too often get a stiffer sentence for the same things that a man would be sent to jail for [the twelve hour jail-time]. They get a stiffer sentence for domestic vio-lence than a man does. They are much more likely to go to jail over that, than a man is. So, all of those things, I think, affect advocacy.

Dual arrest is gendered in multiple ways. First, according to some advocates, women are treated more harshly than men, possibly because they are violating traditional femininity by defending themselves, and aren't "playing the good victim" of the passive, helpless woman who does not defend herself (Ferraro, 2001; Osthoff, 2001). Second, dual arrest often represents "gender neutral" policy, which is in fact gender biased in that it ignores the gender dynamics of domestic violence, as well as the relative size of men and women (generally), and women's consequent reason for using an object to defend herself. Third, such policy further oppresses women when the dynamics of their abuse are ignored and an arrest is made. These findings are consistent with prior research— victims may be arrested for retaliatory battering and self-defensive battering under pro-arrest laws, as the law states that an arrest should be made if either partner has inflicted physical abuse against another (Hart, 1995; Ferraro, 2001).

Similar to Jean, Cheryl described situations in which her clients were arrested, sometimes as the primary aggressor, in dual arrest situations due to abusers' manipulative behaviors:

> Yes definitely we have had some of our clients arrested as well, where police have gone in and not really known who the perpetrator is and so will arrest, or there are many situations where the police go and by the time the police get there the man is so in control and is so calm, and so she looks like the crazy one, she looks like the one that is out of control and needs to be arrested. Because it gets very emotional and she gets emotional and her emotions just weren't able to be put back in check as quick his were, and so he is used to being the manipulator and being cool and calm to everybody else, and yeah, so the police come and "ohhh my god Mr. Nice Guy, she's the crazy one." "I don't know what's going on here, she just attacked me!"

According to advocates in this study, this is a pattern among abusers, who are characteristically savvy and manipulative. They know how to make the victims appear unstable and therefore discredited. Advocates explained that officers were more likely to arrest an individual who appeared to be emotional or out of control.

Another way advocates indicated a dual arrest might occur was when abusers threatened their victims with significant harm and victims perpetrated a "preemptive strike" to avoid a beating. Vicki used an example to illustrate how this dynamic may unfold:

Actually I just had one the other day. She showed up at the home, and he said, "I want my baseball bat out of the car!" Threatening-like. She walks up to the house with the baseball bat and an assault ensues. Probably what she did was more self-defense than anything, but at that time I guess the officers didn't want to wade through it so they both were arrested.

When asked, "What do you do with those cases then?" Vicki replied:

It's really hard. It's really, really hard. A lot of times we'll look through it just to see what kind of history there was, and there was a history between the two of them. So then obviously we know that it was more self-defense kind of thing. So then, at that point, we just try to make contact with them and apologize, for sometimes that happens. It becomes a "he said she said" kind of thing. Sometimes you might get a good officer and then other times you get one that doesn't want to wade through it.

Moreover, Summer indicated that a "pre-emptive strike" might occur at times when there was no immediately imminent danger. She described such cases as rarely occurring, but described one case in which a victim saw no escape from the abuse, and attempted to kill her abuser:

Women perpetrators, who have withstood violence for years and years, decide to do something about it, and when they do it's usually a stabbing or something that's a much higher degree of lethality than the violence that they have undergone over the years. The majority of the second degree domestics where we have women perpetrators, at that moment, it's not in self-defense. It is, "He's asleep right now and I'm going to stab him." Yeah we have had a few of those happen. Not to a lethal degree, not that the person has been killed, but we have had a handful where they have been [close]. Those cases, the women are arrested, they are brought in, the charges are sent over to the prosecutor's office. Fortunately our prosecutor that handles our domestic violence reports is also very well-trained in domestic violence. So she gets it, understands the dynamics, understands why those things may happen, now that doesn't always mean that she has the choice not to charge someone when it is something as serious as that or not, but it's definitely taken into account. It varies on a case-by-case basis and oftentimes the men victims of those assaults don't want to prosecute and will not be an active participant in any type of prosecution. So a lot of times those cases are dismissed because we can't even get the men to make any kind of statement. It's because they know what their background is. I think it is "I had that coming and eventually it was going to happen, so how can I go forward now with trying to prosecute her . . . With that track record . . . when I have done all of these things." Rarely do we have a man that makes a statement or wants to prosecute a female for a domestic violence. And it's because he has all these charges, and knows it wouldn't stick or he doesn't want to be exposed for his battering in open court.

Although this was not a situation of dual arrest, the aftermath shows similar dynamics to dual arrest. Like Summer, Jasmine described dual arrest as rare in rural Glawe County, but challenging to advocacy when it did occur, "[After] review of the case later it's a lot more clear who was at fault, who started things and all of that in self-defense." Jasmine said that the dual arrest charge, in cases where a victim was arrested, would work itself out by the time it reached the courts. When dual arrest happened, advocates used survivor-defined collaborative responses to get the best outcome for victims. A review of individual cases and criminal histories provided a clear picture of who the primary aggressor was. Summer further described that in such cases, it was generally found that the male "victim" had a long history of abuse with the current partner/victim and with previous girlfriends. This should not be confused with "real" male victims, who advocates did work with, although they described this occurrence as rare. Both the Department of Justice and the National Crime Victimization Surveys find that approximately 15 percent of domestic violence victims are men.

Summer, Vicki, and Jasmine described the process of working with the prosecutor's office to drop charges against victims in cases of dual arrest involving self-defense. Consequently, while pro-arrest sometimes resulted in a dual arrest involving a victim, the victim was rarely charged. Vicki said that once the collaborative response with the prosecutor's office was underway, and charges were dropped, "So then, at that point, just try to make contact with them [victims] and apologize." Yet, the victim was still revictimized by the system that was supposed to protect her—because her call to police resulted in her own arrest. This is not survivor-defined, and justification of the arrest by suggesting that such arrests were rare, were not charged, or apologizing and offering services after the fact does not address the problem. Further, some advocates indicated that victims who were arrested when calling the police for help were less likely to call police for help in the future. Anais described her clients' reaction to dual arrest:

> Certainly threats. Lots of threats that law enforcement has made. I've had women say that they don't want to call police again because they were told if they called police again they'd be arrested even though they didn't commit a crime, that's certainly common . . . I've had women call the police and she had warrants and she was arrested.

In this case, Anais indicated that women can be arrested not just in relationship to the domestic violence, but for outstanding warrants unrelated to the call for help. When women are arrested when they are the real victims, it is problematic for survivors and their advocates. Amy illustrated this dynamic in dual arrest situations:

> We will see some cases where they will arrest both of them. Sometimes it was justifiable and it was mutually violent, sometimes it wasn't, where with whatever happened she got arrested, the victim got arrested as well. We don't like that because it makes the victim, I think, see the system as unfair, it doesn't believe her. "Why call the police I'm just going to get arrested too or they are not going to believe me. If I even try to fight back or defend myself, I don't want to get arrested."

In this example, Amy also indicated women who were actually victims in dual arrest cases were less likely to call the police in the future, following their own arrest.

Social Change Practices

Efforts toward social change in Faulds County were clearly related to feminist identity, feminist coalitions, and to feminist-informed social change activism. Emily described conducting police trainings in which one of the focal points was dual arrest:

> In the trainings that we do, we say "don't do it, don't do it, don't do it" [dual arrest] but there are of course, legitimately, there are some situations where they cannot determine the primary aggressor or where both were the aggressor, but there are far fewer of those.

In Faulds County, advocates worked to provide education to officers about the gender dynamics involved in cases of domestic violence as an effort towards eradicating dual arrest involving a victim. This training, or a related collaborative response, was not described by advocates in Glawe County. Thus, again, there is a pattern of social change apparent in Faulds County, and not in largely nonfeminist Glawe County. Recall in chapter 2 the ways feminism related to social change activism, and the lack of feminist identity, programming, and coalitions in Glawe County. In Glawe County, they dealt with dual-arrest after the fact as opposed to working toward systemic change to prevent its occurrence. So while advocates in both regions supported the policy, they dealt with the negative latent consequence of dual arrest in different ways.

Advocates in Faulds County generally supported pro-arrest. They did not wish to change it through activism, as it was their feminist activism along with the [State] Coalition in the first place that resulted in the policy. Pro-arrest itself often takes control of arrest away from victims, and can result in revictimization when dual arrest involving a victim occurs. They responded to the challenges the policy presented only through looking at criminal histories and working with prosecution to drop charges, and police education and training related to dual arrest.

Thus, advocates' responses were gendered in multifaceted ways. The activism and support of the policy was feminist, because they were seeking improved justice system responses and recourse for battered women, thus facilitating women's agency on a societal level. The goal of societal change to promote gendered socio-cultural change resulting from the policy was also feminist. At the same time, advocates reproduced patriarchal approaches by supporting the policy, because they recognized that the policy at times resulted in nonsurvivor-defined practices that denied agency to some individual battered women who did not want their partners arrested for a variety of reasons. Thus, while simultaneously recognizing the policy as *not* survivor-defined, they related the policy *to* survivor-defined practices and social change consistent with feminist advocacy.

No-Drop Prosecution

Prior research finds that while arrest rates did increase with the implementation of mandatory/pro-arrest, batterers initially were rarely prosecuted. For example, one study found only 15 percent of arrests resulted in being charged with a crime (Goodman & Epstein, 2008). Batterers could get their partner to drop charges through threats of violence or through apologetic manipulations (Nichols, 2011). The result was implementation of "no-drop" policies, where the prosecution became the property of the state rather than the victim (Goodman & Epstein, 2008). Advocates worked through coalitions to accomplish this, including the coalition in the state in which the current research occurred. The idea was that if responsibility for prosecution were moved from the victim to the state, abusers would be less likely to retaliate, could no longer intimidate their partners to drop charges, and prosecution rates would consequently increase. Empowerment of victims was a goal of this feminist activism through victims' increased access to recourse through the justice system. Societal change was another goal of advocates, where the justice system could clearly indicate that domestic violence would not be tolerated (Goodman & Epstein, 2008). A consequence of the "no-drop prosecution" policy was increased prosecution of batterers (Goodman & Epstein, 2008). No-drop policy can take the form of a "hard" no-drop, or a "soft" no-drop. With "hard" no-drop policy, prosecution will occur regardless. With a "soft" no-drop policy, there is some discretion, and cases may be dropped in some cases at the request of the victim (Nichols, 2013c). The state where this research takes place is generally a "hard" no-drop state, although the prosecutor did have discretion to drop some cases and there were a few loopholes surrounding no-drop policy. This section examines how advocates interpreted and dealt with no-drop prosecution, highlighting social change and survivor-defined practices.

Survivor-Defined? The Empowering Nature of No-Drop Policy

Advocates described no-drop prosecution and its relationship to survivor-defined advocacy in two competing ways: 1) it empowers victims by providing recourse through the justice system, and removes responsibility of prosecution from the victim to the state; 2) it is disempowering because it denies victims' agency, and can result in both systemic and batterer-based revictimization.

First, some advocates described no-drop prosecution as empowering, because victims may otherwise be coerced or threatened by their abusers into not testifying. No-drop prosecution removes blame from the victim for prosecuting, thus she can prosecute without her abuser holding her responsible. Kari, in rural Glawe County, elaborated:

> Especially if the guy's on probation, the probation officer takes that over and it's like, "It doesn't matter that she doesn't want anything done!" Like, "You violated probation, we're doing something about it." So, at first they [abusers] don't seem to get that, or they at least try and intimidate the victim to make her think that it's not the case, but I'm sure that they figure it out eventually when they see that sometimes it's just not working. Like they are calling everybody, they are making her call everybody and it's not working.

Importantly, Kari noted that the victim was still being intimidated by her abuser, regardless of "state control" of the situation. Similarly, Teresa indicated the way they addressed cases with high-risk abusers in metro Faulds County:

> I think its [no-drop prosecution] benefit is definitely that it takes the pressure off of the victim. The offender is the one that can go back to them [the prosecutor's office], [who says] "she had no abilities to stop this, we're going to go forward anyway." It also gives the victims the ability to do it anyway. So, what they [victims] will do is they will go to the Circuit Attorney and say "I'm really afraid of him. If he knows I'm prosecuting I want you to tell him I'm not prosecuting and they are forcing me." They [Circuit Attorney] will go along with that even though she is being cooperative; they will still act as [if] they are forcing her so that she is safer from him. So I think that's a benefit that the Circuit Attorney and everybody is working towards keeping her safe, so that no-drop prosecution makes it a lot easier.

Similarly, Liz stated that she explained to victims and abusers that it is the state that is prosecuting, because state laws were broken. Like Teresa, she indicated that this worked as a safety net for victims, because prosecution was removed from their control. In fact, a majority of advocates in the justice system made statements similar to Liz, Teresa, and Kari—that the policy could empower victims who may otherwise drop prosecution because of threats, intimidation, or coercion from their abuser. Thus, advocates believed in such circumstances that no-drop prosecution could reduce batterer-based revictimization. In addition, advocates also professed that systemic revictimization was reduced because the justice system was actually prosecuting cases that they would have dropped prior to the implementation of the policy. Again, like pro-arrest, some advocates related no-drop prosecution to feminist social change that would result in improved responses for battered women, consequently facilitating women's agency on a socio-structural level. Charlotte, a feminist in the Faulds County justice system, applied a feminist interpretation to no-drop prosecution. Charlotte, a battered women's movement veteran that worked to get the policy, said:

> If you go with the approaches, I mean there are many popular approaches, but if you go with the popular approach that says if the victims say they don't want to prosecute, then we shouldn't prosecute—this guy still committed a crime and should be held accountable for the crime, especially if it involves a serious assault. We used to always compare domestic violence with robbery victims. People don't ask to become robbery victims, most of the time they don't know the perpetrator who's robbed them, but we don't go in and say "okay, now would you like to prosecute this person?" We don't even ask that question of robbery victims. It is assumed that yes you are going to prosecute this person if that person is caught. So why do we change the rules for DV, when we shouldn't be?

Charlotte was then asked, "Well, Why do you think we do?" Charlotte replied:

> It all has to do with the relationship. I think the relationship dynamics are what change that and then of course, societal all of the societal history of men's dominance, male centered society that kind of thing. A lot of those things carry over even looking at our police force we have a lot of women on our police force, but there are still some real inherent beliefs about relationships and I think as a result of how we apply our frame of reference about relationships that makes a difference in how we view crimes that involve domestic disputes.

While a majority of feminist advocates related survivor-defined "empowering women in society" social change perspectives to feminism, they simultaneously related "what's best for the individual" perspectives to feminism. Thus, feminist interpretations of no-drop prosecution took different forms. For example, while a majority of feminist and nonfeminist advocates (all but one) in both regions and organizational contexts described support for the policy, a majority of the advocates that supported the policy (all but two) also stated that the victim's individual interests should be supported over the state/social change interests.

Basically, they were arguing for a pro-prosecution policy with discretion controlled by victims as opposed to mandatory prosecution. They supported survivor-defined approaches, respecting the agency of victims. While no-drop prosecution appears to be standardized with little room for survivor-defined approaches, prosecution was in fact dropped in some cases at the request of the victim. Advocates indicated that their primary goal was to support victims, in some cases they worked through loopholes in the system to drop prosecution or to support not testifying if it was in the best interests, and desires, of survivors they worked with. For example, Amy stated:

> When we do get that phone call or if we do talk to her and she says I don't want to do it. I just want him to leave me alone, or, I don't want to go through this anymore. I have already done the grand jury but I just don't want to do it. It's usually re-traumatizing. They just can't go through it. I completely understand. Especially if it's a sexual assault case or strangulation, they just don't want to do it. From my position I completely support them. Now, through the legal standpoint, I think either charges won't be issued or the punishment will be maybe less severe because they don't have the witness to the crime, so in the end I think it helps the offender get off easier, or charges don't ever get issued, but I think as long as she feels comfortable with it, and she knows all of her options, then I will support her.

No-drop prosecution is not survivor-defined when victims do not have control of prosecution. Individual victims may have various reasons why they do not want to prosecute including fear of and financial dependence on the abuser. In situations where victims did not want to prosecute, advocates did not directly resist the policy, as the advocates described the policy as having more benefit than detriment. Instead, they worked with victims through their individual-level practices.

For example, one loophole that some advocates used to respond to no-drop prosecution in cases where the victim did not want to testify was spousal immunity. [State] law includes a Spousal Privilege Statute, in which a wife can choose not to testify against her abusive husband or vice versa. [State] is one of four states that include this provision, and advocates used it in recommendations to victims as a way of relieving them from testifying in court if they did not want to. However, unmarried women were not able to use spousal immunity, and were consequently subpoenaed to testify against their abusers, even if they did not want to.

In order to avoid testifying, victims could also invoke the Fifth Amendment to avoid testifying against their abusers. Some advocates were able to inform victims of these loopholes in survivor-defined practices.

Survivor-Defined? The Disempowering Nature of No-Drop Policy

While some advocates described no-drop prosecution as empowering, because victims may otherwise be coerced or threatened by their *abusers* into *not* testifying, they simultaneously described no-drop prosecution as *dis*empowering, because victims may otherwise be coerced or threatened by the *justice system* into testifying. Advocates stated that no-drop prosecution sometimes resulted in both batterer-based and systemic revictimization, leaving advocates little room to provide survivor-defined advocacy because of its centralized control. So, while a majority of advocates supported the policy, in what seemed to be a contradiction, a majority also stated that victims should not be forced to testify because they can be revictimized in the courts by both judges and their abusers.

Eve indicated that forcing women to testify against their abusers could result in batterer-based revictimization. She described how the process had a negative effect on victims in the courts, which problematized advocates' ability to provide empowering advocacy. Four advocates indicated that when women are forced to testify, being in the same room with the abuser can be traumatic. For example, Eve described a situation in which an abuser used religion to keep his wife from leaving their relationship. When she made the decision to leave him and to prosecute him for domestic battery, he brought a Bible into the courtroom, and displayed it for the victim to view. This is an example of systemic and batterer-based revictimization. It is batterer-based revictimization because the batterer was psychologically abusing the victim through religious control mechanisms. It is systemic revictimization because the victim was required to be in the courtroom with the abuser in order to prosecute, which continued her trauma and exposure to batterer-based psychological abuse.

Eve provided another example of how an abuser worked to intimidate one of the women she had been working with who was forced to testify in a similar way. In court, he brought the victim roses, with the black cord he used to strangle her with sticking out of the bouquet. The abuser wanted to threaten her, and to make her appear hysterical to discredit her. Eve stated the importance of survivor-defined practices in such instances:

> If you think about it, a survivor of domestic violence is probably the most amazing person you're ever going to meet in the world. She has survived years of abuse and control, and judgment made against her that was not favorable. Having to walk a line of it's got to look really good in public. I have to keep up my front, my face, but she has also kept him at bay. So who knows her abuser better than she does? She is the one that has had to survive. So we need to listen to her, so when he brings a box of chocolates to court, or he walks in with this bible, and she is hysterical, let's think about why?

Eve noted that it is important to understand the nature of domestic violence and coercive control, and the ways abusers can continue their abuse in a courtroom setting where victims are required to testify in the presence of their abusers. These experiences resulted in revictimization of the victim within the courtroom. No-drop prosecution could be viewed as a "patriarchal" gender-based policy, because the victim was denied agency and choice, out of a "we know what's best for her" ideology and was forced to testify ultimately resulting in her revictimization.

Further, advocates in Glawe County said that one judge essentially revictimized abused women by not taking their cases seriously. Jasmine said that prosecution sometimes resulted in an informal reprimand to the abuser, which revictimized those victims who had agreed to prosecute and wanted recourse for their victimization:

> For example, I can give you several, here is a common example: [The Judge said] "now the prosecution has proven that you were guilty, but I'm going to find you not guilty. And you need to work things out and leave her alone and dah dit da dit da." But to say that in open court they have proven their case, but it means nothing. So that is devastating to witnesses and victims, and law enforcement, because what's the point? Also to someone who's had prior assault charge and had done probation for that, [Judge said] "So I see you've had prior assaults, okay I'm going to give you a $50 fine and don't do that anymore." Okay, that's not even legal, but that's less than a speeding ticket, but [sarcastically] hey that's alright. So those kinds of things, and it was very damaging. To tell a woman with an order of protection to tell someone who had been stabbed by some guy, "you two just need to get along" . . . So these things I have seen with my own eyes, and so when I was sitting

there and I was like, criminal court side of things is pretty odd here! I was like that's kind of weird but didn't say anything until like the second time, that I was seeing especially, "I'm going to find you not guilty even though they proved you guilty." That was beyond my canon! It was just crazy and you just—there is no winning when you have a judge like that. So eventually with the blessing of the prosecutor she started asking for a change of judge. So now that judge has no longer anything to do with [prosecution] except he still does orders of protection, unfortunately!

Such revictimization at the hand of one judge in Glawe County certainly disempowered victims, and is antithetical to the empowering practice of the survivor-defined component of feminist advocacy. Prosecution rights were intended to be empowering to victims, it was the victim's right to have legal recourse. Yet, revictimizing practices in the courts have sometimes manifested, which are not empowering. Further, Belinda noted that while ostensibly responsibility for prosecution is moved to the State, abusers may not make that connection, and may still blame their partners:

You know in St. Louis County our county prosecutor has a do not drop policy. Well, very often after he's been arrested the victim has been prevailed upon after he got out with bail or whatever, has been prevailed upon to drop any charges or not testify and that again puts her in danger if the prosecuting attorney is so insistent upon a do not drop policy and he's not looking at things logically, he's not wanting to be accountable, so he's trying to put the blame on his abused partner, or he or she, so if she goes to the prosecuting attorney's office and asks them to please let it go, or I will not testify, I think there is still going to be pressure to bear on her and her abuser is going to see it as the key person in whether or not they will move forward in the legal process. So in some cases that might threaten her safety. Ohh my goodness yes! That's the whole point, that's my concern. And yet, at the same time, we want to hold abusers accountable. I just want the most extreme consideration to be given to her, so that . . . I do know that sometimes there's an effort made to keep her as a witness in a safe place, a confidential location, that sort of thing; but we also remember the woman who begged for a safe place to stay and wasn't provided it, not by the St. Louis County prosecutor but by a prosecutor in the City and she was murdered in front of her children. You know, it is extremely complicated, and always that potential for harm is there. Sometimes more obviously, sometimes not as obvious, but you have to be very aware that potential to harm. It's a constant threat!

Belinda's example notes the importance of survivor-centered advocacy, and meeting victims' needs. This involves listening to battered women to learn what their fears and their needs are. As stated previously, advocates are experts on domestic violence, available resources, and safety planning. Victims are the experts of their situations and in their knowledge of their abusers. Thus, if victims state that they need a safe place, and that prosecution is a risk for them, they are probably right. Belinda's example represents systemic revictimization, as the system did not protect this woman when she clearly indicated that her safety was at risk. Survivor-defined advocacy considers such input, and leads to needs-based collaborative advocacy. However, other stakeholders, such as prosecutors' offices, must also listen to battered women to engage in *systems* of advocacy to avoid revictimization—and homicide—of battered women in the prosecutorial process.

Moreover, when victims did not want to prosecute, and were subpoenaed, in rare cases women could be jailed for not testifying. In both counties, supported by state law, if victims are served a subpoena and they fail to appear on that subpoena, then the prosecutor can go to the judge and issue what is called a body attachment to make sure victims appear in court. The body attachment gives judges the legal right to jail victims who do not appear, so the victims will be forced to appear at the rescheduled court date. Vicki said:

> Then, they will serve that body attachment and they [victims] go sit in jail. It's never been for more than a day or two, but it's just kind of an eye opening that I think everyone takes domestic violence seriously, and even though you might not be, we're in fear for your safety and we need you to help us prosecute so that way this person is held responsible and doesn't do this again. You know at times it is just eye opening, that people are going to take it seriously; because for so long you didn't show up on a subpoena, "ehh no big deal!" You didn't worry that there was going to be a repercussion, or, if you didn't show up for court who cared? "I have the right to choose if I'm going to prosecute or not," and that's the trend that we're trying to get away from. It doesn't happen a lot, it's very far and few between, but you know the serious felony cases where you're looking at domestic assault second, and they've had repeated things I think sometimes it is helpful. I think other advocates would strongly disagree . . . Some advocates are completely against

that, [they say] "it's revictimizing," but, I guess I'm not. If you repeat-edly are getting abused and then fail to do something and they can take a remedy that might help you, I guess I'm okay with that.

Vicki did not appear to incorporate a feminist perspective recogniz-ing the agency of battered women. In fact, her perspective is patriarchal gender-based in denying women agency with a "for your own good" mentality. Vicki further indicated that her goal was offender accountabil-ity, as well as victim accountability in prosecuting and did not relate it to social change or feminist perspectives. However, none of the other advo-cates in Glawe County, besides Vicki, supported the body attachment.

When asked, "what if a victim doesn't want to testify?" Jasmine, a feminist, offered an alternative perspective to Vicki's. She indicated that body attachments were "revictimizing" and she viewed them as "a retali-ation by the court system." She further noted the importance of survivor-defined practices to uncover women's reasons for not showing up or not wanting to prosecute, "we don't know why she's not coming forward, or she's not showing up or even if she was able to show up, we don't know." Jasmine did indicate that enforcing this policy was rare. She said the courts had a right to, but did it infrequently—primarily in felony cas-es that were perceived as high risk. In total, twenty-four advocates (the majority) in this study did not support the practice of body attachments. The two that did support it were nonfeminists—one in Glawe County and one in Faulds County. Those advocates that did not support body attachments or forced testimony in court developed strategies to address them. In order to deal with the batterer-based and systemic revictimiza-tion involved in no-drop prosecution, advocates used social change prac-tices.

Social Change Practices

Advocates in Faulds County worked toward system change to deal with the revictimization of battered women in the courts. Four advocates described extensive trainings with police officers with the aim of evi-dence based prosecution in cases where victims did not want to testify as an alternative to subpoenaing victims to testify. This worked to repro-duce the feminist goal of the policy—social change and improved re-sponses for battered women—but simultaneously worked to resist the patriarchal elements of the policy—the practice of revictimization in the courts, body attachments, and forced testimony. Charlotte said that the system has gone toward evidence-based prosecution, in which victims are not required to testify in order to prosecute. She described the social change activism around this practice, and trainings of officers towards system change through evidence based prosecution. Evidence-based prosecution involved 9-1-1 recordings, excited utterances, police reports, witnesses, and testimonials. With evidence-based prosecution, victims are not required to appear in court. Thus, they can avoid the trauma of the courtroom experience, and potentially avoid the batterer-based and systemic revictimization described in Glawe County. Similarly, Liz delineated system change resulting from a community-based response team in Faulds County:

> In the spring of 2009, as a result cf a collaborative domestic violence task force, we actually trained over 1,000 police officers. We did a full day where they had sexual harassment [training] in the morning, then they had an overview of advocate roles, the DVDU [Domestic Violence Detective Unit] role, and then they had four hours of specific training put on by the attorneys, both the domestic violence resource prosecutor from the [State] Office of Prosecution Services who designed the curriculum, with the assistance of our prosecutors in our unit. They all took turns because this lasted from March until June. It took that long to do all of the trainings for 1,000 officers.

Charlotte clarified the goal in such trainings:

> We value training, extensively. I think that the value in it is that our goal was that we want the police officers to write more comprehensive police reports, collect better evidence so that when we go to prosecute—if by some chance, we don't have the cooperation from the victim—we have plenty of other evidence that we can put on. We also believe that by the police officers' first response and their dedication to collecting the evidence they show the victim how concerned they are about the victim's safety; and by advocates putting on a part of that training, the police officers got to hear the importance of connecting victims to resources, and why this can make a difference in making that kind of planting a seed, or interrupting that cycle of violence; because a lot of times the officers are just—they are burned out on going to the same house seven to ten times. They don't see any change happening. We wanted them to see how they could be a change agent. As an advocate I can tell you that in numerous times there's a lot of frustration

that's experienced when law enforcement and our investigators and our attorneys can't find this victim, who they need for a hearing or for a trial, and bottom line, it's the advocate that says "Yeah but she had to do this in order to stay safe, to survive. It's not because she's trying to be a pain in your butt, it's because she's trying to survive. You have to accept that she is trying to survive, and this is the step that she has chosen to take."

Thus advocates in the justice system in Faulds County believed that training officers related to evidence-based prosecution would alleviate some of the latent consequences of systemic revictimization involved in no-drop prosecution, as well as provide means for prosecution that did not require the victim's participation.

While Jasmine, in the justice system in rural Glawe County, indicated that educating judges in domestic violence would be desirable, and her only feminist counterpart in Glawe County said it would be wonderful to have a Domestic Violence Court, neither advocate was able to create social change. This was a recurring pattern for the feminist advocates in Glawe County. Without the social support of a coalition, and without feminist understandings of social change within the local advocate community, their feminist ideologies did not result in social change. In fact, it was the prosecutor, with the input of one feminist advocate, who worked to no longer have cases heard by the problematic judge, not the advocates.

In sum, while no-drop policies may help some women, they can be harmful to others who may be revictimized by their batterers or through the practices of judges and prosecutors in the justice system. Victims can be subpoenaed to testify against their abuser, and can be held in contempt of court, and can even be jailed, if they do not. These findings are consistent with prior research, where prosecutors threatened victims with reports to child protective services and consequent custody loss of children as well as jail time if victims failed to testify against their abusers (Moe, 2007; Lyon et al., 2008, Goodman & Epstein, 2008). Social change activism was lacking in Glawe County, and largely limited to practice-level system changes in Faulds County. As Faulds County advocates' past social change activism resulted in the development and implementation of the policy in the first place, with the goal of societal change and recourse for battered women, they did not work to change the policy on a state-level. The issue with the policy was basically in its standardized "one size fits all" format, which was a problem because the relative benefits of the policy varied from case to case.

Advocates thus reproduced both feminist and patriarchal gendered practices in their support of the policy, through their social change activism that resulted in no-drop prosecution, while simultaneously resisting patriarchal gendered practices, such as revictimization in the courts, through use of spousal immunity, trainings for officers on evidence-based prosecution, getting prosecutors to drop charges, and calling abusers to describe the [State] law to displace blame from the victim to the state.

Conclusion

In sum, a majority of advocates in rural and metropolitan contexts—including both justice system and traditional advocates—supported the use of protective orders, pro-arrest, and no-drop prosecution while simultaneously recognizing the limitations and challenges that could foster the revictimization of battered women. Advocates developed strategies to avoid potential systemic and batterer-based revictimization resulting from these challenges.

In line with Acker, gendered practices (patriarchal and neutral) were found in the justice system that some advocates countered using their own feminist practices. Some of advocates' practices were reminiscent of early feminist advocacy, such as collaborative, intersectional, survivor-defined, and social change models. Such findings relate to Acker's theory of gendered organizations, as Acker called for recognition of policies and practices as gendered, not simple genderless mechanisms of organizations. Feminist advocates were able to recognize negative consequences of patriarchal or "neutral" policies and practices, and targeted them for change. Policies that are not survivor-defined, such as pro-arrest and no-drop prosecution, in some cases represented patriarchal policy by denying women's agency, and resulting in further gendered inequalities and revictimization of battered women. Yet, at the same time, feminist advocates considered these policies to be feminist in their overall goal of social change, and provision of recourse for women's victimization. This is why they advocated for them in the first place, and continued to support them while addressing the latent negative consequences. They pointed out that domestic violence was all but ignored prior to implementation of the policies. Advocates' practices to mitigate revictimization were also gendered. Social change activism worked to correct gendered inequalities, as did survivor-defined and intersectional practices. Such approaches countered policies and practices that, at times, could be patriarchal or revictimizing.

Feminist identity of advocates in addressing revictimization of battered women was directly related to their system-change actions. Feminist advocates worked toward system change to avoid dual arrest, to train officers in evidence-based prosecution, and to address patriarchal practices of officers and judges. Feminist coalition activity was significantly related to social change activism, and was consequently related to regional distinctions in system change. Glawe County had less organizational and community support for system change, making activism less likely to occur and to be successful. In addition to social change activism, only feminist advocates used intersectional practices as well. Feminist advocates used such practices to determine whether a protective order was a good option, to assist women with gaining an order of protection, or to address systemic bias in the courts. Nonfeminist advocates did not recognize such biases, nor did they recognize how intersecting identities could impact women's experiences with abuse and with justice system interventions. In turn, all advocates, whether feminist or not, and in all regions and organizational contexts, used survivor-defined practices to mitigate revictimization of women in the protective order process, enforcing orders, no-drop prosecution, and in pro-arrest and dual arrest situations. Survivor-defined, intersectional, and social change practices are all feminist-gender based practices, as they facilitate the agency, empowerment, and safety of battered women.

Chapter 4

Advocacy in Child Protective Services

Organizations that handle cases of child abuse and neglect, such as Child Protective Services (CPS), the Children's Division or Family Courts, or the Department of Children's and Family Services (DCFS), are labeled as gendered organizations, as many of the policies and practices are "neutral/biased" or "patriarchal." Specifically, chapter 4 examines the policies, practices, and related dynamics involving CPS systems identified as having a negative impact on battered women—charges for failure to protect, lost custody, abuser's manipulation of CPS systems, and mandatory parenting classes. This chapter also examines advocates' survivor-defined and social change practices associated with these challenges. Some advocates dealt with such challenges by resisting them. They accomplished this resistance largely by facilitating collaboration with and soliciting survivor-defined approaches of caseworkers on behalf of the battered women they worked with. Feminist advocates were more likely to recognize how gender and domestic violence interacted with child abuse and systems that aim to protect children from abuse, which resulted in feminist advocates resisting challenges and seeking ways to advocate for the interests of the women they worked with in such circumstances. Nonfeminist advocates were more likely to accept victim-blaming behaviors of CPS caseworkers. Although both feminist and nonfeminist advocates used survivor-defined practices, feminist identity, ideologies, or participation in feminist coalitions largely predicted social change practices in all organizational and regional contexts.

Threats of Lost Custody

All of the advocates stated that abusers sought to control their victims and to manipulate CPS systems through threats of lost custody and false claims of child abuse. Advocates noted that it was important to address any concerns women had over their children through survivor-defined practices, as advocates unanimously stated that one of victims' greatest fears in leaving their abusive partners was that their abusers would gain custody of the children. Survivors thought losing their children was a possibility for a variety of reasons. The most common reasons included survivors' lack of financial resources, and abusers' threat to make false claims of child abuse.

First, one reason why women feared lost custody was because they lacked the economic resources to support their children. Advocates indicated that abusers commonly isolated victims from sources of independence—education or a source of income—to keep them dependent and less likely to be able to leave their abusive homes. Abusers used this lack of financial stability to threaten their partners with lost custody. Jean illustrated this dynamic:

> Well the other way that they [abusers] often use the children is if they're the primary earner and she doesn't have a job, she's providing or taking care of the children in the home, she's a homemaker, or even if she's working but it's part-time and she's not making very much money. He'll say that if they divorce, if she leaves, or if she tries to get a divorce, that he will get the children. Because of course, he's making more money, he can provide them a stable home, and she can't.

Advocates consistently pointed to absence of financial freedom as a barrier to leaving an abusive relationship, particularly if there were children involved. In addition to serving as a barrier more generally, abusers used their knowledge of this dependence to instill fear of lost custody as a form of psychological abuse and control. In this way, they were able to manipulate women into staying in abusive relationships. Advocates further indicated that abusers simultaneously placed barriers to accessing financial independence in the way, such as sabotaging or otherwise controlling survivors' employment and education opportunities.

Another reason why women feared lost custody, aside from lack of financial independence, was abusers' threat of making false claims to CPS/DFS. Advocates described how an abuser would call or threaten to call Family Services and falsely claim that the mother was abusing the child. This type of manipulation of the system was experienced by a majority of advocates in this study. Delia stated:

> I work with women all the time where their batterer has said they were going to call CPS and say that she's beating them and they'll get taken away. They use that as a threat-like. It's a control mechanism. That isn't true, but then they are still afraid of it. They see him as having the

power to do whatever. So they don't want to piss him off, and will do what he wants because they are afraid they will lose their kids.

Importantly, Delia noted that this manipulative behavior is an extension of abuse; it is another form of psychological abuse with the aim of control. Women believed that they would lose their children, because they saw their abuser as having the power to make it happen, as their abuser had been able to coercively control other aspects of their lives. Thus, threat of lost custody was a way for abusers to get what they wanted. In addition, advocates noted that many survivors believed that when CPS/DFS was contacted, that they would automatically lose their children. They did not always understand that there was a process or an investigation, and if they were not abusing the children, then they would not lose their children.

Advocates all dealt with the threats of lost custody and fear of false hotline accusations by using survivor-defined approaches. They worked with each woman's individual case, needs, and situation. They explained the law and the process of a DFS visit to the women they worked with to alleviate their fears. Providing information related to women's goals and needs is a central tenet of survivor-defined advocacy that proved to be important to women with fears of losing their children. For example, Kari said:

> I even have lines for my response to that [false hotline calls] because we get that so often. For the "he's going to call DFS on me and is going to have my kids taken away" I will be like "no, he's not going to get them taken away. DFS is going to do an investigation, if you're not doing anything wrong, don't worry about it." Then, I usually say, "are you afraid of him continuing to hit your kids? If you are living together, and if that's the case, we have shelter for you." So we can go that route. As far as taking custody of the kids, I will say "you know what, we have attorneys that will a lot of times do work for women in your situation for free, why don't you give them a call?" Because they always think that he has the right to come and take custody and all of that. I'm like "wait a second!" especially when they're not married and they have never had paternity tests so a lot of times she thinks that he has a right to see the kid even though there has been no established…There is no legal right there. So then we're like "no no no no, he's not going to come. He's not going to take custody."

Chapter 4

Similarly, Summer explained that abusers may threaten to make a variety of allegations to CPS. Like Kari, Summer illustrated a survivor-defined approach in such circumstances:

> That is always a threat. I would say probably half of the perpetrators tell their victim that, "if you leave or if you try to go from here and you take the kids, I'm calling Children's Services and I'm going to tell them that you did this, that you do drugs, that you drive drunk," that and a million things. That is always a concern when we're dealing with victims and usually one of the first things that we try to address with them, because they are scared that they are going to lose their kids. So we quickly address that. [We tell them] "He can make all of the phone calls that he wants. He is free to make them, if Children's Services shows up, you will do the right thing and you can't stop someone from making those hotline phone calls, but again, probably just threats. If there is nothing that you've done, there's nothing to be worried about and as a victim of domestic violence, again, you're the victim and don't let him tell you that . . ." So we definitely try to address that, because it is a real concern for many of our victims.

Summer and Kari indicated that advocates can provide information, resources, and emotional support for women with fears of losing their children due to abusers' manipulations and threats involving Children's Services. Survivor-defined practices to address women's fears of losing their children in such circumstances were practiced by all advocates in both regions.

In a related dynamic, advocates indicated that women not only feared lost custody, but they feared joint custody and visitation rights as well. Such fears prevented many victims from leaving their partners. For example, when asked if abusers used children to manipulate their partners, Eve replied:

> Yes! All of the time. They're told every time, every single time. You leave me I am going to get your kids taken away from you. What happens? Every time that they go on a visit he's right. Then, dad's visiting with the kids and mom's not there...

In this example, Eve notes that in an indirect way, women's children are taken from them when their former partners are awarded visitation rights. If victims leave their partners, they are unable to monitor their children's safety. Eve indicated that this dynamic prevents many women from leav-

114

ing abusive relationships, because courts will still award visitation and oftentimes joint custody to fathers, even if they have a record of abusive behavior directed toward the mother. By staying in the relationship, many women feel they have more control over abusers' interactions with their children, and that they can better protect their children (see Rhodes et al., 2011). In addition, Eve also pointed out that when abusers do have joint custody or visitation, they can gain information from children to continue the abuse directed toward the mothers. She said, "Dad's pumping the kids for information and sometimes the kids just give it to make him shut up." Women's fears of visitation or joint custody proved challenging to advocacy. Awarding abusers custody or visitation could be seen as a gender "neutral" policy, as dynamics of the mothers' abuse were not always considered in the custody arrangements in both Glawe and Faulds Counties.

Failure to Protect

Despite survivor-defined approaches, advocates reported that at times, particularly when the abuser was abusing the child as well, abusers were successfully able to manipulate CPS. Women would indeed lose custody of their children, and could be charged with Failure to Protect as well. Failure to Protect charges developed in many states to protect children from abusers. The idea was that holding mothers accountable for their children's safety would improve the safety of children in abusive homes. Policymakers believed that women would be more likely to leave their abusers if they were legally responsible for the abusers' actions toward their children. Failure to protect charges are most commonly filed against mothers whose children witness the abuse of their mothers, or whose children are also abused by their father. In both Glawe and Faulds Counties, advocates reported Failure to Protect as the most difficult problem they experienced with CPS systems. Such charges developed in a variety of different ways, detailed below.

Abusers' False Claims of Abuse

Advocates noted that in cases where CPS became involved, women could be charged with Failure to Protect, and very well could lose their children. For example, Anais indicated that failure to protect charges were common among the victims she worked with, and noted that this charge was often facilitated by abusers as another form of abuse. She described a pattern in which abusers abused the children, and then called DFS falsely stating that the victim was abusing the children. Even when caseworkers figured out that the abuser was really the person inflicting the abuse upon the children, mothers were at times still charged with failure to protect as opposed to being charged with child abuse:

> It's a recurring theme here. An abuser will threaten the mother and say "I'm going to call Family Services and say you're abusing the kids so you'll lose custody" as a way of controlling her. We see that frequently. Absolutely! Yeah because it will be her fault [Failure to Protect] and she will lose the kids and he will end up with the kids even though he's the abuser. I've seen the cases. Absolutely! At minimum he ends up with unsupervised visitation. He controls every move she makes around that because she's the one that is in trouble with Children's Services. Yeah! It's common.

Thus, abusers have discovered how to use CPS/DFS systems to continue their patterns of control and abuse directed toward their victims.

Abusers Report Themselves for Abusing the Children

To complicate matters, abusers not only made false claims about victims abusing the children, but they also called CPS and told them that they, the batterers themselves, were abusing the children or abused the mother in front of the children, and the mother did nothing to stop it. In such cases, victims were subject to charges for violating failure to protect laws. Ingrid stated:

> I had one case that was really difficult. The abuser called DFS, and said that he was abusing the kids, and it was the mother's fault because she knew he was doing it and let him do it. That wasn't true. The abuser is the abuser, it's the abuser's fault. It was his way of controlling her. She was making plans to leave him, and he knew it, but [she] didn't have the money yet. It was like a, "you don't do what I want, you think you can leave me, then I will make you pay, see what I can do." And he made the whole situation into "it's her fault." He got probation because he was seen as a good boy for seeking help, and she was charged with failure to protect and lost her kids. He didn't care that they were lost, he

116

didn't get them either, but he didn't care. It was all about using them to get to her. She didn't get them back until she took parenting classes and did some other things. And she had to like say she was wrong and had problems when she didn't. She was humiliated at having to be seen as this bad person and bad mother who lost her kids. It was like she was the abuser, but she was the victim!! Unreal!! But it was him abusing them to get to her, and he totally played the system to terrorize her. And he still has visitation!! Unreal!!

Thus, abusers could use the children to control both CPS systems and their victims not only through false claims of abuse, but through manipulations of CPS and failure to protect charges for their own admitted abuse of the children. Abused women were being held responsible for the abuse that their batterer inflicted upon them as well as their children. This was labeled by advocates as another form of abuse intended by the abuser. Further, it represents systemic revictimization, as abused women were being punished by an institutional policy that held them responsible for their abusers' behaviors when they "called for help." Ironically, Aileen noted that the opposite happened if abused women called CPS for help:

Which is why if there is an issue where we think we have to have them [Child Protective Services] involved [because of mandatory reporting laws], we think through it very carefully, we prefer that she makes the phone call so it's obvious that she's the one who is saying, "I'm a responsible person and I'm reaching out for help in this situation." It's never going to be about domestic violence. Her reaching out to say, "I have an abuser and I need help, and I need help protecting my children [from the abuser],"...They will come in [CPS] and lay down this: "well you can't have contact [with the abuser], the kids have to go to him [for visitation], but you can't facilitate it, or you're going to, we're going to hold you responsible if the kids get hurt of if they witness anything." It's a nightmare.

Thus, if women called CPS on their abusers, or to get assistance from CPS on behalf of their children, they could potentially lose their children or be charged with failure to protect. Consequently, on the face, this represents gender "neutral"/biased practices, as both men and women "seeking help" may lose their children. However, it is in fact gendered, because one person seeking help is an abuser and the other is a victim, yet they are both treated as abusers. The policy ignores the gendered nature of domestic violence and parenting. First, mothers are predominately the caregivers of children, and consequently will likely retain custody and care of their children. Similarly, they are also given responsibility for children's outcomes. Abusers are generally not primary caregivers, and according to advocates, don't care if they or their partners lose custody. Further, the gender dynamics of domestic violence hold that most victims are women and most abusers are men; thus, policies that punish victims in the same way that they punish abusers clearly fall along gendered lines. Failure to Protect charges are another extension of the "blame the victim" mentality that serves to further oppress victims of domestic violence. Such practices are reflective of the "gendered organization" that, intentionally or not, serves to further oppress women. As Jean noted, "Batterers, men, are very seldom ever charged with failure to protect in domestic violence cases." In fact, the latent consequence of the policy is that it is highly gendered, to the extent that it is almost exclusively a woman's charge. Because men are largely perpetrating the abuse in co-occurring child abuse/intimate partner violence, the partner that fails to protect is almost always going to be the female victim.

Victim Exposes Children to the Abuser or Fails to Report

Moreover, Aileen's quote above illustrated the challenging dynamic of policy contradiction. Women were required to relinquish children to their abusers for visitation or they could be charged with kidnapping. Simultaneously, in a direct contradiction, women who relinquished children directly to the abuser could be charged with failure to protect if the abuser harmed the kids, despite the custody arrangements.

Not surprisingly, women did not want to disclose situations in which the abuser was abusing the children, because they thought they might lose their children. Gillian provided another case of a survivor who experienced failure to protect charges because she did not report his abuse of her child, and lost her children—even though she had ended the relationship and he was not living in the home after the incident. In this example, the mother was held responsible for her abuser's behavior:

> Just recently I was working with a woman, and she was in a relationship with this man and they were together four or five years, a couple of kids. He assaulted her, broke her jaw. She split with him for like a

week or so, two weeks, went back, again [because she had] no job that kind of stuff. So we're working with her helping her get a job, and then I want to say it was Memorial Day weekend, there was an incident where he had really significantly spanked one of the kids, I don't know if it was with a belt, but . . . mom saw it, apparently it must have happened in the morning, mom goes somewhere all day, work I guess, comes home in the evening, the dad leaves to go and he doesn't come back until the next day, but meanwhile that's when she sees the marks on the kid. Dad comes home the next day, she tells him, "get out!" So he leaves, then I think it is the holiday weekend, because the kid goes to visit a relative. The kid that he beat was not his kid, it was her older kid. So he [the abuser] was the dad of the other kids that she lived with. So she says "get out of here I am really mad at you." Then she sends the kid with the marks to an aunt's house. The aunt on his dad's side. They see these marks on the kids butt, they take the kid to the hospital. The hospital hotlines mom, gets called by the aunt that they have taken the kid to the hospital, she shows up at the hospital, but mom immediately goes into a little bit of cover for dad mode. They end up putting the kid in foster care, and she's totally freaked out, but when mom goes into cover up mode, they see that as a very negative thing. So mom is now being punished, as well as the guy. So there was a hearing later that week, maybe the beginning of the following week that I went to with her, and they chose to keep the kid in foster care. We have a hearing at the end of this week, again, that's the next time that she's been to court in which time she has a long to do list of things that mom will be graded on doing these to-do lists. Now, mom was not the person who whacked the kid. She was the person who may not have been completely forthcoming about what she knew about him whacking the kid. So she's responsible. Absolutely, failure to protect. So, again, the shared goal [between advocates and CPS caseworkers] is the kid doesn't get whacked anymore but the difference is accountability for that, and really holding moms accountable for protecting their kids from the other party in a way that is really harsh. I even said and the lawyer said "Dad's out of the house," but because she wasn't truthful with them, they now say, "we can't necessarily believe that she'll keep him out of the house."

Like Gillian, Aileen noted a similar situation, in which the mother was held responsible for exposing the child to the abuser. However, in this case, the mother was required to provide the abuser with visitation of the children by the Family Courts, but simultaneously was prohibited from exposing the children to the abuser by DFS:

Chapter 4

Well, if we have a Mom whose abuser is the father of her children and she enables the abuser to continue to have visitation with the children, we believe that's a risky situation. It becomes her fault, I mean [says sarcastically] clearly it is her fault for putting the children at risk of harm rather than it being his fault for being the person who abuses. This is an ongoing immovable sort of response with Family Services, and my response is get him out of the house. If he's the one abusing Mom and the children are witnessing it, why is it Mom's fault? Why isn't it his fault? He's the one causing the violence, get him out of the house. Stabilize her in that house and help protect her, that's never what it is—she ends up homeless, she's still trying to . . . the children are wanting to see Dad typically because it's so extremely complicated for the kids, or the courts have ordered it, or the courts have not or there is nothing barring it so she is believing that the best way for her to be safe and the kids to be safe is to hand the kids over and it keeps him happy and she knows what's going on. It's her fault! It's never his fault. The risk of harm is from her exposing . . . why isn't it risk of harm for him? I don't get that! I am just not getting that at all. This is kind of a reoccurring theme with women being held responsible for either the batterer also abusing the children or the children witnessing the abuse of the mother. Absolutely! Absolutely! If you stop him from having contact it's going to go away. Totally! We've been saying this for years and we've not been able to really change the fact that Mom is completely responsible for the well-being of those children, but Dad has a right to have them, to have access to the children. Those are in complete conflict with each other!

When asked, "Do you think that has anything to do with gender dynamics?" Aileen, a feminist in metro Faulds County, responded:

Totally! It's completely! The man still has a right he's entitled we reinforce this entitlement issue. He is entitled to his family, he's entitled to the children, he's entitled to sex, he's entitled to her income, he's entitled to run everything, but it's her responsibility to fight against that entitlement. When he beats her he tells her, we hear this all of the time, "I have to discipline you, I have to, I'm entitled to, you owe me"... but then, we lay all of the burden for safety for that in that framework, in that hell that we have created in this structure, this family structure, all of the responsibility for protecting everybody is on her! That doesn't make sense! We are not getting anywhere with that.

Aileen indicated that some policies were contradictory, and the system set up women to fail. In this example, the courts gave the abuser visitation rights, and the battered woman was responsible for upholding her end of the custody arrangement by making sure that the abuser had access to picking up the kids for his visitation. If she did not comply, she could be subject to kidnapping charges. Yet, if anything happened to the kids in the abuser's care, the mother could be charged with failure to protect, and she would be violating her agreement with CPS. In such cases, advocates, working in transitional housing, made arrangements where there was an intermediary to connect the abuser to his children. Oftentimes, this occurred through their local police department, and in a policy loophole, women could then not be held responsible for exposing the children to the abuse. Thus, the systems that required women to provide abusers access to the child were in direct contradiction to the systems that punished the mother for providing abusers access to the children. This contradiction of systems and policies was problematic for abused women and their advocates. Aileen described this dynamic as woman-blaming:

> That dynamic right there, the one we're talking about the woman blaming. We are so familiar with how that's going to play out [CPS], we really don't want them involved in our families at that level . . . So there's definitely a shared vision among the staff here that we don't want them involved, because it's too dangerous. It will end up with her losing the children if she doesn't tow the line in a way that doesn't make sense.

Similar to Aileen and Gillian, advocates consistently noted that abused women were held responsible for their abusers' behaviors. When women were held accountable for abuser's actions toward children, advocates noted that they had to "jump through hoops" to get their children back or to keep their children in custody. Eve described such policies as problematic for her advocacy:

> What comes up the most frequently as a problem with Family Services is taking children away from mothers. Because of Failure to protect! And then making her..... forcing her to walk a fine line, and again, she is always held accountable. The fine line, the psych eval that is just ridiculous! Supervised visitation, when the only reason why you have removed a child from their mother, is failure to protect and she is in a domestic violence shelter, the child should come back to the mother

immediately! You have full time staff, we have a full time therapist [at the shelter]. If there is anything going on here, we're the place for that those families to be. You have a family that is in distress, dad goes this way, mom goes that way, the children are just put out there. Children of domestic violence suffer so many behavior problems. Then, when you have uprooted those children from the one person that's been the consistent in their life, and you expect her to jump through hoops it just makes it too hard. There are too many times when Children's Division is aligned with the batterer because he's a batterer! He is good, he is manipulative, and he knows what to say.

In this example, Eve also noted that abused women are perceived as mentally ill, and must obtain a psych evaluation. This is another example of a gendered policy, as abusers were not required to obtain a psych evaluation in Glawe County to retain visitation. Eve provided another example:

We have a woman right now that DFS took her children away from her because of her failure to protect from him. She left her home, and she is living in a domestic violence shelter and is currently having supervised visitation because she was a victim of domestic violence. We have no idea when she will get her children back! So far they've been gone from her for probably a month.

In these examples, Eve found victim-blaming attitudes among those they worked with in Children's Division in rural Glawe County. Mothers staying in a domestic violence shelter with no contact with the abuser frequently lost their children, according to advocates. Eve's experiences were somewhat different from the experiences of advocates in Metropolitan Faulds County, which was characterized by a higher level of community collaboration and informal/formal relationships. Eve did state there was some collaboration with the director of Children's Division, but individual caseworkers were problematic to work with. She relied on using survivor-defined approaches with the director to improve outcomes for the battered women she worked with in her shelter. Eve stated:

Fortunately for us, we can do that. I can pick up the phone right now, and call the head of the Children's Division and that's great, and I'll say, "what is going on here?" but I cannot battle every single case worker. And I found myself having to do that over and over and over again. Those that have been there for awhile have moved out and they are in management. I think that they forget that component of that new person coming in out of school or whatever. You don't have that background in domestic violence because it's not taught in schools.

Similarly, Jean also described survivor-defined practices by collaborating with victims and with DFS caseworkers in Faulds County. She was able to solicit survivor-defined practices of caseworkers by educating them in the dynamics and needs of each woman's case:

Yeah! and they are kind of strategic planning meetings too. Where they sit down with the woman with her family, friends or whoever she wants to bring in her advocate, if she wants to bring an advocate. So, most of my contact with DFS has been with that light. I help them make their case plans. Collaborating with the DFS people.

When Jean was asked to elaborate on what collaboration and survivor centered approaches looked like in such instances, she replied:

The kinds of things that I would talk about as a domestic violence advocate would be their concerns are always about keeping the children safe. So, I would point out what her plan is to keep the children safe and women always have plans to keep the children safe. Whether it's going to a neighbor's, if he comes around, or if he is living there and gets violent, but, generally he is not living with her if DFS is involved. I would just go into her plans and talk about her strengths; that she has used resources such as our Domestic Violence Agency, other Domestic Violence Agencies, that she has called the police and 9-1-1 when she's needed to, and that sort of thing. I think part of the problem with DFS is that in the family situation where they are dealing with a mother, father and the children they only really have access to the mother and the children. The father is never involved. She is always the one who is held responsible for the domestic violence that is occurring because he's not going to show up for those meetings, he doesn't care. So, the person who really needs help from DFS . . . Isn't there!

Like Jean, other advocates worked to bring about system change by educating caseworkers and other stakeholders in the Family Court. These interactional-level collaborative practices were an extension of survivor-defined advocacy and were practiced by both nonfeminists and feminists in both counties. Yet, feminist identity was associated with social change activism. In the courts, feminist justice system advocates in Glawe County were the most active in attempting to address system change. They wanted to improve all victims' experiences with CPS, to engage in systems of advocacy, as opposed to continued change-seeking in each individual case. Their social change activism included training, and availability of advocates to work with victims in CPS and the Family Courts. Emily illustrated:

> I was available and we had advocates available kind of to do the same types of work that we do here. Helping them through the system helping them with other options and just having kind of an outside person from the court, because a lot of times in a situation like that where kids are out of your care and you're just afraid that anything you do or say is going to be one more reason for them to not come home, it's really hard for them to really admit that maybe there is violence in the home. So we wanted to have an outside person available to assist them through that. It was not as successful as we had hoped because we found that they were still worried about that. So, we got a chance though to do some trainings and build a little bit of a relationship with the family court and some of the workers.

Nonfeminist advocates in Glawe County and Faulds County used survivor-centered practices in their collaboration with CPS caseworkers, but did not generally seek system change in the way that feminist advocates, like Emily, did. However, both feminist and nonfeminist advocates in Metro Faulds County also participated through their local feminist coalition in a large-scale grant funded Greenbook initiative (see chapter 1), with the aim of collaboration as a central part of system change. Thus, coalitions facilitated social change activism in this case, among nonfeminist and feminist advocates. Greenbook was not described as successful by advocates in Faulds County; this dynamic is described in another section of this chapter.

Systemic Revictimization in CPS Systems

Abuser's Manipulation of Women's Personal Histories

Some advocates indicated that abusers used women's personal histories, or emotional states, to discredit victims' allegations of abuse. At times, abusers were successful in doing so, as caseworkers were not able to recognize the extension of abuse in such circumstances, and to recognize that abusers were "playing the system." For example, Gillian described a situation in which a client she worked with had a history of childhood abuse, and her abuser knew about it. The woman had sought help from a therapist to deal with her childhood trauma. The abuser then used this information as a part of his abuse and control over her in CPS. Gillian stated:

> The perpetrator uses a woman's personal history because she's been honest with him. [The abuser will say] "This really didn't happen [the abuse], but this was her issue as a child, so now she's saying I'm doing it. She's really the one that's gotten psychological help, and see, these are all just her issues."

Caseworkers failed to recognize dynamics of abuse; women coming from abusive households are more likely to enter into abusive relationships themselves. Further, child abuse co-occurs with intimate partner violence in more than a third of cases (Banks et al., 2008; Nichols, 2011). Thus, abusers presented challenges to victims and their advocates when they manipulated CPS systems by using women's personal histories to discredit their allegations of abuse, which was further complicated by CPS caseworkers' lack of knowledge in the area of domestic violence. In fact, advocates reported that caseworkers frequently failed to recognize dynamics of abuse that impact abused women's interactions with CPS. Gillian described another case where an abuser used his victim's psychological history to discredit and institutionalize her, with the end result of the abuser gaining custody of the children:

> I think the hardest one for me in light of the whole court system is when children are involved and the whole custody, all of the custody battles. Well, that's always a threat that's used for women if their partner doesn't want them to leave or knows they are getting ready to leave. Who will get the children? "I will make you pay! You will never see your children!" Then, women continue to stay and it just gets worse. Then, the crazy making around that of wanting to protect the children and using that whole thing against them, they are obsessive about their children, or they are crazy. So more like an emotional type of abuse with the kids. I have one woman who her husband committed her to a psychiatric ward, I mean she was there for 18 hours and she didn't need to be there. There are things that she doesn't know how to handle, and the anxiety it just compounds all of the issues, and finan-

cially he can afford to have a high class attorney, she can't. She does not have her children now. His family does, and her children are very, very young. All of those issues, and usually it's the one that can support them the best who will get them. It is not true that the mother always gets the children. Especially in domestic violence. Yeah, right! So then you run into the things, the father's rights etc. Who has the most money?

Thus, women could lose custody of their children due to abusers' manipulation of CPS systems and using their partners' history of abuse or anxiety, and even their helpseeking by going to a therapist, against them. This represents systemic revictimization, as the system actually facilitated the abusers' continued abuse and control of their victims. Systemic revictimization occurred not only in the context of psychological abuse and discredited child abuse allegations, but occurred in mandatory collaborative sessions with CPS as well.

Collaborative Sessions

Some advocates reported that women were required to attend collaborative sessions with CPS caseworkers and their abusers in order to retain or regain custody of their children. This requirement exposed women to further batterer-based revictimization. Many advocates described that the psychological abuse was so intense, and abusers were so good at manipulating the system, that they could make victims appear hysterical or emotionally unstable in front of caseworkers in collaborative CPS sessions. A majority of advocates reported that caseworkers repeatedly failed to recognize the extension of abuse in both joint supervised visits and in collaborative planning sessions. For example, Aileen stated:

It is a problem where Family Services has provided the supervision of supervised visits with Dad, Ohh my God, those can be just unbelievable, where it's their interpretation of what they are seeing. We've had where there should be no contact between Mom and Dad, where in fact they are supervising this joint visitation thing and he spends the whole time threatening her in this very passive aggressive sort of way. Mom comes out of there hysterical and then the write up about it is, well Mom is completely inappropriate and emotionally unstable! A nightmare!

Like Aileen, other advocates also noted that the abusers' presence can be traumatic for victims in such circumstances. Further, when abusers intimidate or threaten victims, they are continuing their abuse, even after the woman has left that relationship. For example, Ingrid stated:

So, one of my ladies, she had come into the emergency room, and he had beaten her pretty badly. I don't want to get into the gruesome details, but he used a hammer. She had experienced abuse for a long time, but stayed in it because he had this bad upbringing and family life, and she felt sorry for him, and thought that he was the way he was because of his own abuse. Well, she thought he would change when he realized she wouldn't do that to him. Well, after the hammer, she decided to leave him. Except the courts gave him supervised visitation. And, she had to be there. She wanted to be there because she felt like she needed to protect her kids. She didn't trust it to the caseworker. And, she told me he would just stare at her. And when the case worker looked away, he'd do one of these [angry face with quick forward movement] or, he'd cock his head to the side and just stare. Now, you might be like "so what" but, hey, this guy took a hammer to her. She's scared for herself and for her kids. So, she looks a little nuts in front of the caseworker because she's freaking out. She is nuts, she's freaking out, and she should be—you'd be too. But with DFS, they don't see the domestic violence side of it, she just looks nuts and like she's freaking out and that's what they see.

Again, this example depicts ways abusers can continue their abuse through CPS systems, and also how CPS systems can fail to recognize dynamics of domestic violence. Eve, a nonfeminist (but who held strong feminist ideologies, see chapter 2) responded to structural problems in the system, where victims were exposed to their batterers in collaborative sessions or supervised visitation, by refusing to go to sessions where the abuser was going to be present:

I think it is a lack of understanding and education, and actually their knowledge of domestic violence is, what a woman has to do to protect herself and her children, and I always say to every case manager that I work with, "Who's safety plan is it? You need to listen to her. She has been surviving this for the last ten years. You need to listen to her." You need to have your family team meetings separate! You should never ever have the victim and the abuser in the same room at the same time talking about the same parenting plan. It should always, always be separate. One women come to us, and I have even worked with women outside of Woman's Safe Home to do family support team meetings and I won't attend a family support team meeting where the batterer is present. I just will not! Because his level of power is still there. She is not going say . . . she's not going to tell you the truth in front of him. And he's going to continue to have that control over her because he still has contact, and she knows he has told her all along you mess with me I will take your kids away from you! And that's exactly what happens!

By refusing to attend, and educating caseworkers on why collaborative sessions could be revictimizing, Eve was using survivor-defined advocacy. Like Eve, other traditional advocates in both Glawe and Faulds Counties attempted to contact caseworkers or their directors to address these challenges. Justice system advocates in Glawe County reported rarely working with CPS systems, and justice system advocates in Faulds County were working largely with the Family Courts to seek system-wide changes through expanded availability of advocacy in the courts, training, and collaborative sessions between CPS and advocates.

Mandatory Classes

Some advocates described judges that might mandate victims to certain types of services, such as parenting classes or counseling, to maintain or to regain custody of their children. This represents patriarchal gender-based policy, as such judges assumed there was something wrong with victims of abuse, not just their perpetrators. As a result, mandatory classes were reminiscent of the "for your own good" mentality typical of patriarchal gender-based policy. For example, Eve, who did not self-identify as feminist, but held strong understandings of gender inequality on a societal level as well as in cases of domestic violence, illustrated:

I feel that, first of all, domestic violence does not necessarily mean that she has something wrong with her, and it's not an illness or a disease that needs to be fixed. It's a whole social issue. I believe that batterers need to be held accountable, and there is not enough accountability. An abused woman will hold herself accountable, in fact, she takes the blame for everything that happens to her. So for her, she does need some help that *she* is open for! But to court order her—just because she is a victim of domestic violence doesn't mean that she is a bad mother. Just because he is a dad doesn't mean that he is a good one. My opinion is anybody that would beat their child's mother or physically and emotionally or financially harm her, is not a good parent or a good role model.

Eve further delineated that while mothers were required to go to counseling or to take parenting classes in rural Glawe County, batterers were not. Batterers could retain visitation regardless of whether they were assigned to or completed such classes. In this way, such policy is gendered because it ignores the gender dynamics involved in domestic violence and also in parenting—the vast majority of advocates' cases involved a female victim and a male perpetrator. The women wanted their children and the abusers didn't seem to care. Jasmine, a Glawe County feminist, stated:

> There are cases where the batterer is ordered to a parenting class. Okay? But there is no teeth in it. There is no follow up with it. So they might be ordered but they might not go, whereas victims want to keep their kids so they're more likely to go. But batterers still get visitation whether they follow through with what the courts have said, or not. Do you see any equality in that then? No! No absolutely not! I don't! Batterers are not held accountable and until they are, you can have all of the programs in place . . . that's what I meant in equality, in the sense of the batterer gets the advantage. And he does by doing nothing! The batterer has all of the advantages by doing nothing.

Advocates reported a similar dynamic in the metropolitan Faulds County. For example, Jean stated:

> I do know that sometimes the abusive partner has been told that he has to attend parenting classes, but he doesn't attend; because he doesn't care if he gets the kids back or not.

Again, at face value, the policy of requiring parents in abusive households to take parenting classes appears to be gender neutral. However, it fails to recognize that one parent is the abuser and the other is the victim. The terms "family violence" and "abusive households" are thus misleading, and result in ignoring gendered realities of domestic violence. Thus, treating an abuser and a victim equally is gender "neutral" yet it is clearly gender biased in reality, as most victims are women who wish to keep their children. Further, abusers retained visitation regardless, while victims would lose their children if they did not attend the classes.

Required Tasks Related to Economic Access

In some cases, women could be charged with child neglect for not having electric, water, or heating resources in their homes. Women could lose their children, and would then be required to gain these resources in order to regain custody of their children. In such situations, advocates worked to address these challenges through survivor-defined practices, and facilitating such practices among caseworkers as well. There were some distinct differences between feminists and nonfeminists in their descriptions of such requirements. For example, Belinda, a nonfeminist stated:

> I think the folks that are responsible for these cases they are over-worked, underpaid, under constant duress, and it's been my experience if you treat them with respect they will listen, if they can get a quick minute to just listen. It's been my experience that they want what is best for the children, that's their number one responsibility. They don't want to be punitive toward the victim, and they try to work with the parents too, even if they have to take the children away, I mean it seems like their first investment is trying to restore the family, try to get some services for the family. Let's face it if they feel like the child is endangered they're sometimes are going to have to make tough decisions. I used to participate in like a community team approach and I remember one in particular where they had to take the children. Over time it worked out because she worked hard to get her children back. She did the things that were in a plan.

When asked, "Like what kind of things?" Belinda replied:

> Get some parent education, get her water turned back on, get her light turned back on, just certain things like that. She worked hard to do that but I was there the day they had told her the decision was to [take her children away] and I don't know if you heard it, pretty much that wailing cry, it comes from the depths of your soul that grief. I will never forget it. I will just never forget it, but that also showed how deeply she loved her children, and she obviously did, because she did the things she needed to do to get her children back.

Yet, at the same time, Belinda did not acknowledge the possibility that the mother could have kept her children while simultaneously accomplishing the required tasks. Further, the reasons why her water and electric were not on were related to her abuse—isolation from economic resources and control of household arrangements by her abuser. Moreover, Belinda suggested that abused women need parenting classes.

In contrast, Gillian, a feminist, noted the specific dynamics of abuse in one case, where the abuser was not allowing the victim to get trash service. Instead of recommending parenting classes and the removal of her children until she could get trash services, Gillian recognized the gender dynamics of abuse, and the impact on her client and her client's children.

> Very frustrating! It's frustrating because you see what it is doing to this person, I mean to really all of them. And her children too. So those are extremely frustrating situations, and all of the legal things. How do people pay for attorney fees? They can't! Especially if their abuser has prevented them from working, or getting a job. Even if they do have a job where has the money gone? They may not have access to it. I mean we get the whole economic spectrum of women who come here and they may live in [affluent suburb], in a brand new home, and still have no money and no access to money. In fact, we had a woman who came here several years ago who all of her utilities were turned off and she lived in a very nice house. She could not even—her trash—she would go out at night to put it in someone else's dumpster, and the police were called because someone saw her putting her trash someplace else. I mean all of those things happen and it's really because of lack of understanding. People don't understand the issue.

Responses such as Belinda's and Gillian's were typical of nonfeminists and feminists, respectively. Feminists consistently understood that the safety of the children was tied to the safety of the mother. Feminists also recognized the impact of domestic violence in such situations—mothers may appear to be neglectful for not having water, trash pickup, or electric, but it may be a manifestation of abusers' control over them, their economic resources, and their children. Thus, feminist identities and ideologies were important in recognizing the impact of domestic violence on economic resources, resources associated with neglect in CPS systems, and related barriers to leaving abusive relationships. While a majority of both feminist and nonfeminist advocates did not support removing the children from their mothers, nonfeminists were more likely to support the idea that abused women should be required to take parenting classes, while a majority of feminist advocates felt it was paternalistic and unnecessary. Nonfeminists were more likely to hold victim-blaming attitudes and punitive responses, and they acknowledged them as benefitting victims and their children rather than punishing them. Feminists were more likely to see it as a punishment.

Victim-Blaming among CPS Caseworkers

Victim-blaming within CPS systems and advocates' responses to them are described below in the context of social change/system change activism. Jean, a feminist in Faulds County, noted that CPS/DFS held paternalistic attitudes toward abused women. This represents systemic gendered practices, lending itself to a gendered organization. Because women are more likely to be abuse victims than men, they are more likely to receive paternalistic behaviors from caseworkers. When such behaviors are typical in organizations, they reflect and reproduce gendered oppression of women. For example, Jean stated:

> Well, certainly DFS and Child Protective Services because again, it's the same situation, she's in this mess that is having to deal with them, DFS, or CPS because she's either blinded by love, she's a softy, she's a woman, she doesn't know how to keep herself safe, she doesn't know how to take care of her kids. I think again, there is a patronizing attitude instead of holding this man accountable who's beating them up when that is the issue, as it sometimes is.

The same dynamics were uncovered in rural Glawe County as well. Eve also described systemic biases experienced by abused women. When asked, "What are the pros and cons to working with Family Services?" Eve replied:

> They are biased against women victims of domestic violence. There is more buy-in in Child's Division for the male than for the woman. I believe that, in my opinion, working with Children's Division they have to be won over every single time. The victim is always the one at fault. She is always the one that has to prove herself the most. She is held more accountable and I believe that they do not have a good understanding of the nature and dynamics of domestic violence. I know that

due to the large turnover through Children's Division they don't always get the knowledge that they need, but I think that it should be mandatory for them, because the majority of their cases are domestic violence and they just don't even know it.

When I asked her for an example of gender bias in CPS systems, Eve described an experience of one of the women staying at the Glawe County Shelter:

Currently . . . yes I can we had a case that we worked with very closely and the little girl mom and dad had domestic violence, the little girl told her mom that daddy was doing some uncomfortable things to her when they would go on visits. The child was pretty graphic in what she was saying. I don't know how much details you want on that, bath times for a little ten year old girl was becoming very stressful for her at her dad's house. She felt that dad did not need to bathe her, was not giving her privacy. There was other things going on, she reported it to her mother, her mother went straight to DFS and told them about that, and mom was treated like she was vindictive, a liar, hostile and in fact her child was taken away from her. She made sexual assault allegations, sexual abuse allegations toward her ex concerning her child and Children's Division stepped in and took it upon themselves to talk with the judges and her child was removed from her and placed in foster case. She was only given supervised visitation with her child, the abuser was not. So he could visit with his child. He could visit with his child unsupervised. His visits went on the way it was court ordered. Hers were not.

Similarly, Jean stated, "I see a lot of that. Where the assumption is that she is lying unless she can very specifically prove otherwise." Eve and many other advocates also noted suspicion of women who disclosed their abuse in CPS/related systems:

Yes! I truly believe that Children's Division you are not innocent until proven guilty, you are guilty until you prove yourself innocent! I see it all the time!

Eve further tied the victim-blaming mentality and consequent systemic revictimization to a lack of understandings about domestic violence and the safety of the mother. This type of response was typical of advocates with feminist ideologies:

The difference that I saw when I was doing that work was that the CPS worker and the Family Court personnel their goal is best interests of the child, that's the whole frame work. So, I think while my perspective is that the best interests of the child include the best interests of the mother and the parents I think that part gets lost sometimes from my perspective with the CPS workers. They are very focused on services for the child.

In metro Faulds County Linda also recognized lack of understanding about domestic violence as a problem among CPS caseworkers, and education and training as a solution to the problem of victim-blaming:

You know shockingly I think what surprised a lot of people is that the lack of knowledge about domestic violence in the frontline social workers from Children's Division. Actually just social workers in general I think sometimes, some of these investigators in Children's Division who go out and investigate child abuse didn't have more than a cursory understanding of the nature of domestic violence. We were really surprised by that. I think that over the last, certainly 5 years, they have done a better job of training some of these front line workers in a better working understanding of domestic violence and the dynamics that exist within these families and blended families that keep that cycle going, and why women don't necessarily report, and why from the outside it would look like she's putting her children at risk, but here's the reasons why. So I think that's been a benefit too. There has been a more concerted effort to train some of these frontline workers.

Further, Linda suggested cross-training, between advocates and CPS caseworkers as a potential solution to some of the victim-blaming problems that arose in CPS systems:

Family Services, their number one job is to keep the kids safe. And we would want the children to be safe, too. I think that they often consider domestic violence even if an advocate is not present in their cases. I do. All of us, I think, have made an effort to try to . . . I can't say cross fertilize, that would be just too much because we don't do their job, they don't do our job, but we do try to connect and there are opportunities to do that. I think it raises sensitivity on both ends. I realize how large their case load is, I realize how much pressure is on them, I realize things if I hadn't spent some time talking with people in that discipline maybe I wouldn't make snap judgments and say "well obviously they just don't care about the victim, they care about restoring their family or whatever." So it helps to get a better picture of the whole picture if you have that collaboration. Okay.

Advocates in Faulds County, as a part of the local feminist coalition and joint grant funding endeavors, participated in the Greenbook Initiative (see chapter 1) as a means toward system change. Belinda described the benefit of informal relationships that the project helped to facilitate, while simultaneously indicating that the project was flawed and disorganized:

> Collaboration with Family Services is pretty formal. I did Greenbook. And that was one and actually I was going to review cases at one time for them, but they never called me. I mean I went to the training that they had, and so then when they called again, I just said no I can't just be on call and never be called to review cases. I have had situations where a worker was called into situations where there was domestic abuse and the father pushed or hit another child and then police came and Family Services was called in because the abuse affected some of the children, and because I knew the worker from being on community response teams and we had that in Oakwood and we also I went to Apple Valley, and I just got to know workers. So when this worker was called to this house and she found out that the woman was already coming here because of abuse, she called me. We talked about what was going on in that home and . . . having the informal relationships is helpful because then you can . . . Because in a sense it gave her a picture of what was going on even before the child was involved, and really it was the child that was really trying to protect. So that's . . . ohh yeah I think any kind of relationship like that really helps.

Belinda and other advocates described that during the training, the project showed merit, but after the training period, they did not get calls from DFS to review cases. In fact, Greenbook was described by advocates in this research as largely a disaster. Advocates who participated in Greenbook suggested that it did provide them with some helpful informal contacts, but it did not lead to any kind of significant system-wide change or a real increase in referrals from CPS. Thus, collaboration with CPS remained a problem in both regions. This is consistent with prior research, which indicated that the success of Greenbook varied widely between sites (see Banks et al., 2008).

Chapter 4

Conclusion

In sum, advocates relied on survivor-defined practices to improve the outcomes of the women they worked with. This included collaborating with women, listening to their assessments of their situations, needs, goals, and fears, and addressing them. Advocates supplied information and resources so survivors could make their own informed decisions. In addition, advocates met with or otherwise collaborated with caseworkers on behalf of the women they worked with to get better outcomes for them. Sometimes this collaboration resulted in advocates educating caseworkers about dynamics of domestic violence, or their clients' specific cases. At times, advocates, victims, and caseworkers met and worked together to develop a case plan. Essentially, advocates worked to educate and collaborate with CPS caseworkers through survivor-defined practices to address the goals of battered women.

Advocates largely resisted CPS policies and practices that had a negative impact on the women they worked with through survivor-defined approaches, and worked collaboratively with victims and with caseworkers to get the best outcomes for the women they worked with. At the same time, advocates with feminist ideologies were those who largely worked to bring about system change. These attempts were limited, and had limited success as well. It is unclear why advocates were more successful with social change endeavors in the justice system compared to CPS systems. Perhaps it was because they already held a strong presence in the police departments and the courts, but did not have a recognized presence in CPS/DFS systems. Nonfeminist advocates did not individually work toward social change, although some advocates participated in Greenbook due to their local feminist coalition activity. This again suggests the importance of strong local feminist coalitions in working toward social change, although problems arose with Greenbook. Advocates described Greenbook as never really taking off. A shared goal, system of referrals to advocacy, and mutual understandings of the interrelated nature of domestic violence and child abuse were never established. The only positive result of Greenbook in Faulds County involved the limited development of some informal relationships that assisted advocates when problems arose in some of their cases.

Collaboration with CPS in community based responses to domestic violence is greatly needed in order to mitigate both batterer-based and systemic revictimization of battered women. Since over one third of CPS cases involve domestic violence, collaboration is desirable (Banks, Landsverk, & Wang, 2008). However, challenges can arise because CPS social workers generally provide gender "neutral"/biased policy and service provision (Saathoff and Stoffel, 1999; Findlater and Kelly, 1999). As discussed in chapter 1, the goal of CPS is the safety of the child, without specific recognition of how abuse of the mother may influence the safety of the child (Banks, Landsverk, & Wang, 2008). The ideology that the safety of children is inextricably linked to the safety of the mother is central to the feminist gender-based perspective that is more likely to be held by feminist domestic violence victim advocates (see Whitcomb, 2002). This was definitely the case in Glawe and Faulds Counties.

Acker's theory of gendered organizations points out that reproduction is inherently gendered. This leads to sociocultural dynamics that influence women's roles as mothers, as well as the societal expectations that mothers are largely responsible for all aspects of their children's lives. Such societal expectations are different for fathers, who are held to a dissimilar standard. This is clear when examining CPS interventions, such as failure to protect, visitation, and mandatory parenting classes. Thus, the policies, practices, and outcomes of such interventions are clearly gendered. Moreover, gendered expectations of parenting are institutionalized in these CPS policies, which both perpetuate and reinforce such expectations. While laws vary from state to state, CPS policies and practices are affected by gender "neutral" child abuse laws.

Prior research finds that child abuse laws hold women accountable for the abuse of children when they have failed to protect children from the abuse, or when children are exposed to the abuse of the mother. This is evidenced through lost custody, charges of criminal child abuse, or charges of failure to protect children from the abuse (Whitcomb, 2002; Nichols, 2011). In addition, a mother may be charged for exposure to abuse if her partner beats her in front of her child, if she has not shown an effort to leave her abuser (Whitcomb, 2002; Nichols, 2011). The research presented in this chapter supports prior research. Advocates consistently noted failure to protect and neglect charges as problematic for victims and for their advocacy. Women lost their children in such cases, and had to attend parenting classes, develop safety plans, accomplish various tasks, and attend collaborative sessions in order to get their children back.

Another problem with CPS policy that prior research suggests is that abusers are learning how to manipulate the system in order to continue their patterns of abuse or avoid accountability (Lyon, 2002). For example, Lyon (2002) noted abusers threatened to tell CPS that the children were being abused if the victim called the police or filed for an order of protection. Other researchers have found the threat of lost child custody deterred some women from utilizing services (Findlater & Kelly, 1999; Lyon, 2002). The research presented in this chapter finds overwhelming support for this work. Yet, chapter four additionally finds other ways abusers are manipulating the system—through false hotline calls, using women's personal histories, and threatening women in collaborative sessions. The chapter additionally notes the benefits of advocacy in such circumstances. Advocates can facilitate survivor-defined approaches of caseworkers by educating them about women's unique situations, and dynamics of abuse.

Further, in addition to Failure to Protect, abusers manipulations, and continued abuse, CPS systems themselves revictimized battered women. Advocates noted victim-blaming behaviors of caseworkers directed towards abuse victims. CPS workers at times assumed women were lying when disclosing abuse. Advocates also found women were required to attend parenting classes, were held responsible for lack of resources such as heating, electric, and water that were controlled by their abusers, they were exposed to their abusers in collaborative sessions and in supervised visitation, and were caught between contradictory policies—upholding visitation and not exposing children to abuse. Advocates were challenged to negotiate these gendered policies and the practices that enforce them in order to maintain the safety of abused women and their children. A few advocates refused to have abusers present in collaborative sessions, and worked on behalf of victims to avoid batterer-based revictimization in such circumstances. Others contacted individual caseworkers or directors in CPS. Feminist advocates worked towards social change through the Greenbook Initiative, and collaboration and training with the Family Courts. Advocates' practices aimed to mitigate the gender "neutral" revictimization of battered women through survivor-defined and social change practices. Yet, their accomplishments were limited. The current system—including the policies and practices presented in this chapter— gives batterers an incentive to intimidate victims, and allows them to control their partners and their outcomes through threats, "playing the system," and making those threats a reality. Basically, these policies and practices enable such abuses.

Chapter 5

Advocacy in Shelters

In the previous chapters, the gendered policies and practices advocates encountered in the justice system and in child protective services were examined. Such organizations at times reflect policies and practices that are "neutral/biased" or "patriarchal." Yet, shelters are gendered organizations as well. Shelters are traditionally feminist organizations; their actors, leadership, and clientele are almost exclusively women. However, shelters simultaneously maintain feminist, "neutral/biased," and patriarchal gendered policies and practices as well. Specifically, chapter 5 examines the shelter rules that have been most contentiously debated in the practitioner-based literature: accepting adolescent boys into shelters, confidentiality, curfew, mandatory classes, entrance requirements, and chore assignments. This chapter also examines advocates' survivor-defined, intersectional, and social change practices—or absence of such practices in some instances—associated with the policies. Advocates both resisted and reproduced different forms of gendered practices. They were reproduced when advocates supported patriarchal or neutral shelter policies that facilitated revictimization of battered women. Yet they were simultaneously resisted through survivor-defined, social change, and intersectional feminist practices. Thus, the gendering of shelter organizations is complex, contradictory, and challenging for domestic violence victim advocates.

Adolescent Boys in Shelters

Some shelters maintain a policy denying shelter to mothers who have teen sons accompanying them. Prior literature suggests the policy developed out of an expectation that boys contribute to a lack of appropriate privacy and put women and girls at risk of sexual assault (Patterson, 2003). Further, teen boys were seen as a source of potential violence because of the perception that boys who witness domestic violence are more likely to be violent (Patterson, 2003; Nichols, 2011). Yet, boys who witness such violence are often not violent themselves, and standardized policy consequently discriminates against teen sons and their mothers (Nichols, 2011).

Moreover, the policy is not supported by the National Coalition Against Domestic Violence, or the [State] Coalition Against Domestic Violence. The policy is slowly being eradicated around the nation, and is now the exception to the rule in the State that Glawe and Faulds Counties were a part of ([State] CADV, personal communication). The national and state coalitions work to provide education and training to coalition-member shelters on best shelter practices. In fact, there was a triple homicide in [State] three years ago because a woman returned to her abuser with her two children when the local shelter would not accept her teen son; upon returning, the abuser killed them all. Because of this incident, the state coalition made it a priority to educate shelters, aiming to eradicate any existing policies barring teen sons or to provide alternative emergency shelter in a local hotel ([State] CADV, personal communication). However, despite this work, the shelter in Glawe County continued the policy.

In rural Glawe County, there was only one shelter, and this shelter had a policy of not accepting teen boys. This created a challenge for advocates working outside of the shelter in the justice system. All the advocates in the justice system in Glawe County described the policy as problematic, as the policy commonly resulted in victims returning to their abusive homes. For example, Vicki explained how the policy barring adolescent sons from shelter made finding a safe living space difficult for victims, and consequently contributed to women going back to their abusers:

> I think the age is 11 or 12, after that they [adolescent boys] can't go into the shelter. So a lot of times people won't want to leave [their abuser]. They're not going to leave their son behind or they don't have somewhere else to go. So that does create issues and transitional housing usually isn't an option to go right into.

The policy resulted in systemic victimization, as the shelter policy created a barrier to accessing safe shelter. The policy also resulted in the potential for further batterer-based revictimization upon the family's return to the abuser. When asked how many women ended up going back to their abusers because shelters would not accept their teen sons, Kari replied, "I really can't say a number but I can say that it is very common." She then said:

They may stay with a friend for a week or so, out-stay their welcome, and then it's time to go. And then they go back. Or they don't want to uproot their kids. A lot of them, especially for the older kids [women say] "they only have a year left in high school and I don't want to move them to a new high school now," and I understand that.

If women couldn't get into the local shelter because of the policy excluding teen boys from shelter, and they did not want to move to a new location where their kids would be displaced, they returned to their abusers because of lack of alternatives.

In metropolitan Faulds County, there was once a policy barring teen boys from shelter. Jean described how, as an advocate, she experienced specific challenges in finding space that would accept victims with their teen sons:

That's such a difficult situation for a mother ... Some women really don't have any other options and what I've found is that women who cannot find another place for their 16 year old, they usually end up having to go to a homeless shelter. They have to go with their whole family, and they may have kids who range, the 16 year old boy may be the oldest and their youngest is a four year old. Most of our [homeless] shelters in this area are in unsafe neighborhoods. The shelters themselves are often unsafe, a lot of stealing goes on. Of course, some have more problems with that, some less, but it's not a place where you want to go with your family. You have no privacy. It's extremely difficult to go to a homeless shelter with your whole family. Also if confidentiality is of any importance in your situation, you're certainly not in a confidential location if you're concerned about an abusive partner looking for you in [homeless] shelters.

She indicated that the alternative, the homeless shelter, was unsafe and undesirable for families, and it posed a safety risk because of lack of confidentiality. When asked, "Have you ever had a case where a woman didn't go to a shelter because she couldn't take her teen sons with her?" Jean replied:

Yeah, I had one woman that I was working with who was living in her car. She had her teenage son and her other children staying with family and she stayed in the car because she could be closer to her children that way. They didn't have a lot of room and the kids were all sleeping on the floor in the living room and it was a very tiny house. It was not a good situation. Certainly many women who have a 16 year old son and can't get into a shelter, well they may not have any other place to go. So they would be staying home with their abusive partner, and that does certainly happen. I've worked with several women who have done that.

In this case, the woman was perhaps at an even greater risk staying in her car, which would be visible to her abuser should he find her. In addition, family members' homes are common places of refuge, and thus likely places to be found by an abuser. A car parked in front of a family member's house is certainly not a confidential or safe location. Thus, the policy barring teenage boys from staying at the shelter with their mothers can contribute to further batterer-based revictimization if the abuser finds the victim because she is staying in an identifiable and consequently unsafe place.

Since women generally maintained primary care of children, and were not willing to leave their children alone with an abuser or move far from their communities, they and their teen sons returned to abusive homes. Advocates responded to the challenges in different ways in rural Glawe County and in Metro Faulds County, and the varied responses also coincided with feminist identities and related practices.

Advocates in the Glawe County shelter, who were all nonfeminist, were asked about the policy where shelters might not accept boys over a certain age. Eve replied, "That's tough! . . . boys need to be with their moms and they need safety and security." Yet, she indicated that the shelter she worked in did not accept boys over age twelve. She described issues with teen boys and girls staying in close quarters and privacy as the primary concern with accepting teen boys. She stated that there were other places to refer women with children to that had a better structure for families. Her approach to this challenge was exclusively through referring these women elsewhere:

> There are other shelters that take children, boys over the age of 13. They have a different setup than we do. There's a wonderful, wonderful shelter that is almost like a resort type area and they have cabins. So families don't live in one room together, they have their own little cabins. When you come to a shelter, space is tight. Families share a room so you know you've got an 11 year old girl, you have a 13 or 14 year old boy, you have to worry about modesty . . . Children have it hard enough living in a domestic violence shelter without having to worry about children going through puberty and sexuality, and everything else.

Eve also cited transitional housing as a better option for women with children:

> Transitional housing is absolutely the most wonderful thing that they have ever come up with, and we work closely with our transitional housing program [in a neighboring county], that is the best of all worlds. If you want to know the truth, after a woman leaves and her immediate safety needs are met and you work with her and find out where she wants to go, and then to be able to go into a housing program where she can stay, but still have the support groups and the advocacy, I can't even talk good enough about it.

The other advocates in Glawe County also responded by referring victims to shelters in neighboring counties—and even other states— nearly an hour away. For example, Kari described the policy barring teen boys as a challenge, and strategized by making referrals to other shelters that did accept teen boys:

> I do know that our shelter here cannot accept males over 12. So when I have a woman who does have a male over 12, I know the other shelters that do accept those kids, so I will tell her directly about those shelters.

When asked how far away the other shelters were, Kari further described that distance and rural mentalities were additional barriers to accessing shelter for women with teen sons, even when such shelters accepted them:

> The nearest one [shelter] would be like 45 minutes south of here. So you're talking pretty far out. There is a couple in the [Faulds] City [an hour away] or within that metro area that will do it but you know a lot of our women are used to Glawe County or a more rural experience, so they're afraid to go into Faulds City. So if that one shelter 45 minutes from here doesn't have . . . [space] they are a lot of times . . . "no I think I'm just going to try and stick it out [stay with the abuser] or stay with a friend."

The policy and coinciding practices excluding such women from the shelter are not survivor-defined. Advocates worked around the policy, but they clearly recognized that the result was often returning to an abuser due to lack of alternatives. Further, one issue with both of the alternatives advocates mentioned—transitional housing and a cabin-style shelter in another county—was that they were located nearly an hour from Women's Safe Home. This proved difficult for women whose employment, children's schools, and community resources were in the county, and those who were not willing or able to make the move. Additionally, in the transitional housing program, women generally cannot go directly into it; women need a shelter stay first before they transition over. Availability in the cabin-style shelter and with transitional housing is also an issue; such options are very limited. Thus, this policy and advocates' attempts to circumvent it do not necessarily consider individual cases, specifically family-related needs, which are key to survivor-defined advocacy. While advocates did consider women's individual cases in recommending shelters that *did* accept teen boys, the policy itself did not consider women's needs, and had a negative impact on women's agency by potentially denying shelter if women were not willing to leave their communities, jobs, or if there were no spaces available. Basically, it limited women's choices compared to women without teen sons. The gender "neutral" policy that ignored the socio-cultural gender norms of mothering guided the similarly gendered practice. At the same time, the policy is gendered by labeling all adolescent boys as a threat. The assumption of violent masculinity is gender-biased in regard to boys seeking shelter with their abused mothers. Thus, the policy is both gendered and gender "neutral" at the same time, depending on whether the concept is applied to the individual experience of the mother or the boy.

Intersectional practices were apparent to some extent—but only in the context of recognizing a mothering identity as a trigger to refer women with teen sons into shelters that accepted teen boys. Or like Kari above, advocates recognized women's rural identities and reluctance to go long distances to stay in a city shelter. Yet, simultaneously, intersectional practices were limited, as women's social backgrounds of mothering identities were ignored in developing and sustaining this policy. In other words, if advocates recognized that mothers were returning to their abusers because the shelter did not accept their teen sons, and the alternatives were problematic, the policy itself was not informed by intersectional or gendered ideologies. None of the shelter advocates identified as feminist, and only one expressed gendered ideologies of domestic violence. They did not have intersectional perspectives or approaches.

The theory of gendered organizations maintains that organizations perpetuate the relegation of women to private spheres through gender "neutral" policies that both reinforce and ignore gender resulting in inequality. Acker (1992, p. 567) indicates that neutral gendered policies and practices contribute to a gendered understructure: "reproduction, the domain of female responsibility, is relatively invisible..." This policy serves to perpetuate inequality by ignoring existing societal gender dynamics. Women are generally the primary caregivers of children, and comprise the vast majority experiencing intimate partner violence. Policies which bar abused women with teen sons from shelter can thus result in batterer-based revictimization. This further complicates leaving a child with an abusive partner. The gendered nature of intimate partner violence and mothering, i.e., reproduction, is not considered in gender "neutral" exclusionary policies. In turn, the perception of teen boys as a danger solely based on their gender as opposed to their individual qualities and histories is also gendered. Teen boys may experience re-victimization as well under such policies. Thus, a policy can be gendered in multiple ways, with effects varying according to individual gender identity.

Feminist identities were associated with survivor-defined and intersectional approaches related to this policy, and social change activism as well. Social change activism relating to policies barring teenage boys from shelters was not practiced in Glawe County. The majority of advocates in Glawe County (all but one) saw it as a challenge but did not question the policy itself. Such advocates did not speak of changing the policy, as indicated in the narrative quotes above. The advocates did not generally express social change perspectives relating to this policy, although they saw it as problematic. Social change activism is important to note here, as the rule of not accepting teen boys puts women and their sons at a safety risk, and advocates were not active in seeking change. This was the case for all nonfeminist advocates, and was also the case for one feminist advocate in Glawe County. The other feminist advocate, Kari, stated, "I don't really have control of the policy; I've complained— I have a really good relationship with the director so I can do that—but I don't have the support of anyone else, so, no-go [the policy was not changed]." It should be noted that the only two feminist advocates in Glawe County worked outside of the shelter in the justice system, and likely had less control over the rules. Recall again that there is no strong local feminist coalition, which appeared to have a negative impact on social change activism.

In contrast, in Faulds County, none of the shelters or transitional housing programs that participated in this study had a policy against taking adolescent boys. When asked about policies against accepting teen boys, Shelli stated that at one time, there was a restriction on accepting teen boys in the shelter she worked in, but they changed the restriction, and they did not experience any subsequent problems. This change occurred because of social change activism regarding this matter in the local feminist coalition:

> So we've been taking boys as long as they are accompanying their mother and they're still considered minors, we'll take boys of any age. We've had boys who were 18 in here, we've had a couple of boys who were older, 19, 20 because they were still living at home with mom . . . but there is no problem, we've really had no problem.

In Faulds County, advocates used survivor defined, intersectional and social change practices to resist the gendered practice of denying teen boys shelter with their abused mothers. They clearly recognized individual cases and needs in their advocacy, and specifically used intersectional approaches by recognizing mothering as an important factor in regard to this shelter rule. The policy was not present in Faulds County in the shelter/housing in my sample because of the activism in the area that worked to eradicate the policy. This is likely related to the majority of feminist identities/ideologies among Faulds County advocates and the strong local feminist coalition.

Confidentiality

In the case of confidentiality, shelter residents cannot be dropped off by anyone, even a cab driver they do not know, within two to six blocks of the shelter (depending on the shelter). Residents also cannot tell anyone where they are staying, or give the phone number of the shelter to anyone not approved of by the shelter director. This includes family members, employers, friends, and others in addition to the abuser.

Advocates had mixed responses about the confidentiality policy. Some advocates felt it was imperative to women's safety, to avoid further batterer-based revictimization and supported the policy in their practices by expelling women for violating confidentiality. Others thought it put women at more risk for both batterer-based and systemic revictimization, as women could be expelled from the shelter for violating confidentiality rules. The benefits of confidentiality generally were described as

146

safety for the victim and other shelter residents, protection of privacy, and psychological benefits. The challenges were disconnecting from social supports, and getting expelled from the shelter for violating confidentiality. Interestingly, there were no regional or organizational distinctions regarding this practice. Whether confidentiality was seen as beneficial or problematic varied from advocate to advocate; there was no distinct pattern, thus the responses varied as well.

When asked about the benefits and challenges of confidential shelter location, Shelli responded:

> It gives them a sense of peace, when you tell them [victims] that it is confidential, you can't tell anyone where you're going, and that's for safety reasons . . . At least for her emotionally, it brings a sense of peace, that when I'm in there, this is a safe place. No one knows where it is, it's not published . . . it's very, very helpful for her.

In addition to the psychological benefit of confidentiality, Shelli highlighted safety as the primary reason for a confidential location:

> . . . I would say for the overwhelming majority of the women, he [the abuser] probably wouldn't find us because he's not going to go through all of that trouble to do that, so it does bring her safety. It literally keeps her safe. So we're going to make sure that it's not in her neighborhood before we take her, that kind of thing. So there's a real physical safety issue that it brings.

In contrast, when asked about confidentiality policy, Glenda illustrated the challenge of confidentiality policy and expulsion to her advocacy as an advocate working outside of a shelter:

> I can see the shelters' point-of-view, and I know why they do it, for the safety of the women and everybody in there. I also know that women have been put out of the shelter because they said where they were. It seems a little harsh especially if you want your children to know where you are or . . . but, I guess what I found is that they really stick to it. There's no bending.

Ingrid found the rule about maintaining a confidential location through a drop-off point a safety risk, and described it as a challenge to advocacy:

I don't see how that makes any sense either because if an abuser is following her, and she gets dropped off at the drop off point, then she's walking back to the shelter, isn't he still going to see her? Yeah! I really don't understand it. It doesn't make any sense!

Confidentiality is supposed to keep victims safe, yet when women are expelled for violating confidentiality rules, their safety then drops to zero. The policy, or at least expulsion for violating the policy, appears to be counterproductive. So, while serving as a strategy to mitigate revictimization for some advocates, it provided challenges to others.

Revictimization was also described within the context of intersectional practices. Ingrid illustrated intersectional approaches to advocacy when working to get women shelter. She described talking with women about their various identities to plan for safety and confidentiality in shelter. For example, she said sexual orientation was important:

I worked with a lesbian woman whose partner pretended to be abused so she could track her down at a confidential shelter. It wasn't anything I would have thought possible, but there it was. They were both kicked out, including the victim, because confidentiality was violated. I always ask now, it's important to see how someone's background might impact their safety.

Jean described another example of intersectional practices related to confidentiality policy:

Another woman that I worked with, she also broke the confidentiality rule. What happened is she took a cab and she had them let her off too close to the shelter. There's usually a drop off location, and in this case, she's a disabled woman and has trouble walking. She can walk and has walked from that pickup spot to the shelter. But I think in this case she was tired, she was hurting and she had the cab driver drop her off in front or very close to the shelter. She was also asked to leave. Also went back to her abusive partner.

Jean's example indicates confidentiality as potentially problematic for disabled women, who may have more difficulty physically accessing the shelter in a confidential manner. She indicated challenges for women of limited English speaking ability, as they may face language barriers in understanding shelter rules:

Several people that I've worked with have had to leave a shelter because they had not followed the confidentiality policy. In one case it was [a] Chinese immigrant who didn't understand what they were telling her about when they explained the confidentiality rules. She didn't understand it. So, unfortunately she had to leave the shelter and she went back to her abusive partner. You know, our goal is supposed to be to help keep people safe, to keep women safe. I feel like we don't do a very good job of it sometimes.

Jean, Ingrid, and the majority of advocates in Faulds County expressed that intersectional approaches were important to advocacy, in keeping victims safe and avoiding systemic victimization in shelters. When women were expelled from shelters because their individual social backgrounds were not identified and understood in relationship to confidentiality violations, it resulted in safety risks by increasing the likelihood of further batterer-based revictimization. Importantly, such ideologies and resulting intersectional practices were not expressed by nonfeminist advocates in both Faulds and Glawe Counties. Feminist identity in both regions was highly related to intersectional approaches in regard to shelter practices, with the exception of one feminist director in Faulds County.

Anais specified that women who went to the shelter were making a choice to leave their abuser, thus confidentiality served to reinforce that break. She related survivor-defined advocacy to confidentiality:

We believe in providing a safe place for the victim and a lot of times that means separating her from the abuser—we don't make that decision, the woman has to make that decision . . .

The victim makes the decision to enter, yet she does not really make the decision to keep her location confidential—she has to accept confidentiality as a condition of receiving shelter. Thus, it is not entirely survivor-defined. Anais was asked if the confidentiality policy posed any problems for advocacy:

So two years of living in a confidentially located setting is really hard. It's very hard ...They can't come on site, they can't be here. They have to go elsewhere. The women live here with all of the freedom they need to go elsewhere. The idea is for them to have a safe space to have refuge and we have to—that's problematic. It's just hard to do. So it's a constant struggle. It's a constant struggle . . .

Chapter 5

Confidentiality is thus complex. It can provide safety, psychological benefits, protect privacy, and reinforce broken ties with abusers. Yet, it can also isolate women. This is consistent with prior research. Haaken and Yragui (2003) note that confidentiality policies separate abused women from their communities, and cut them off from social support networks instrumental in helping them leave their abusers. In addition, this policy puts some women at risk of systemic and batterer-based revictimization if they are expelled for violating the policy. It was clear that it was a struggle for advocates, too, to weigh the relative pros and cons of the policy.

Advocates used survivor-defined practices to determine whether a confidential location was the best option for the women they worked with. The practice of confidentiality is to some extent patriarchal because it assumes that women may be in need of protection, and it is the standardized shelter rule that determines confidentiality, not the woman. Thus, the practice is not really survivor-defined either, as it is a standardized response. Therefore, advocates who preserve confidential location in their practices may be simultaneously reproducing patriarchal gendered responses, as well as feminist gendered responses focusing on empowerment through safety and confidentiality. Regardless, expulsion is not survivor-defined and puts women at risk. Advocates who did not support confidentiality because of the safety risk of expulsion responded through social change practices.

Eve described attending state coalition meetings, where she was exposed to a variety of different shelter rules. She discussed some of these rules when asked what was problematic about shelters that were confidential: "First of all, a victim—what kind of jeopardy are you putting her in if you drop her off five blocks from her safe place and she's got children and you know he's out there looking for her!" Eve stated that Women's Safe Home in Glawe County, the only shelter in the rural county, was once a confidential location, but adapted to become semi-confidential over time. Eve illustrated:

> Okay, here at our shelter we are the new term "openly hidden" we are not an undisclosed location [but] we don't put a sign out. I feel that there are no cons to that at all. We are more visible. The police department, sheriff's department they know where we are, the community knows where we are . . . We are more accessible to the very victims that need us, and one of the things that it did, it made us re-examine our safety policies. So we got cameras. We have alarms.

She indicated that the [State] Coalition Against Domestic Violence educating toward social change was instrumental in the changes at her shelter. In addition to loosening confidentiality rules, she also indicated that the shelter adopted a flexible curfew policy, and did not have mandatory classes per the influence of the state coalition (detailed below). This is interesting, because the state coalition also suggests accepting teen boys, so social change at this shelter was somewhat contradictory as this shelter did not accept teen boys.

In Faulds County, the advocates had very mixed perspectives on confidentiality. Some advocates believed the benefits of the policy outweighed the challenges. The advocates that did not support it responded by working with directors to advocate for change and for the woman they were working with, and were all feminists. The results were mixed—the policy was not changed, but at times individual women were allowed back into the shelter. However, in other cases women were not allowed back in the shelter, or did not want to go back because they were embarrassed or upset about being asked to leave. Such advocates also described bringing up the issue in their local coalition community meetings in the context of what Gillian and Jean described as "hotly contested policy debates."

Curfew

Curfew policies generally include a time shelter residents are required to return to the shelter for the night. Women may also be required to sign in and sign out of the shelter, disclose where they are going, when they plan on returning, and leave a contact number. Advocates expressed mixed responses about curfew policies. Some advocates indicated curfew was an available strategy to reduce the likelihood of batterer-based revictimization: the benefit was safety. In addition, some advocates indicated that curfew was necessary for group living, so other residents would not be disturbed by comings and goings at night.

In Glawe County, the practices surrounding curfew were survivor-defined and flexible. They did have a curfew, but the policy was tailored to the individual needs of each woman residing in the shelter. Eve illustrated the complex realities of curfew and safety:

Our shelter here only has one staff working in the evening into a mid-night shift. Staff need to know who's coming and who's going ... Safe-ty reasons, plus it's not safe for her to be out at night and he's looking for her and we can't get to her.

Yet Deb stated that while they did have a curfew, there was some flexibility in the policy that did address individual women's needs and allowed women to decide:

We suggest at 10 p.m., but there is ways . . . truly if a woman is some-place visiting her parents or her sister and she's safer to spend the night, I would prefer for her to spend the night and come back in the morning. If she has a job where she gets off of work at like 10:30 p.m., it's not . . . a big deal.

So, even though Women's Safe Home had a curfew, it was flexible and survivor-defined. In addition, women were not generally expelled for violating curfew, unless they were gone for several days without com-municating with an advocate so the shelter could open a bed to another survivor. Eve, the director, also described taking issue with other shelters expelling women for curfew violations, and why survivor-defined flexi-ble approaches were better than standardized responses:

You know maybe the bus is late, maybe there is an accident and she doesn't get back to the shelter in time, she's passed curfew so she's kicked out! Okay, the very system that said that they would help her is now working against her! Again, it's more power and control!

Such systemic revictimization can also result in batterer-based revictimi-zation, as policies may interfere with a victim's ability to retain shelter and leave an abuser.

While in Glawe County, curfew was survivor-defined and flexible, in Faulds County, it varied. One of the organizations in Faulds County that participated in this study was a shelter that had standardized curfew with few exceptions, and rules surrounding the exceptions. In contrast, the other organization from Faulds County that participated in the study was a transitional housing program that did not have curfew requirements for residents. In one shelter in Faulds County, Shelli, like Eve, described curfew policy as a benefit to women's safety:

> If there is no curfew, we don't know if something happened to her ... If we know that everybody is supposed to be back by ten and so-and-so's not back by ten, we go into action; but if there is no curfew we might not know that something happened till ten o'clock the next morning, because there's no curfew.

She also indicated that there was some flexibility in the policy, but women would be expelled for violating curfew rules after the third violation. Shelli described curfew as imperative to safety. However, other advocates described curfew as representing a patriarchal policy, resulting in systemic revictimization. For example, Jean described working with clients staying at shelters that had flexible curfews for women with jobs. However, other requirements surrounding curfew and the workplace posed some challenges:

> The only problems, [ways] that curfew has really limited some of my clients are, I could say a couple. One is if they have a job. They are going to get in maybe 11:30 or 12:00 and they're required to have a note from their employer [confirming] that they're working until such and such a time, then . . . if a person [victim] asks for this [note] what do you say to your boss, "I need a note to work late." To show who? Well, now you're telling them that you're staying at a shelter? That you have domestic violence problems? This isn't stuff that you necessarily want to share at your workplace.

So while shelter curfew may be seemingly flexible, in this case considering women's work schedules, requiring a note to verify their whereabouts is patriarchal because it assumes women are lying otherwise to extend curfew, and violates personal confidentiality because they will likely have to disclose to the boss that they are in a shelter and that they are victims of domestic violence. This is certainly not a survivor-defined policy/practice, and contrasts sharply with the practices of early feminist advocates. Shelli described having mixed feelings about the policy herself, and tried different techniques with problematic results:

> When we had it at different times, or did not have a curfew, it became very disruptive to the women who still wanted structure and the routine. Because the woman who didn't want that and would come back at all hours of the night would wake other people up. Because all of the sudden she's in the bathroom, she's in the kitchen, she's talking on the phone . . . and the other person in the bedroom, "I didn't sleep, she

woke me up at three o'clock in the morning." So it's not fair for those
who want the structure.

Thus, it was clear Shelli struggled with her decision-making over the
policy. She wanted to give women freedom and empowerment, but experienced significant problems when she did that negatively affected some
of the shelter residents. Her example indicates the complex realities of
group living. In addition, she said:

> We firmly believe that with structure, when you're coming from trauma
> and chaos, you absolutely need structure to bring tranquility! It's a fact!
> You have your habit. Kids especially need structure. They need to
> know what is expected: that this is when you go to school, this is when
> dinner is, this is when bath time is, it gives them a sense of security and
> peace.

This practice appears to be a patriarchal practice, in that the shelter
director is determining such matters as opposed to the mother. Many
families not experiencing domestic violence do not have regular bath and
dinner times. However, the shelter has determined that this is the best
family structure, thus denying women's agency. This is contrary to survivor-defined feminist models emphasizing empowerment through control of decision making. At the same time, shelter rules are grounded in
the realities of group living—having multiple children needing baths
with no schedule over bathtub use is problematic. Further, Shelli indicated the potential benefits to children. In addition, no curfew was disrup-
tive to the other women and children's sleeping patterns. This complicated feminist advocacy. On the one hand, survivor-defined advocacy
works to empower women on an individual level, but what about when
an individual negatively affects other women in shelter? Then *those*
women's experiences are not survivor-defined. Thus, survivor-defined
advocacy becomes complex and challenging, and this is likely why advocates themselves were so mixed in their perceptions of this policy. In a
contrasting view to Shelli, Jean stated:

> Curfew is based on a patronizing attitude treating adult women like
> children. It's really all about control stuff. Needing control and project-
> ing how they feel comfortable onto others rather than a feminist coop-
> erative woman-defined model and method of dealing with problems.

Another advocate also offered a perspective from an organization that provided housing and had no curfew. Anais stated, "We don't have a curfew policy. The women and children are pretty free to come and go." Anais then explained that they did not have problems associated with not having a curfew. The setting of Safe Harbor is in separate apartments, so curfew did not pose an issue with disturbing other residents the way it did in shelters with group living. Thus, survivor-defined models can be tempered by complex realities of group living as well as patriarchal attitudes.

Flexible curfews were part of the "best practices" model advanced through training by the [State] Coalition. Shelli explained how the coalition facilitated system change in her shelter. She also described experimenting with curfew policy, doing away with it, and then bringing it back for practical reasons:

> So it's worked out for us, there's a time period there where we were like, I think it was, we went six months where we had this no curfew experiment, it was a statewide thing that all of the shelters were doing. It was total disaster for us. Total disaster for the residents who were actually serious in working on their goals, the women who were just using us had a ball! But not the ones who needed the assistance. We will stick with curfew.

Shelli noted that the [State] Coalition Against Domestic Violence was important in shifting curfew rules to a more flexible and survivor-defined approach. Yet, she stated that this approach did not work in her shelter. She seemed to have the perception that if women were not "working the program" they were problematic. It is likely that curfew did not have successful social change surrounding it in Faulds County because advocates themselves were somewhat divided. In Glawe County, it was not a problem because it was a much smaller group and they all agreed. This suggests that the [State] coalition, as well as the local coalition community, was an agent of social change in efforts to change the policies on a broader level. However, advocates must convince others that changes are warranted (and that they work) for those changes to occur.

Chapter 5

Mandatory Classes

The rural Glawe County shelter had many classes and programs available to women, but they were not mandatory. In Faulds County, one shelter participating in the study had mandatory classes. The transitional housing program in Faulds County had multiple classes available, but they were not mandatory. Classes generally consisted of individual and group therapy, and parenting, budgeting, and job skills classes.

When discussing mandatory classes, anything that is mandated could be perceived as patriarchal in nature, because it denies women's agency and assumes women need the classes regardless of individual needs or wants. This reflects a "for your own good" mentality consistent with patriarchal policy. Further, mandatory classes are not survivor-defined, because they reflect a standardized practice that does not consider specific needs. Yet, when asked about mandatory classes, Glenda, a feminist in Faulds County working in a traditionally feminist organization described their benefit:

> Well the thing is everybody has to want it, or it's not going to help... But I guess a part of it is you want to give people whatever skills they can acquire to be able to maintain a good life ... so I guess like they need some skills, otherwise they are not going to make it ... So, that's the value that I see within a shelter with support groups, it gives them a sense that they are not alone in this issue, there are other people who have these same issues, and they have these same problems with their kids. You can make it! I see value in it. It's hard for me not to see that it shouldn't be mandatory.

However, Glenda assumed that all women who have experienced abuse "need skills." She related these skills to empowerment, but simultaneously assumed that women were not able to determine which classes they needed and which they did not need. This response was expressed by most advocates who were not feminist but only two (out of eighteen) who were feminist. This suggests that feminist identity is related to feminist survivor-defined practices in this context.

In contrast, when asked about mandated services, Anais, who identified as a feminist, said:

> There are no mandated services here! Periodically, we will mandate a housing meeting, where we've got to get information to them and you

have to come. If you don't come, then you have to make arrangements to meet with somebody; but that's not participating in services . . . But as far as her individual sessions, her group stuff, engaging with the legal process, she does not have to do any of that. We inform her all of the time, "here are your options." We may go as far as to say, "this is why I think it's a good idea," but it is her decision.

In Safe Harbor, a transitional housing program, survivor-defined approaches were used to determine whether to recommend a particular service, and women's agency was respected as they had control over what classes they chose.

Eve also described flexibility in the policy regarding class attendance at the shelter in Glawe County, illustrating survivor-defined advocacy:

We individualize every family here. So we work a program that suits their needs . . . The benefit to that is we have people that are more comfortable being here, we're not forcing them to lie. We are not controlling their lives, we're giving them options and they are more successful. We have more resources because we are zeroing in on what they need and they're not having to conform with what we think they need.

Eve described the benefits of updated training and education through the [State] Coalition as facilitating the survivor-defined model of advocacy. While Eve did not self-identify as feminist, she expressed feminist ideologies (see chapter 2) and maintained best practices recommended by the [State] Coalition Against Domestic Violence. When asked how she thought it would look if advocates did not have background or training in domestic violence, and she replied:

It would be horrendous! It would be absolutely horrendous! One of the things that nobody really wants to talk about—but it is out there now, and we are addressing it—is power and control in a shelter setting. The coalition has come up with a wonderful power and control training for us and we will refer to that. You know, people do it, it's just like anything. You get job burnout. You get cynical. You become judgmental, and as an advocate you can't! So I don't care if you have heard one story or you have heard fifty stories today she demands the respect, time and attention, but working in a shelter where you're working 24/7 it gets hard, and you do get tired, but everybody is held accountable. You have to remember why you are here.

Chapter 5

The [State] Coalition was apparently facilitating the survivor-defined component of feminist advocacy through their extensive education and training programs of all their member organizations, including suggesting such approaches to classes and services.

When asked about mandatory classes or support groups, Jean, a "traditional" feminist in Faulds County, described working with shelters that did have mandatory classes as problematic for her advocacy:

> Almost every woman that I've worked with who has, for instance stayed at a shelter, has appreciated the shelter that it has been a place to stay while she's making a plan to start her new life, or whatever, [but] has also been mandated to attend parenting classes . . . And if she doesn't attend the parenting classes or whatever that the shelter wants her to, there are repercussions. Well, she's not going to meetings, she's not showing up, there's something wrong here. She's much less likely to get into long-term housing from that shelter. The more she cooperates, the more that she does what they want her to do, even if it's parenting classes, or whatever, the more likely she is to get the help that she needs.

Jean described further challenges with mandatory classes. In relationship to mandatory nature of the classes not being survivor-defined, they sometimes were not even relevant to individual cases:

> The other thing is, one woman that I was working with was single and I was trying to make plans to meet with her and she said, "I can't because I have to go to this parenting class." And I said, "You don't have any children do you?" She said, "No I don't!" And I said, "Well why are you going to a parenting class?" and she said "Well, it's one of the things that I'm supposed to do while I'm here at the shelter."

Mandatory parenting classes are thus not survivor-defined. The policy guides advocates' practices inside and outside of the shelters. Attending mandatory classes may prevent women from meeting with their advocate outside a shelter, or from following a plan in looking for a job or otherwise because they have to meet the mandatory requirements as a condition of receiving shelter. Five advocates, all feminist, indicated that classes at times interfered with job searches and finding housing. For example, Gillian said:

She might have two weeks to three months, you know, to find a job, to get a place to stay, to move her kids to a new school, and so much other stuff—and they throw these classes on top of it? I mean, I see the benefit, but sometimes it isn't realistic and she's better off using that time to do what she needs to do in that limited time she's got at the shelter.

The challenge most advocates expressed with the classes was not the classes themselves, but that the classes were mandatory (depending on the shelter). Jean said:

I think what's so bad about it is just that . . . it's one thing to offer them, that's fine. To encourage someone or to indicate that if they're a good parent, or want to be a good parent they will go to these classes, because they really need to—well it indicates that you think that the mother is not a good parent. Women feel that, and I think that's doing them a disservice.

Jean further described that some shelters treated women like children through rigid rules:

In a shelter, women often feel that they are treated as children. They are told when to wake up, when they have to be in, when to go to bed, what programs they need to attend, what classes they need to go to, et cetera et cetera. If they don't, they are in trouble. I do think that there is sexism. I think that women are often treated in a patriarchal way, we're patronizing women. They are the victims. We have to take care of them, they don't know how to keep themselves safe so we need to tell them how to stay safe. So I think that is very patronizing toward women. I see it in domestic violence agencies and so I think that is sexism coming through.

In addition, women can be expelled from shelter for not attending the mandatory classes because they are perceived as uncooperative and "loafing." Vicki, a nonfeminist, described women getting expelled from a shelter for "not trying hard enough." She said this could occur when there was evidence of:

Them not [being] willing to work the program, kind of just wanting to use it as a loafing in between kind of thing, not ambitious to find a job, not always there for their groups and different things like that.

Nonfeminists were significantly more likely to have this perception. There was only one feminist in the sample who believed women who did not "work the program" did not take their situation seriously. Further, some of what might be perceived as "loafing around" may actually be indicative of deeper psychological/emotional troubles. For example, Ingrid said:

> There is a failure to recognize depression, especially in women who aren't working the program, are sleeping too much, missing meetings. The tendency is to label them as lazy, not serious, and not worthy of advocacy, housing, and other issues.

Prior literature finds that depression and PTSD often accompany domestic violence (Goodman & Epstein, 2008). Consequently, it is possible that Ingrid's perception of symptoms of depression interfering with mandatory classes is correct. Since women may be expelled for not taking their classes, which may be related to depression or PTSD, this practice of expulsion is not survivor-defined. Jean had another perspective on the consequences of "loafing" when a client of hers was expelled from a shelter for missing classes:

> You know, in terms of leaving a shelter and going back to an abusive partner, I also worked with another woman who was told to leave the shelter because . . . well, she had slept late and missed a few classes that she was supposed to attend. Anyway, she was asked to leave. She was told the third time that she slept late and missed her class . . . she would probably be asked to leave. Well, she missed that third time and she was asked to leave and they do try to sit down and plan with them for a safe place where they will go. So, they asked her where she would go and she said she was going to go home to her mother, but she wasn't going home to her mother. She was too embarrassed to tell them that she had no place to go, that it was either the streets or her abusive partner. So, they took her to the train station so she could go back to her mother. As soon as they left, she didn't even have a train ticket, of course, she left the train depot and was walking the streets with her little daughter, who was four years old at the time, until she ended up at [a mall parking lot].

Jean further described how this woman and her daughter were found by mall security walking with trash bags full of their belongings. Jean had been her advocate working out a hospital program, and referred her to shelter. In this case, the woman and her daughter were dropped off by police at the hospital, and she saw Jean the next morning. Jean was able to get them into another shelter. Jean further discussed how advocates worked hard in shelters to keep women safe, but this perception of safety was sometimes implemented in counterproductive ways through patriarchal practices.

> The thing is that I know it's hard at shelters, and they try to do things and I know they are trying to keep women safe. So, what goes wrong when a woman decides she's going to leave the shelter and go back to her abusive partner? Women have told me that they feel that the shelter is like their abusive partner, because they are controlling them, they are telling them what they have to do all of the time. Making a lot of demands on them. Sometimes they will get so frustrated they leave and figure I'm better off just going back and being with him.

Advocates used intersectional feminist practices related to referring women to shelters or housing that had mandated services. Gillian described the limitation of shelter space, and how waiting lists were often problematic for women leaving their abusers. For an example of intersectional approaches related to mandated services, Gillian said another option in the community was a faith-based boarding house. In order to get shelter at the boarding house, it was also mandatory for women to receive services—women had to attend three hour-long sermons a day. Another advocate, Jean, said:

> I know that there was a faith based shelter nearby and one of the requirements of shelter was that the women had to attend several sermons a day even if it interfered with some of the things they needed to do with job search and things like that.

Gillian said she used intersectional approaches in order to learn whether this boarding house might be a good option for some women. Although she did not frame it herself as an intersectional approach, it worked to recognize intersecting identities of gender and faith and advocate to those individual identities. Gillian said:

> God love him, but he's upfront about it. It's good to know because I'm talking to women who that may be an option for and I'll say, "Are you a church person or not a church person? Because here's the deal, this is what he expects of people who are there. If you're on board with that,

great!" But Minister Kline is a private guy doing his thing. He can create whatever kind of model that he wants, I'm okay with that. To me it's different when you are operating a Domestic Violence Shelter specifically to serve woman who you know are escaping from a relationship at the core of which is power and control. So I would want those programs to not engage in practices that really are kind of about power and control. What Minister Kline does to me, it's like I don't need this to be for battered women advocates . . . I have never met the guy, I know people who have stayed there and thought it was lovely. I know people who stayed there and you know, couldn't get the heck out of there fast enough. Because it's not everybody's cup of tea. But that's true for any of the residential services that we use. Whether they are other boarding houses, whether any of the domestic violence shelters, it's just not everybody's cup of tea.

She again explained how it was important to advocate for women's individual cases and needs. In some cases, women might not mind or even want mandatory classes or sermons, and in other cases they might be seen as offensive and undesirable (Nichols, 2011). When measuring women's needs in shelters, Lyon et al. (2008) found that 72 percent wanted counseling, 57 percent wanted help with budgeting and handling money, and 57 percent needed a job or job training. The findings indicate many women do want these services and classes and find them helpful, but others do not. This calls mandatory services into question, and highlights the element of choice, consistent with feminist gender-based advocacy (Nichols, 2011). The mandatory classes represent patriarchal gender-based policy, as the choices of the survivors are not considered.

Substance Abuse

Policies regarding substance abuse are not uncommon; many shelters have policies restricting access to those who have substance abuse problems (Moe, 2007; Lyon et al., 2008; Goodman & Epstein, 2008). Macy and colleagues (2010) also note that many shelters "require women to be substance free as a condition for shelter admission." However, some abused women may use substances as a way of coping with their abuse (Osthoff, 2001). Yet, abused women who have substance abuse issues, many of whom have co-occurring PTSD as a result of their abuse, can be denied access to services that would provide valuable resources for leaving their abusive situations.

Substance abuse was not indicated as a barrier to accessing shelter in Glawe County, but in Faulds County it was described as a problem, depending on the shelter, as some shelters in Faulds County accepted individuals with substance abuse issues and others had a zero tolerance policy on substance abuse. Different policies resulted in different practices. In rural Glawe County, it is generally known that methamphetamine abuse and alcohol abuse are problems associated with the area. When asked about substance abuse, Vicki said they had a substance abuse program as a part of their coordinated community response in Glawe County, and the shelter could refer women with substance abuse issues to get help from this community resource. This is progressive, as national research indicates that substance abuse is a barrier for some women in accessing shelter, and the majority of shelters nationwide do not address it in terms of offering substance abuse resources as a part of the shelter experience (Lyon et al., 2008, DeJong & Burgess-Proctor, 2006). Nonetheless, women could still be expelled from the Glawe County shelter for actively using drugs or alcohol. Kari and Vicki both recalled having clients who were asked to leave when they were consistently high or drunk and caused problems for others in the shelter.

In contrast, at one shelter in Faulds County, there were very strict rules related to substance abuse, as it had been a problem in the past. As a result, the policy was standardized as opposed to survivor-defined and caused some problems for shelter residents and their advocates who worked to keep them in a safe place. Part of the standardized policy related to substance abuse was that all medications had to be turned in to the shelter staff upon admittance, and could be requested when needed. Gillian, working in a traditionally feminist organization that was not a shelter, said:

> I think the shelters have some rules which are not good in trying to protect people, and I mean I have an example of a woman who would not go to a shelter because of what she had to do. She had to give up all of her medications, when she went into a shelter. One of her medications was an inhaler. She said, "why would I give up my inhaler? I'm going to leave because I'm afraid I'm going to die there, and I don't have my inhaler when I need it, I will die. I can't wait for somebody to bring me my inhaler."

Consequently, Gillian had to work to find a different safe place for her client that would allow her to keep her inhaler. As shelter space is limited, Gillian found this policy to be challenging to her advocacy. Further, Jean, who worked with Gillian, indicated how such a standardized admissions policy related to substance abuse impacted her advocacy:

> When I am working with a woman who needs to get into a DV shelter, before she does the admission interview with them over the telephone, I tell them what to expect, what kind of questions they will ask, so they won't be offended because they often ask if they have mental health problems, if they've had alcohol or drugs in the last few days to two weeks depending on the shelter. One shelter does drug screens on admission. But women aren't expecting that, and are offended. Sometimes they just want help and they feel like they are being treated like there is something wrong with them, like they are criminals.

Ingrid described how a more feminist collaborative approach to advocacy, that is survivor defined, worked to produce better outcomes for the women receiving advocacy:

> It seems like mental health or substance abuse issues are something that could be dealt with after admission if needed, or at least in person with the attitude of assisting as needed with issues.

In this manner, women who needed help with substance abuse would get it instead of being denied shelter, and women who did not need the help would not feel demeaned or otherwise controlled (a patriarchal practice), as was the case when Gillian's client was not allowed to have her inhaler and Jean's clients were offended by being required to take drug tests. Ingrid was suggesting substance abuse policy in shelters take the form that the Glawe County Shelter had already put into practice. Assistance with substance abuse was offered when such issues were uncovered through survivor-defined advocacy. Advocates worked collaboratively with victims, and assessed what their challenges and goals were. At times, the result was referral to their community partner for help with substance abuse.

Advocates countered substance abuse policies by calling the directors of shelters that had rigid policies and working with them to get better outcomes for victims. In one case, Jean described contacting a director and getting a client back into the shelter after the shelter resident had been expelled for giving another resident a Tylenol. Three advocates also indicated bringing up policy debates in community meetings, which sometimes resulted in change. Importantly, Gillian said that she knew of two programs that were working on getting funding to address substance abuse, thus, it appeared that changes were in progress in Faulds County related to substance abuse. However, such changes had not manifested yet at the time of this study.

Other "House Rules"

Amy described shelter rules as challenging to some of her clients, while simultaneously recognizing the complex realities of group living and safety:

> I've had some [clients who] have been in shelter before and don't want to go back, or are in one right now and are not enjoying the rules. The rules are . . . leaving a controlling situation, sometimes they find them-selves being told what to do and they have a curfew and they have to clean their room, and they have to come down for dinner and what not. I completely understand there has to be shelter rules, there's got to be curfews because if you're gone until three in the morning, we're wor-ried about your safety, but I also see that being difficult for victims who are trying to leave and want some freedom and are being told that they need to do chores and they need to be home at this time, and check in with people. So I've had several victims I've talked to who are like "I've done shelter before and I do not want to go back. I did not like it."

In the interviews, a "cup story" had become somewhat notorious in the community. Gillian said, "Are you interviewing Jean? If you talk to Jean, ask her about the cup." Jean's cup story is as follows:

> At one shelter a woman that I was working with, she was supposed to . . . that [story] was about people were cleaning up the kitchen after dinner, and then, for this woman that I was working with she got in late after her job. She would finish her job, then she would pick up her child, who was staying at, I believe, at a daycare or a family member's, she would pick up her child, she came back. She was in the kitchen and poured some chocolate milk for her daughter. She had something for herself, they were having like a little late supper or snack together; and she left the rest of the milk sitting out on the table and the cups. She was asked to leave. I was told that the reason that she was asked to

leave was because they have a pest problem in the kitchen and people were being too messy and not cleaning up after themselves. So they told everybody, "if you don't clean up after yourself, you're out!" So, she was. When I talked to the director [she said] "this is something that we found we have to do because otherwise they have problems with roaches and other pests." I mean you are talking about the safety of this woman versus pest control!

When asked, "Where did she go when she was asked to leave?" Jean said, "Well, she went back to her abusive partner. Where else would she go?" The policy and corresponding practice of expulsion could be labeled as patriarchal, while simultaneously recognizing realities and challenges of group living. When asked what the problem was with advocacy that was not survivor-defined, Belinda, an abuse survivor and advocate, replied:

I don't like that because that takes her personal power away from her, that says your way is not good enough, you have to make it our way, and she has been told she's not good enough for so darn long. You have to comply. We all have to live within some rules and laws so that we can avoid chaos, but I think there are some times where systems get in the way of woman centered service delivery. Systems like you have to fill out this form before you can do this. You have to talk to this person before you can see a counselor. You have to go through an assessment before we will let you into therapy. Garbage! Garbage! Am I not good enough to take? What is going to make me so much better? What's going to make me so much more eligible for your services if I jump through your hoops? It's diminishing, it's demeaning, it's offensive. I don't like it!

When asked for a specific example, Belinda illustrated:

Well you know I was appalled. Once I was at a meeting and it was some rural shelter. They were talking, do you know what their system does? The woman has to report to the police department in order to be transported to the shelter. She's been arrested sometimes because there were outstanding warrants for her. What if she's being abused by one of the sheriffs in that rural county? I was just appalled! Now, there is a system that makes her jump through that hoop that does not honor her need . . . Now tell me how you are empowering somebody, I don't care if you have the most beautiful shelter in the world, if you're doing that sort of thing I wouldn't want to be a part of that system.

These examples provide additional illustrations of patriarchal policies that deny battered women agency. In the above example, imagine a victim of abuse going to the police department to gain access to shelter, and getting arrested for outstanding warrants that are unrelated to domestic violence. This is certainly an example of systemic revictimization, in further victimizing the victim. Advocates seemed to have a good sense of the feminist collaborative shelters and the ones that were more hierarchal and controlling. In cases where they had a client they perceived as potentially having problems with such a structure, they worked to get her into a less structured setting. In turn, for women they worked with that would appreciate and benefit from the structure, advocates worked to place them in the structured setting. However, this was difficult, as shelter space was a primary concern. The luxury of picking and choosing which shelter to go to was tempered by the reality of lack of shelter space and availability. Community meetings were continuously mentioned as forums for contentious debates regarding rigid shelter rules. Thus, advocates worked together to resolve problems, but the outcomes appeared to be the result of sometimes heated debate.

Conclusion

In sum, shelters and housing had different curfew, confidentiality, entrance and class requirements, and policies. In general, the policies in Women's Safe Home in rural Glawe County were created and altered following the guidelines of the [State] Coalition Against Domestic Violence with the exception of allowing teen boys. Since the state coalition is perceived as feminist, it resulted in policies that were flexible, collaborative, and survivor-defined. The nonfeminist director (who did have gendered ideologies of domestic violence and of societal gender inequalities) of the shelter incorporated survivor-defined policies, and attributed it to the State Coalition education and trainings. However, the policy on teenage boys was not changed despite the trainings. One feminist advocate in the Glawe County justice system (of only two) did advocate for change, but she did not have the support of the other advocates. In Glawe County, social change perspectives were largely absent. Yet, they were progressive in their policies, as their policies were largely informed by the [State] Coalition Against Domestic Violence, which promoted a survivor-defined approach.

In Faulds County, the transitional housing program also had flexible, collaborative, and survivor-defined policies and coinciding practices with the exception of confidentiality. The director was a vocal feminist, and described feminist programming in her housing program. The other shelter that participated in Faulds County had a mix of gendered policies. They mandated classes and had rigid confidentiality; however, they did allow teenage boys and had some flexibility around curfew. This presented somewhat of a contradiction, as the shelter was aimed at empowerment, but simultaneously maintained some rigid "house" rules. However, the feminist director had the perspective that such rules were developed for "the greater good" of those living in shelter. The director's perspective was tempered by her experiences and her ideas of what was best for the majority of women staying in her shelter. Women could be negatively affected in some cases without such rules when other women disturbed their shelter experience—such as when women came in noisily at 3 a.m. In Faulds County, the majority of feminist advocates maintained all the components of feminist advocacy: survivor-defined, intersectional, and social change practices. Nonfeminist advocates did not express intersectional approaches, but the majority did express survivor—defined practices in the context of shelter/housing.

Advocates' narratives indicated the problem with "neutral" advocacy is that it is standardized advocacy, and consequently ignores what women want and need in their specific situations—such as women who are limited in shelter access because of their teen boys, those that may or may not want classes or services, or who do not need a curfew or confidentiality. Patriarchal advocacy can also systemically revictimize women through unwanted mandated classes, curfews which require employer notes, confidentiality that results in expulsion, and inattention to dynamics specific to disabled and limited English-speaking women. Consequently those women who are expelled from shelters for violating shelter rules are susceptible to further batterer-based revictimization. In contrast, feminist advocacy relies on supporting women's agency, choices in services offered, and working collaboratively to address the needs and goals of battered women.

Advocates' descriptions of their experiences were consistent with prior research finding shelter rules simultaneously problematic and beneficial. Confidentiality, curfew, and mandated classes were seen by some advocates as strategies to avoid further batterer-based revictimization, and to meet the greater needs of the group. However, others saw them as patriarchal, resulting in both systemic and batterer-based revictimization. Advocates' narratives call for survivor-defined advocacy recognizing individual cases and needs, supporting women's agency, and allowing women choice in services offered, and giving them control. Access to shelter certainly provides empowerment to women leaving an abusive partner, but when this strategy is blocked due to entrance requirements or expulsion for not following rules, such systemic revictimization can result in batterer-based revictimization in addition to undermining women' safety and denying them agency. In some shelters, safety, though seen as a primary mission, becomes secondary when feminist policies and practices are not followed and patriarchal attitudes and practices dominate. This is not the case in shelters and housing that stick to the components of feminist advocacy: survivor-defined, intersectional, and social change practices. Feminist practices facilitate agency and empowerment, whereas patriarchal or neutral practices deny agency and empowerment, perpetuating gender inequality and the subordinate status of battered women.

Survivor-defined advocacy in group settings is complex. In order to best meet the needs of the women in shelter, some advocates felt rules needed to be supported. For example, while one woman was expelled because of pest control issues, the other women did not have to deal with the pests. While survivor-defined curfew facilitates agency for individual women, if one woman causes problems for the other residents, she negatively impacts the other women. That is, sometimes what works for one woman may conflict with another's needs. Thus, while rigid curfew policies appear patriarchal, they occur within complex living situations that affect multiple women. At the same time, expulsion from shelter for violating these rules posed significant risks to women's safety, and undermined their autonomy. The result was conflicting views among advocates, who disagreed with one another, and at times struggled with their own perspectives on such policies.

Chapter 6

Implications for Theory, Policy, and Practice

The research described in the preceding chapters is generally a study of feminist advocacy in anti-domestic violence organizations. More specifically, it is a study of feminist identities, ideologies, and practices as components of organizations that both resist and reproduce various facets of gender. The gendered organizations theoretical framework draws attention to different aspects of gender in organizations. Feminist identity, ideology, and practices were the theoretical components under investigation. The criminal justice and child protective services interventions and the shelter rules that were examined were not genderless mechanisms of organizations; rather, they were gendered in complex and competing ways. Consequently, advocates' practices responding to such policies and practices in shelters, child protective services, and the justice system were also multifaceted, sometimes in conflicting ways. In fact, advocates' interrelated identities, ideologies, and practices were gendered, and were influenced by and influenced other actors in their organizations. The final chapter draws from the research presented in this book to highlight implications for gendered organizations theory and the practice of advocacy.

Theoretical Implications

This section delineates potential theoretical developments based upon the dynamics uncovered in the previous chapters. First, contextual differences between regions and the importance of such distinctions for gendered organizations theory are examined. Second, contextual comparisons between advocacy in traditionally feminist organizations and advocacy in masculine (or "gender-neutral") organizations are drawn. Third, an extension of the gendered organizations framework by exploring actors' practices countering gendered processes is suggested and detailed. Last, an intersectional focus and its contribution to theoretical development are described.

171

Chapter 6

Context: Regional Distinctions

Regional distinctions were related to feminist identities and gendered ideologies of domestic violence. Advocates working in rural areas were much less likely to identify as feminist. Disassociation with feminism may be a product of a rural environment, as advocates in this study who worked in rural areas reported living and working in areas where feminist identity was not generally accepted. Further, there was no local feminist coalition, and fewer opportunities for feminist education in rural Glawe County. As feminist practices are guided by feminist identities/ideologies, rural advocates were much less likely to incorporate intersectional and social change practices in their advocacy. The opposite was the case for advocates in metropolitan contexts. Regional distinctions in feminism and feminist advocacy suggest that regional contexts may impact gendered processes. Some regions, such as metropolitan regions, may facilitate feminism more easily than rural regions. Cultural acceptance of feminism, local feminist coalitions, and feminist-informed education were all defining factors.

This finding does not suggest that patriarchal and neutral processes are not present in metropolitan areas, as patriarchal and neutral processes were present in both rural and metro areas. However, it is the feminist responses resisting these processes that were much less common in rural contexts. So what does this mean for a gendered organizations theory? Simply, contextual differences may account for differing research results in different regions. Prior research lends some support to this argument, that rural-located advocates are less likely to incorporate feminist social movement philosophies (Lehrner & Allen, 2009; Macy et al., 2010). The gendering of organizations in this study varied by region, as metropolitan-located advocates were more likely to identify as feminist and practice feminist advocacy. Consequently, researching gendered organizations must involve a comprehensive examination of the contexts in which gendered dynamics of organizations take place, and the contextual dynamics that may inform the gendering of organizations as well as the gendering of resistance.

Implications for Theory, Policy, and Practice

Context: Feminine and Masculine Organizations

This book is somewhat distinct in the realm of gendered organizations research as it involves advocates working in traditionally feminist organizations, and also offers comparisons of advocates working in such organizations to advocates working in the largely masculine justice system (see Haney, 2010; Britton, 2011). The bulk of gendered organizations research takes place in organizations that are traditionally masculine in their structure, workforce, hierarchy, and leadership (Martin, 1980; Jurik, 1985; Jurik & Musheno, 1986; Britton, 1997, 2000, 2003; Chesney-Lind & Pollack, 1995; Williams et al., 1999; Dellinger & Williams, 2002; Williams, 2006; Webber & Williams, 2008; Williams & Connell, 2010; Kruttschnitt & Gartner, 2004). In contrast, this book examined gendered processes within feminist organizations whose leadership, clientele, hierarchy, and workforce were female-dominated. Advocacy in these traditionally feminist organizations was compared to advocacy in the justice system. Justice system organizations are labeled masculine because the workforce, hierarchy, and corresponding gender attributes are usually male-dominated and masculine. In addition, this book examined co-optation—the idea that one organization's goals, identity, and ideology is lost or reduced when collaborating with another. Specifically, feminist advocates' collaboration with individuals, policies, and practices in masculine or "neutral" organizations was explored.

First, the findings suggest that "neutral," feminist, and patriarchal policies and practices can be present in traditionally feminist organizations as well as in traditionally masculine organizations. There were inconsistencies in gendered policies and practices both within and between traditionally feminist organizations. Feminist policies and practices were present within some traditionally feminist organizations, and a mix of gendered processes existed within others.

Yet, what does it mean when feminist organizations have "neutral" or even patriarchal practices within their own feminist organizations—that are dominated by women, directed by women, have exclusively women workers, and largely serve women? Feminist organizations do not exist in a vacuum; they are part of a gendered world and interact with masculine actors and masculine organizations. Advocates are exposed to gendered assumptions from society, and abused women to some extent may reflect "the other," they are the women that need to be protected—

even against their will. While a minority of advocates maintained this perspective, it did translate into practice in at least one shelter: the shelter with mandated classes and rigid rules.

Second, what happens when those from feminist organizations interact and collaborate with those from masculine organizations? Are they co-opted? Do they "lose" feminism? Advocates both resisted and reproduced gendered (feminist, neutral, and patriarchal) practices, identities, and ideological assumptions in such contexts. It is important to note that there is not an exclusive binary system of feminists in feminist organizations or nonfeminists in masculine organizations. A vast majority of feminist advocates working in the masculine justice system retained their feminist identity, ideology, and practices. In fact, advocates working within the justice system were *more* likely to identify as feminist than advocates in feminist organizations.

At the same time, in concerted efforts to present themselves as "neutral," advocates reported toning down or hiding various representations of feminist identity and ideology within the justice system (see chapter 2). However, their outward presentation of "neutrality" did not impact their practices with individual women or with their social change activism, which remained fully committed to their feminist ideology. For example, when officers' practices interfered with victim safety, or implemented controlling practices, these advocates were not co-opted at all; rather, they became social activists within their organizations—but they did it using "neutral" language. To some degree they worked within the confines of the existing system, but it didn't change their feminist practices or ideologies. Thus, in some contexts advocates reproduced the gender dynamics of the masculine organizations they collaborate with, and in other cases they specifically resisted them. Ultimately, feminist identity, whether in the justice system or in traditionally feminist organizations, was a better indicator of feminist advocacy than the organizational type. This generally counters co-optation concerns involving gendered organizations, and suggests the importance of other factors such as a feminist background/education, related training, and strong local feminist coalitions to the practice of feminist advocacy. More generally, the dynamics that impact feminist identity may be important in countering gendered processes in any organization.

In addition, the research presented in this book is unique in that, to some extent, it examines co-optation working "the other way around." It works to answer the question: are masculine organizations ever co-opted by feminist organizations? The answer to this question was complex; co-optation of the masculine justice system by the feminist advocacy organizations was mixed and intimately linked to feminist advocacy, specifically, the social change component of feminist advocacy. For example, in Faulds County, advocates were able to make some dramatic policy changes in the justice system generally over the last few decades. The masculine organizations were to some extent "co-opted," as changes did occur as a result of the interactions of feminist advocates within the masculine justice system: such as training, using hierarchal channels, developing the Court Watch program, and communicating with individual officers. But in Glawe County, there really was no evidence of co-optation of masculine organizations by feminist organizations, save changes in state law that were advocate-driven (but not by Glawe County advocates). Thus, such research offers a distinct contribution in examining how feminist organizations my impact masculine organizations through coalition-sponsored social change efforts as well as interactional-level social change practices.

Resistance

Advocates not only were impacted by gendered practices, but they also responded to them. Interaction includes not just action, but reaction. How these reactions both resist and reproduce gender is an important theoretical extension in the area of gendered organizations. First, advocates resisted both co-optation and gendered processes while they were simultaneously impacted by them. In previous chapters, I concluded that the institutional setting may be less important than the feminist background, education, and experience of the individuals in the organization. Individuals are not passive recipients of social conditioning present in organizations. Rather, individuals possess unique social backgrounds and perspectives, causing them to react differently to environmental stimuli. To some extent both nonfeminist and feminist advocates reproduced patriarchal or neutral-gendered practices, although only feminist advocates resisted them through social change activism. The end-goal of system change was important to feminists—in order for their presentations, education, training, and system change approaches to be acceptable to officers, advocates used different language to accomplish it. Thus, advocates reproduced "neutrality" in education, trainings, and interactions in order to resist and accomplish feminist/gendered system change. Feminist identity was important in identifying gendered practices, particularly identification and resistance to gendered practices through feminist social change activism.

Many researchers have identified gendered practices within organizations, but there has been less systematic focus on how actors react to or counter gendered practices, especially when said actors recognize them as gendered practices. In other words, we know to some extent how gendered processes are reproduced, but less about how they are resisted. The research presented in this book suggests specifically how advocates resist gendered practices through survivor-defined, intersectional, and social change practices. Findings indicate generally, how actors can *resist* gendered practices *through* gendered practices. Actors can resist patriarchal and neutral practices through feminist practices. Feminist identity, corresponding ideologies, and practices can be central to resistance. This seems like a fruitful avenue in extending gendered organizations theory.

Further, intersectional practices can resist patriarchal or "neutral" practices. First, the previous chapters indicated that practices are simultaneously gendered, raced, classed, sexed, and based on disability and limited English-speaking ability. Intersectional perspectives can be combined with a gendered organizations perspective to provide a more nuanced theory. Acker briefly mentions race, sexuality, and class in her original treatise (1990), but it is not often incorporated in gendered organizations research, limiting development of the overall theory in *how* intersecting identities work in gendered organizations, particularly in terms of resistance (see Britton, 2003, 2011).

Within the present research, evidence of intersectional ideologies and practices in advocacy related to shelters and the criminal justice system was found. Feminist perspectives can lead to intersectional perspectives, which can lead to resistance of simultaneously gendered, raced, classed, and other practices. For example, when feminist advocates identified biases toward limited English speaking clients, they worked to change it. A majority of advocates with feminist perspectives identified how intersecting identities impacted practices. Similarly, a further extension of gendered organizations theory could focus on how intersectional feminist perspectives can direct targeted organizational change. More work is needed in this important area of study.

Implications for Policy and Practice

The ways gendered policies and practices may contribute to revictimization of battered women is of central importance. For example, Martin (2005, p. 152) found that rape victims experienced revictimization through organizations that "prioritize the organization's interests over victims' interests" through policies and requirements. Martin took Acker's conceptualization of practices—that practices in organizations can be gendered and lead to inequality—a step further to highlight how gendered policies and practices can lead to not only inequality, but revictimization. Similar to Martin (2005), the previous chapters explored how gendered practices can lead to the revictimization of battered women in various organizations and how advocates worked to mitigate such revictimization through practices associated with feminist advocacy.

Uncovering gendered processes of police, judges, the courts, shelters, child protective services, the family courts, and advocacy that may revictimize battered women through patriarchal or "neutral" policies and practices is an important focal point. This is why a gendered organizations lens is important. The revictimization of battered women is rooted in gendered processes; *identification of such processes leads toward directed organizational change* (Britton & Logan, 2008). Britton and Logan indicated that identifying gendered policies and practices is a necessary first step. Eradicating or changing such policies and practices is based upon such recognition. Without this identification, system change is unlikely to occur. Following this framework, gendered policies and practices identified in this study led to a number of recommendations for advocates and the anti-domestic violence stakeholders they work with.

Eliminating Policies & Practices Constraining Women in Shelter

Policies that may serve as a barrier to entering a shelter, such as policies excluding women with substance abuse issues or shelter policies preventing adolescent boys from staying with their mothers should be revisited. First, shelters could offer assistance with substance abuse while offering women shelter (Lyon et al., 2008). This is the policy in the Glawe County shelter and of some of the shelters/transitional housing in Faulds County, but is not the policy of at least one shelter in Faulds

177

County. In a comprehensive review of domestic violence literature and Coalition guidelines, recommendations for best shelter practices included offering substance abuse services to women using shelter services (Macy et al., 2010). Based on her evaluation of 215 shelters, Lyon (2002) also recommended that service provision related to substance abuse is needed in shelters. Other researchers have noted the co-occurrence of PTSD and substance abuse and thus recommend trauma-informed substance abuse treatments, as abused women may have substance abuse problems as a way of coping with their abuse (see Macy et al., 2010).

Findings indicated in chapter 5 support the extant literature, and suggest that substance abuse can be a barrier to advocacy. Advocates report that women may feel as if they are being treated as criminals when applying to stay in shelters. They may have to take drug tests, and may have to answer multiple questions about drug use. Second, women that do have these problems cannot access much-needed shelter. Third, such policies can develop into very rigid policies that are counterproductive— for example, at least one advocate had difficulty finding shelter for a victim who would not turn in her inhaler to shelter staff, and another advocate worked with a client who was expelled for giving another woman in the shelter some Tylenol for a headache.

These issues related to substance abuse are all gendered practices— denying entrance to those that do have substance abuse issues is gender "neutral" because it ignores the gender dynamics of domestic violence and the association between substance abuse and victimization. Removing substance abuse from the context of domestic violence is problematic for that reason. In a domestic violence shelter setting, the Glawe County shelter's practices serve as a model. Women are not denied entry for substance abuse problems, and receive treatment if they want it upon entry.

Second, the shelter/housing in Faulds County did accept teen boys, but in Glawe County, the only shelter did not accept any teen boys, regardless of their histories. Not accepting a teen boy is also a gendered practice (see chapter 5). Boys' masculinity is associated with violence and sexuality in the Glawe County shelter, hence the continuation of the policy. The policy is thus based on gendered assumptions removed from boys' individual characteristics and personal histories. The policy is gender "neutral" because it ignores the gender dynamics of mothering and that women experiencing domestic violence with teen sons need a safe place to stay but may not leave their mothering roles to do so. If a teen boy has no history of problematic behavior, he should be able to find safety with his mother in a shelter. If he does have a history of problematic behavior, this shows that he is in serious need of help. The National Coalition Against Domestic Violence, as well as the [State] Coalition, and Macy et al.'s (2009) comprehensive review of the research literature, recommend accepting adolescent boys. Many shelters offer services for children. In cases where there is no history of violent behavior, then there is no issue. In cases where there is a history of violence, services for children could expand to address such boys' needs. Safety in shelter and access to resources should be available for all children. If a teen boy poses a real threat to others, alternative shelter, such as emergency placement of the family in a hotel, or direct movement into transitional housing, should be an option. Some shelters and outreach services already have cooperative agreements with hotels, and are prepared for such circumstances. In addition, transitional housing may be an option for women with adolescent sons as well. Although this would call for a lot more of this type of facility, this is an alternative to shelter that has proven successful on many other fronts (Nichols, 2011).

Third, confidentiality policies that limit women's access to community resources and social support networks should also be revisited. The Glawe County shelter adopted a flexible approach to shelter rules, in which the director worked with each individual woman to find a set of rules that worked for her. If she needed confidentiality, any phone calls to her at the shelter would be screened for her, and she would not tell anyone where she was. Because of the loose confidentiality, they got better locks, security cameras, and developed a collaborative relationship with local police in case an abuser did appear. The Glawe County Shelter also implemented a flexible curfew and worked with women on their individual work and social schedules, so they knew women were safe if they chose to stay out past the recommended curfew. Mandatory classes should also be revisited, emphasizing "what makes sense" in each individual survivors situation. The element of choice facilitates ownership of decision making and empowerment consistent with feminist advocacy.

Strict confidentiality and curfew policies perpetuate notions that abused women cannot determine what is safe in their situation. They do not get to choose; thus it is not survivor-defined. The patriarchal policies assume women are in need of protection and deny women's agency. Confidentiality and curfew policies, as well as mandatory classes, that inhibit a woman's ability to work, seek education, or otherwise limit her freedom should be reconsidered to allow for discretion in the practiced enforcement of the curfew policies. Further, screening for depression among women who appear lethargic, apathetic, or who otherwise display signs of depression is recommended. Some women may need more resources other than the counseling and group therapy that is typically offered.

Increasing Training and Cross-Training

The research findings also support the recommendation of educating justice system and child protective services stakeholders about domestic violence. Advocates in both sites reported that working with detectives, police, prosecutors, judges, and CPS/DFS caseworkers who were educated in domestic violence was better than working with untrained caseworkers, officers, or judges. Further, advocates reported a distinct difference in outcomes depending on the caseworkers, judges, or officers with whom they worked. Such individuals who were uneducated in domestic violence problematized advocacy through their patriarchal or neutral practices.

Consequently, extending education and training to the additional stakeholders who are involved in efforts to combat domestic violence is recommended. According to Acker, ideology can inform policy and practices. Some researchers suggest cross-training and educating various service providers in one another's areas as a means of improving service provision in community-based approaches (Macy et al., 2010). Zweig and Burt (2006) provided one such example of successful cross-training. They found that when law enforcement worked with domestic violence victim advocates, the result was increased arrest of batterers, better evidence collection, and more convictions. In contrast, without collaborative settings, victims were more likely to be arrested themselves, felt like they had less control, and were consequently revictimized. Weisz (1999) also found reduced reoffending when officers used protocols developed collaboratively with victim advocates.

First, one of the biggest challenges indicated by advocates in the project was collaboration with judges. This was, in part, due to subjective interpretations of judges, victim-blaming practices, and strong evidentiary requirements to gain a protective order. These issues derive from a lack of understanding about the gender dynamics involved in domestic violence. Advocates indicated that judges who did understand domestic violence were wonderful to work with, and they went out of their way to work with such judges to benefit victims. Cross-training and collaboration between judges and advocates could provide common understandings about the problem of domestic violence and how to address it—from protective orders to prosecution. For example, advocates can influence the court through Amicus (friend of the court) briefs. Amicus briefs are filed by professionals with expertise, credentials, or experience in a particular area, such as domestic violence (Rutkow, Vernick, Webster, & Lennig, 2009). Amicus briefs can be used by advocates when victims are being manipulated or threatened to drop protective orders or prosecution (Rutkow et al., 2009). Advocates can provide information to inform court decisions in domestic violence cases and can thus mitigate a potentially negative impact on battered women. Advocates in Faulds County were able to build informal relationships with some judges, and provided their expertise by directly collaborating with judges. Such relationship-building is recommended.

The issue of body attachments associated with no-drop prosecution was clearly a patriarchal gendered practice. This practice punishes victims for not cooperating in cases where the judge wants to move forward once prosecution has begun and the victim no longer wishes to prosecute. The judge or prosecutor determines prosecution, and further victimizes the victims by putting them in jail. Such practices should be revisited because they are counterproductive, particularly when abusers are sentenced to probation, community service, or limited jail time (See Nichols, 2013a). Having a victim arrested for any period, much less a longer period than her abuser, is certainly revictimizing. As an alternative, training of officers in Faulds County was an effort made by advocates seeking social change related to no-drop prosecution. Evidence-based prosecution removes the trauma of testifying away from a victim, as they do not have to see their abuser in the courts. Police can provide better evidence to prosecutors, through more detailed reports, witness testimony, and statements of the victim at the time of the incident. Based on this, such training of police in gathering evidence with the aim of evidence-based prosecution is suggested. Evidence-based prosecution allows the continuation of advocates' feminist social change agenda while dealing with latent consequences of no-drop prosecution, and is a recommended alternative to forced testimony. One problem that has been identified with evidence-based prosecution is that without the testimony of the victim, jurors are more likely to acquit batterers. Another alternative that is currently being explored is video testimony of the victim. In addition, with pro-arrest, avoiding dual arrest is imperative to avoid revictimization. Officers also should not ask victims if they want an arrest in the presence of the abuser. Training of officers should thus address survivor-defined practices and education in dynamics of domestic violence to avoid dual arrest when possible. Expanded advocacy in police departments is also recommended in order to evaluate dual arrest charges based on criminal histories, and contacting victims to offer advocacy support and resources.

Further, educating and training caseworkers in various systems that address child abuse to identify domestic violence, learn the dynamics of domestic violence, and recognize manipulative behaviors of abusers is important in avoiding both batterer-based and systemic revictimization (Saathoff & Stoffel, 1999; Findlater & Kelly, 1999; Banks, Landsverk, & Wang, 2008; Banks, Dutch, & Wang, 2008). Practices should be survivor-defined and collaborative to get the best outcomes for both abused women and their children. Expansion of domestic violence victim advocacy within such organizations may be helpful. Advocates can help caseworkers develop plans that are informed by battered women's input. Further, understanding and advocating for women who are caught between policies—upholding required visitation with the abuser and simultaneously exposing children to abuse and failure to protect charges—is important. Failure to protect charges should be eliminated, as failure to protect is largely a "woman's charge" that further revictimizes abused women. Prior research notes that the safety of children is inextricably linked to the safety of their mothers (Saatholf & Stoffel, 1999; Nichols, 2011; Rhodes et al., 2011). As such, as an alternative to Failure to Protect charges, the emphasis of CPS should be on simultaneously improving the safety of mothers and children as opposed to punishing mothers for their batterers' abuse directed toward them and their children. They also stated that many women experienced difficulties in leaving their abusers, and failure to protect policy just added another layer of difficulty to leaving abusive homes. Failure to protect charges, and policies that take custody away from mothers, give batterers an incentive to intimidate victims, and allows them to control both CPS systems and victims.

The Greenbook Demonstration Initiative and other research indicates that CPS workers should screen for domestic violence and make referrals to victim advocates and shelters, and shelters should offer services to children (Saathoff & Stoffel, 1999; Findlater & Kelly, 1999; Banks, Landsverk, & Wang, 2008; Banks, Dutch, & Wang, 2008). A study of

3,410 residents of 215 domestic violence shelters found that 79 percent of shelters offer assistance with CPS, and 27 percent of respondents said they wanted help dealing with CPS (Lyon et al., 2008). However, relatively few referrals of clients experiencing domestic violence to domestic violence victim advocates actually come from CPS (Findlater & Kelly, 1999). Findlater and Kelly found two-thirds of caseworkers reported domestic violence as "unimportant" in their case decision-making and just one-third noted the mother's safety as important. Another study of 92 child welfare agencies and 5,501 children and their families found caseworkers reported 9 percent cases of co-occurring intimate partner violence while self-reports from the families indicated 40 percent co-occurrence rates (Kelleher, Gardner, Coben, Barth, Edelson & Hazen, 2006). Kelleher et al. (2006) found few referrals to domestic violence services, and noted that domestic violence assessment was not generally a part of CPS casework. They found variance nationally, with some sites implementing highly coordinated services with higher numbers of CPS workers screening for domestic violence and providing referrals to domestic violence services, but the overall rate of coordination was low. As indicated in chapter 4, advocates noted that this was largely due to the lack of knowledge of CPS caseworkers in the area of domestic violence. Screening for domestic violence within Child Protective Services and offering victims referrals to domestic violence victim advocates would provide better outcomes for abuse victims and their children rather than lost custody and charges of neglect or failure to protect.

Implications for Advocacy Practices

Research suggests that survivor-defined, intersectional, and social change practices produce better outcomes for abused women. Survivor-defined approaches are associated with lower levels of future abuse, higher rates of leaving an abusive partner, further legal action toward an abuser, use of multiple services, and higher satisfaction with services (Allen, Bybee, & Sullivan, 2004; Goodman & Epstein, 2008; Weisz, 1999; Zweig & Burt, 2006, 2007). Social change activism has produced all of the social services and justice system resources currently available to domestic violence victims (Goodman & Epstein, 2008). Intersectional approaches work to increase access to services, address individual and systemic bias, and better meet the needs of women from various backgrounds and identities (Arnold & Ake, 2013; Bent-Goodley, 2004; Donnelly et al., 2005; Richie, 2005; Sokoloff, 2005). Consequently, it is important to facilitate survivor-defined, intersectional, and social change practices in advocacy. The research findings led to implications for developing such practices. The following subsections outline the importance of and ways to cultivate survivor-defined, intersectional, and social change practices.

Prior research suggests that meaning-making guides action (Lehrner & Allen, 2008). In the current study, feminist advocates made meaning of domestic violence and advocacy through feminist perspectives, which supported survivor-defined, intersectional, and social change practices. Nonfeminists did not have intersectional or social change ideologies of domestic violence and advocacy nor did they hold intersectional or social change practices. Thus, feminist ideologies and meanings of domestic violence appeared to be important to the development of social change and intersectional approaches to advocacy. Yet, such ideologies and related practices could ostensibly be facilitated among those that do not identify as feminist, as the research findings also suggest that feminist-informed advocacy can also be engaged by advocates who do not have a feminist background. For example, a strong feminist coalition, training, and feminist programming in organizations facilitated survivor-defined approaches among nonfeminists (see chapter 2). Ostensibly, education, training, and programmatic design inclusive of intersectional and social change ideologies could potentially be successful as well. Further, facilitating feminist meanings of domestic violence and advocacy through these mediums, as well as ongoing participation in local and state coalitions may be important to maintaining or developing survivor-defined, social change, and intersectional practices.

Survivor-Defined Practices

Meanings of domestic violence that support survivor-defined approaches are important to victims' outcomes. The current study found advocates all reported practicing survivor-defined advocacy, regardless of feminist identities or feminist meanings of domestic violence. This finding counters prior work by both researchers and practitioners (Lehrner & Allen, 2009; Macy et al., 2010). Both researchers and practitioners have reported an absence of survivor-centered practices, and instead found victim-blaming and authoritarian practices (Adams & Bennett, 2008; Curran, 2008; Hobart, 2006; Nichols, 2011; Olsen, 2007, 2008; Lindquist, 2008; Tautfest, 2008). Advocates in this study attributed their survivor-centered approaches to feminist ideologies, yet nonfeminists also practiced survivor-defined advocacy largely due to coalition training and feminist programming in their organizations. This finding suggests important implications for domestic violence victim advocacy as approaches to advocacy can be impacted by such factors. Ostensibly, intersectional and social change practices could be impacted by coalition training and programmatic design as well.

Intersectional Practices

Most advocates identifying as feminist expressed intersectional feminist perspectives and recognized inequalities based on intersecting identities. Yet, nonfeminist advocates did not recognize such inequalities. This may be problematic, as advocates who are unable to see biases relating to gender, race, class, sexuality, disability, and immigrant status are unlikely to work to change such biases, and may not be able to advocate to specific needs. For example, an abusive lesbian partner may find her way into a confidential shelter in order to continue the abuse. A disabled woman may have increased difficulty maintaining confidentiality requirements if she has trouble walking two or more blocks to the shelter. Recognition of these challenges is important in addressing them. The focus of the extant intersectional research is largely centered on the biases advocates themselves hold toward victims, or barriers women may experience in accessing services (Bent-Goodley, 2004; Donnelly et al., 2005; Hill-Collins, 2000; Potter, 2008). Findings suggest that when advocates do identify sources of bias specific to intersecting identities, they appear better able to advocate for a victim's needs. An intersectional approach to advocacy works to recognize individual identities and backgrounds and the relationship to domestic violence, and can also work to avoid potential biases within the system. If advocates do not recognize biases based upon intersecting identities as a potential problem, they may fail to identify how such identities influence abuse and responses to abuse. For advocacy to be truly survivor-defined, recognition of each individual woman's place in the matrix of oppression is necessary to determine any potential bias and to address each woman's particular needs.

Further, to respond to domestic violence on a structural level, and to incur real cultural and institutional change, understanding how such changes may specifically be informed by and impact women's intersecting identities is necessary. If advocates find domestic violence is related to other social inequalities, they will advocate for structural shifts and individual needs related to these inequalities. If advocates perceive women's experiences with abuse, as well as the responses to abuse, are impacted by women's specific identities, then advocates' practices will work to address the potential inequalities that women may experience. Thus, providing education, training, and programming in organizations to engage advocates in intersectional approaches to advocacy is suggested. Some state coalitions are already training in the area of intersectional approaches; this could serve as a model to other state coalitions, local coalitions, and organizational programming.

Social Change Practices

Advocates suggested that a strong local coalition rooted in the feminist battered women's movement was important for social change approaches. In Glawe County, feminist advocates who did try to implement change did not accomplish change because there was no institutional or coalition support. In Faulds County, nonfeminist advocates by association with the local coalition became involved in social change efforts, like Court Watch and Greenbook. Based on this, the development of a local feminist coalition seems important in facilitating system change/social change activism and is recommended. If this is not possible due to rural or other cultural norms, many [State] Coalitions Against Domestic Violence provide trainings for advocates and workers that include social change activism and the history of the battered women's movement—perhaps in the same manner the [State] coalition successfully trained advocates for survivor-defined approaches.

Employment of individuals educated in woman-centered advocacy, the dynamics of domestic violence, and the battered women's movement in general had an impact in facilitating feminist identity and social change approaches, and such education either before hiring or through training is recommended. Prior research supports this recommendation, and so does the [State] and National Coalition Against Domestic Violence. In the research presented in this book, advocates performed mandatory training and orientation for new employees in which they were educated about the battered women's movement, the societal gender dynamics of violence against women, and survivor-defined advocacy in Faulds County. This training was provided by the local coalition.

Social change activism was important in directing system change in the justice system. Nonfeminist advocates did not see social change as a part of their advocacy. This was particularly the case in Glawe County, where there was no feminist majority or local coalition. Social change efforts did not work because of lack of organizational and local support, and that is why local feminist coalitions are important. There should be continued efforts by advocates within the domestic violence movement to change justice system and CPS responses and shelter practices that are patriarchal or "neutral" and cause problems for battered women. Lack of social change practices results in a system that supports revictimization. Focusing on the immediate as opposed to social change activism is a Band-Aid for the larger problem, and by ignoring it advocates can contribute to the continued cycle of revictimization of battered women. Targeted organizational changes, therefore, should work to include social change elements in training, education, practices, and policies that support battered women.

The extant research finds social change activism may be in a state of decline among advocates (Lehrner & Allen, 2008, 2009; Macy et al., 2010; Nichols, 2011). The current study supports this research in part; finding social change activism absent among nonfeminist advocates, but thriving among feminist advocates, who composed nearly two-thirds of the sample. Thus, feminist identities and ideologies matter because identity guides their practices. Nonfeminists, approximately a third of the sample, did not recognize gender dynamics of domestic violence and socio-structural gender inequalities. They also did not have social change perspectives, nor did they express social change activism in their organizations or with community-based response partners. Violence against women is primarily the context in which domestic violence occurs and early feminist social change targeted that explanation by developing coalitions, hotlines, shelters, and collaborative responses. If the perception of domestic violence becomes neutral and it is not recognized as largely male-to-female violence, social change efforts and resource allocation may not be targeted accurately. If advocates perceive that domestic violence results from structural inequality, their practices work to address such structural inequalities. If advocates view women's individual needs as a priority and don't focus on structural changes as well; then advocacy will be limited to individual-level advocacy. Consequently, implementing education, training, and programming in organizations that prompts advocates to participate in social change efforts is suggested to maintain structural-level advocacy.

Conclusion

In conclusion, policies and practices that lead to revictimization of battered women should be altered to become as survivor-defined and flexible as possible, while simultaneously facilitating environments where women have autonomy, structural recourse for their victimization, and where violence against women is not accepted. This includes both shelter rules, and child protective services and criminal justice interventions. Advocates should also receive education and training in intersectional approaches and social change activism as well as survivor-defined advocacy from state and local coalitions, as well as their own organizations. Social change and intersectional practices were techniques that feminist advocates used successfully to counter policies and practices that were revictimizing. If nonfeminist advocates had education and training in this area, they may incorporate them in their advocacy. Extending education and training in gender dynamics of domestic violence and survivor-defined advocacy to other anti-domestic violence stakeholders, such as judges and officers, to better meet the needs of advocates and the victims they advocate for is also recommended. In this way, *systems of advocacy* would be present to support victims' needs. Expansion of advocacy and availability of domestic violence victim advocates throughout child protective services and in the justice system is also recommended, to facilitate such systems of advocacy. Examining both organizational and regional distinctions was intended to add to the readers' understandings of context, and how policy and practice can be impacted by the environments in which they take place. Readers of this book are encouraged to read other works in other settings and to consider such contextual distinctions. What works in one context may not work in another. Importantly, the best designed system is still dependent on the actors in organizations. Thus, implementation takes different forms in different sites as well, even with identical policies.

It is important to recognize that advocates, police, prosecutors, CPS/DFS caseworkers, and judges are dealing with a complex problem tempered by complex realities. Group living can be a difficult thing.

Women with substance abuse issues can be harder to work with—and can impact other shelter residents as well. Judges and police may not like seeing victims return to their abusers and continue to ask for the help they later decline. Children's safety is of the utmost importance, and their experiences with child abuse and the abuse of their mothers is a difficult problem for caseworkers to address. The point of this research is not to condemn the work of anti-domestic stakeholders, rather, the point is to use the research—advocates' own policies, practices, experiences, identities, and ideologies—to inform the work advocates do. This research provides an opportunity for advocates to learn from one another in their various regions and organizational contexts to impact their work and the victims they advocate for.

Lastly, advocates' expertise is largely marginalized in the current research literature. Advocates in this study had case-loads ranging from 20 to 170 clients a month. Because advocates are front-line workers with victims, have been through thousands of cases in their experience, know victims' cases perhaps better than anyone else in the system, see the outcomes of victims' cases, and are with them through all of the legal channels including prosecution and protective orders—their expertise should not only be valued, but sought-after. A goal of this book was to give voice to domestic violence victim advocates, who do difficult and important work.

Notes

Chapter 1

1. I use the term domestic violence and intimate partner violence inter-changeably throughout this book. Domestic violence organizations define themselves using the term "domestic violence," such as the National Coalition Against Domestic Violence, and most advocates who took part in this study held the title "domestic violence victim advocate." This is the legal terminology used in the justice system as well. At the same time, in definition, intimate partner violence is the more accurate term, and the term that is generally more popular in academia. Advocates in this study used the terms interchangeably; I've done so as well.

2. I also use the terms "victim" and "survivor" interchangeably, referring to one who experiences or has experienced abuse. These terms are highly debated. Those who prefer the term survivor claim that its use is empowering, and shows what the individual has gone through, overcome, and survived. They claim that the use of the term victim is disempowering and ignores women's agency. In turn, those who prefer the term "victim" claim that the lasting effects of abuse are ignored by use of the term "survivor," and the term also minimizes the violence they have experienced. Many women continue to be stalked, harassed, physically and psychologically victimized by their abusers, regardless of whether they stay or leave their relationships. Since I believe both of these arguments have merit, I choose to use both terms.

3. Intersectional practices were not specifically called or labeled as "intersectional practices" in this early phase of advocacy; intersectional feminist theory was largely developed and applied to intimate partner violence by scholars in the late 1980s and early 1990s (Crenshaw, 1994; Hill-Collins, 2000; hooks, 2000). The term is used here in retrospect, applying the currently widely-used terminology. Advocates in this study also did not specifically label their practices as intersectional practices. Rather, they described practices in detail that reflected understandings of intersectional identities.

4. The hospital program was labeled as a traditional program, rather than as a justice system organization, because it is a non-profit grant-funded non-governmental organization (NGO) program stemming from an initiative rooted in the battered women's movement. Its goal is to support women's safety, assist women in leaving abusive relationships, and support women who choose to stay with their abusive partners through long-term follow-up.

Copyright Acknowledgments

The author acknowledges SAGE for permission for the use of the following material:

1. A portion of chapter 1 was adapted from: Nichols, Andrea. 2011. Gendered Organizations: Challenges for Domestic Violence Victim Advocates and Feminist Advocacy. *Feminist Criminology* 6: 111-131.
2. Chapter 2 and a portion of chapter 6 were adapted from: Nichols, Andrea. 2013. Meaning-Making and Domestic Violence Victim Advocacy: An Examination of Feminist Identities, Ideologies, and Practices. *Feminist Criminology* 8n3:177-201. DOI 10.1177/1557085113482727.
3. A portion of chapter 3 was adapted from: Nichols, Andrea. 2013. Survivor-Defined Practices to Mitigate Revictimization of Battered Women in the Protective Order Process. *Journal of Interpersonal Violence* 28n7.

Bibliography

Abrahams, N., & Bruns, M. (1998). Gendered violence, gendered response. Coordinated community response networks and the battered women's movement. In C. Renzetti & L.Goodstein (Eds.), *Women crime and criminal justice* (pp.148). Los Angeles: Roxbury.

Acker, J. (1990). Hierarchies, jobs, bodies: A theory of gendered organizations. *Gender and Society,* 4, 139-158.

Acker, J. (1992). From sex roles to gendered institutions. *Contemporary Sociology,* 21, 565-569.

Adams, D., & Bennett, S. (2008). Rethinking punitive approaches to shelter. *Washington State Coalition Against Domestic Violence.*

Adler, P., & Adler, P. (2008). The four faces of ethnography. *The Sociological Quarterly,* 49, 1-30.

Allen, H. (1987). Rendering them harmless. In P. Carlen & A. Worrall (Eds.), *Gender crime and justice.* Open University Press.

Allen, N. E., Bybee, D. I., & Sullivan, C. M. (2004). Battered women's multitude of needs: Evidence supporting the need for comprehensive advocacy. *Violence Against Women,* 10, 1015-1035.

Arnold, G. (2011). The impact of social ties on coalition strength and effectiveness: The case of the battered women's movement in St. Louis. *Social Movement Studies* 10, 131-150.

Arnold, G. (1995). Dilemmas of feminist coalitions: Collective identity and strategic effectiveness in the battered women's movement. In M. M. Ferree & P. Y. Martin (Eds.), (pp. 70-84). *Feminist organizations: Harvest of the new women's movement.* Philadelphia: Temple University Press.

Arnold, G., & Ake, J. (2013). Reframing the narrative of the battered women's movement. *Violence Against Women* 19, 5, 557-578.

Avalon, S. (2008). Legal advocacy: Remembering who we work for. *Washington State Coalition Against Domestic Violence.*

Bailey, D. M., & Jackson, J. M. (2003). Qualitative data analysis: Challenges and dilemmas related to theory and method. *American Journal of Occupational Therapy,* 57, 57-65.

Banks, D., Landsverk, J., & Wang, K. (2008). Changing policy and practice in the child welfare system through collaborative efforts to identify and respond effectively to family violence. *Journal of Interpersonal Violence* 23:903-932.

Bibliography

Banks, D., Dutch, N., & K. Wang. (2008). Collaborative efforts to improve system response to families who are experiencing child maltreatment and domestic violence. *Journal of Interpersonal Violence* 23: 876-902.

Bell, M., Perez, S., Goodman, L., & Dutton, M. (2011). Battered women's perceptions of civil and criminal court helpfulness: The role of court outcome and process. *Violence Against Women*, 17, 71-88.

Bennet Cattaneo, L., & Goodman, L. (2010). Through the Lens of therapeutic jurisprudence: The relationship between empowerment in the court system and well-being for intimate partner violence victims. *Journal of Interpersonal Violence*, 25, 481-502.

Bent-Goodley, T. (2004). Perceptions of domestic violence: A dialogue with African American Women. *Health & Social Work*, 29: 307-317.

Boba, R. & Lilley, D. (2009). Violence Against Women Act funding: A nationwide assessment of effects on rape and assault. *Violence Against Women*, 15, 168-185.

Britton, D. M. (1997). Gendered organizational logic: Policy and practice in men's and women's prisons. *Gender and Society*, 11, 796-818.

Britton, D. M. (2000). The epistemology of the gendered organization. *Gender and Society*, 14, 418-434.

Britton, D. M. (2003). *At work in the iron cage: The prison as gendered organization.* New York and London: New York University Press.

Britton, D. M., & Logan, L. (2008). Gendered organizations: Progress and prospects. *Sociology Compass*, 2, 107-121.

Britton, D. M. (2011). *The gender of crime.* Lanham: Rowman and Littlefield Publishers, Inc.

Bybee, D. I., & C. M. Sullivan (2002). The process through which a strengths-based intervention resulted in positive changes for battered women over time. *American Journal of Community Psychology*, 30, 103-132.

Campbell, J. (2004). Helping Women Understand Their Risk in Situations of Intimate Partner Violence. *Journal of Interpersonal Violence*, 19, 1464.

Bibliography

Chesney-Lind, M., & Pollock, J. (1995). Women's prisons: Equality with a vengeance. In A. Merlo & J. Pollock (Eds.), *Women, law, and social control*. Lexington Books.

Corbin, J., & Strauss, A. (1990). *Basics of qualitative research: Grounded theory procedures and techniques*. Newbury Park, CA: Sage Publications, Inc.

Crenshaw, K. W. (1994). Mapping the Margins: Intersectionality, Identity Politics, and Violence Against Women of Color. In M. A. Fineman & R. Mykitiuk, Eds., *The Public Nature of Private Violence*, pp. 93-118. New York: Routledge.

Curran, M. (2008). Moving from rules to rights and responsibilities. *Washington State Coalition Against Domestic Violence.*

Daly, K. (1994). Men's violence, victim advocacy, and feminist redress. *Law and Society, 28,* 777-785.

Daly, K., & Chesney-Lind, M. (1988). Feminism and criminology. *Justice Quarterly, 5,* 497-538.

DeJong, C., & Burgess-Proctor, A. (2006). Summary of personal protection order statutes in the United States. *Violence Against Women, 12,* 68-88.

Dellinger, K., & Williams, C. (2002). The locker room v. the dorm room: The cultural context of sexual harassment in two magazine publishing organizations. *Social Problems, 49,* 242-57.

Dobash, R. P., Dobash, R.E.,Wilson, M., & Daly, M. (1992). The myth of sexual symmetry in marital violence. *Social Problems, 39,* 71-91.

Donnelly, D., Cook, K., VanAusdale, D., & Foley, L. 2005. White privilege, color blindness, and services to battered women. *Violence Against Women, 11,* 6-37.

Dugan, L., D. Nagin, and R. Rosenfeld. (2003). Do domestic violence services save lives? *National Institute of Justice Journal, 250,* 20-25.

Epstein, D., Kohn, L. Bennet, C., Goodman, L., & Zanville, H. (2009). The victim-informed prosecution project: A quasi-experimental test of a collaborative model for cases of intimate partner violence. *Violence Against Women, 15,* 1227-1247.

Ferguson, K. (1984). *The feminist case against bureaucracy.* Philadelphia: Temple University Press.

Bibliography

Ferraro, K. (2001). Woman battering: More than a family problem. In C. Renzetti & L. Goodstein (Eds.), *Women crime and criminal justice,* pp.135-151. Los Angeles: Roxbury.

Findlater, J., & Kelly, S. (1999). Child protective services and domestic violence. *Domestic Violence and Children* 9: 84-95.

Ford, D. A., & Regoli, M. R., (1993). The criminal prosecution of wife assaulters: process, problems, and effects. In N. Zoe Hilton (Ed), *Legal responses to wife assault: current trends and evaluation,* pp. 127-164. Newbury Park, CA: Sage.

Gelb, J., & Hart, V. (1999). Feminist politics in a hostile environment: Obstacles and opportunities. In M. Guigni, D. McAdam, & C. Tilly (Eds.), *How Social movements matter.* Minneapolis: University of Minnesota Press.

Gelles, R., & Straus, M. (1988). *Intimate Violence.* New York: Simon and Schuster.

Glaser, B. G., & Strauss, A. L. (1967). *The discovery of grounded theory.* Chicago, IL: Aldine Publishing Company.

Goodman, L. A., Dutton, M. A., & Bennett, L. (2000). Predicting repeat abuse among arrested batterers. *Journal of Interpersonal Violence,* 15, 63-74.

Goodman, L., & Epstein, D. (2005). Refocusing on women: A new direction for policy and research on intimate partner violence. *Journal of Interpersonal Violence,* 20, 479-487.

Goodman, L. A., & D. Epstein. (2008). *Listening to battered women: A survivor-centered approach to advocacy, mental health, and justice.* Washington D.C.: American Psychological Association.

Guest, G., Bunce, A., & Johnson, L. (2006). How many interviews are enough? An experiment with data saturation and variability. *Field Methods,* 18, 59–82.

Haaken, J., & Yragui, N. (2003). Going underground: Conflicting perspectives on domestic violence shelter practices. *Feminism and Psychology,* 13, 49-71.

Haney, L. (1996). Homeboys, babies, men in suits: The state and the reproduction of male dominance. *American Sociological Review,* 61, 759-778.

Haney, L. (2010). *Offending women: Power, punishment, and the regulation of desire.* Berkeley: University of California Press.

Bibliography

Hart, B. (1995). Coordinated community approaches to domestic violence. *Strategic Planning Workshop on Violence Against Women*. National Institute of Justice.

Heckert, A., & Gondolf, E. (2004). Battered women's perceptions of risk versus risk factors and instruments in predicting repeat reassault. *Journal of Interpersonal Violence, 19*, 778-800.

Herman, J. (1997). *Trauma and recovery*. New York, NY: Basic Books.

Hill-Collins, P. 2000. *Black feminist thought*. New York: Routledge.

Hobart, M. (2006). Changing the script: Thinking about our relationship with shelter residents. *Washington State Coalition Against Domestic Violence*.

hooks, b. (2000). *Feminism is for everyone: Passionate politics*. Cambridge: South End Press.

Jordan, C. (2004). Intimate partner violence and the justice system: An examination of the interface. *Journal of Interpersonal Violence, 19*, 1412-1432.

Jordan, C., Pritchard, A., Duckett, D., & R. Charnigo. (2010). Criminal offending among respondents to protective orders: Crime types and patterns that predict victim risk. *Violence Against Women, 16*, 1396–1411.

Jurik, N. C. (1985). An officer and a lady: Organizational barriers to women working as correctional officers in men's prisons. *Social Problems, 32*, 375–388.

Jurik, N. C., & Musheno, M. C. (1986). The internal crisis of corrections: Professionalization and the work environment. *Justice Quarterly, 3*, 457–480.

Keilitz, S., Hannaford, P., & H. S. Efkeman. (1997). Civil Protection Orders: The benefits and limitations for victims of domestic violence. National Center for State Courts Research Report, *National Institute of Justice*.

Keilitz, S., Davis, C., Efkeman, H., Flango, C., & P. Hannaford. (1998). Civil Protection Orders: Victims' views on effectiveness. National Center for State Courts. *National Institute of Justice*.

Kelleher, K., Gardner, W., Coben, J., Barth, R., Edleson, J., & A. Hazen. (2006). Co-occurring intimate partner violence and child maltreatment: Local policies/practices and relationships to child placement, family services and residence. *National Institute for Justice*.

Bibliography

Kelly, K. (2003). *Domestic Violence and the Politics of Privacy*. Ithaca: Cornell University Press.

Klein, A., & Tobin, T. (2008). A longitudinal study of arrested batterers, 1995-2005 career criminals. *Violence Against Women*, 14, 136-157.

Kohn, L. P., & Wilson, M. (1995). Social support networks in the African American family: Utility for culturally compatible intervention. *New Directions for Child Development*.

Kruttschnitt, C. (2001). Gender and violence. In C. Renzetti & L. Goodstein (Eds.), *Women crime and criminal justice*, pp.77-92. Los Angeles: Roxbury.

Kruttschnitt, C., & Gartner, R. (2004). *Marking time in the golden state*. Cambridge University Press.

Kulkarni, S., Bell, H., & Rhodes, D. (2012). Back to basics. *Violence Against Women*, 18, 85.

Lehrner, A., & Allen, N. (2009). Still a movement after all these years? Current tensions in the domestic violence movement. *Violence Against Women*, 5, 1-22.

Lehrner, A., & Allen, N. (2008). Social change movements and the struggle over meaning making: A case study of domestic violence narratives. *American Journal of Community Psychology*, 42, 220-234.

Lindquist, T. (2008). Mandated to service: How to best serve survivors who are forced to use our services. *Washington State Coalition Against Domestic Violence*.

Logan, T. K., Shannon, L., & Walker, R. (2005). Protective orders in rural and urban areas: A multiple perspective study. *Violence Against Women*, 11, 876-896.

Lyon, E. (2002). Special Session Domestic Violence Courts: Enhanced Advocacy and Interventions, Final Report. *National Institute of Justice*.

Lyon, E., Lane, S., & Menard, A. (2008). Meeting Survivors Needs: A Multi-State Study of Domestic Violence Shelter Experiences. *National Institute of Justice*.

MacKinnon, C. (1987). *Feminism unmodified: Discourses on life and law*. Cambridge, MA: Harvard University Press.

Macy, R., Giattina, M., Sangster, T., Crosby, C., & Montijo, N. J. (2009). Domestic violence and sexual assault services: Inside the black box. *Aggression and Violence*, 14, 359-373.

Bibliography

Macy, R., Giattina, M., Parish, S., & Crosby, C. (2010). Domestic violence and sexual assault services: Historical concerns and contemporary challenges. *Journal of Interpersonal Violence, 25,* 3-32.

Markowitz, L. (2002). Paradoxes of professionalization: Parallel dilemmas in women's organizations in the Americas. *Gender and Society, 16,* 941-958.

Martin, P. Y. (2005). *Rape work: Victims, gender, and emotions in organization and community context.* New York: Routledge.

Martin, S. E. (1980). *Breaking and entering:* Policewomen *on patrol.* Berkeley: University of California Press.

Miller, J. (2008). Violence against urban African American girls: Challenges for feminist advocacy. *Journal of Contemporary Criminal Justice, 1,* 1-11.

Moe, A. (2000). Battered women in the restraining order process: Observations on a court advocacy program. *Violence Against Women, 6,* 606.

Moe, A. (2007). Silenced voices and structured survival: Battered women's help seeking. *Violence Against Women, 13,* 676-699.

Muftic, L., & J. Bouffard. (2007). An evaluation of gender differences in the implementation and impact of a comprehensive approach to domestic violence. *Violence Against Women, 13,* 46-69.

National Coalition Against Domestic Violence. (2011). Retrieved from http://www.ncadv.org.

Nichols, A. (2011). Gendered organizations: Challenges for domestic violence victim advocates and feminist advocacy. *Feminist Criminology, 6,* 111-131.

Nichols, A. (2013a). Survivor-Defined Practices to Mitigate Revictimization of Battered Women in the Protective Order Process. *Journal of Interpersonal Violence* 28n7.

Nichols, Andrea. (2013b). Meaning-Making and Domestic Violence Victim Advocacy: An Examination of Feminist Identities, Ideologies, and Practices. *Feminist Criminology* 8n3: 177- 201.

Nichols, Andrea. (2013c). No-drop prosecution in domestic violence cases: Survivor-defined and social change approaches to advocacy. Paper presented at the Midwest Sociological Society Annual Meeting, Chicago, IL.

Bibliography

Nurius, P., Macy, R., Ijeoma, N., & Holt, V. (2011). Intimate partner survivors' help-seeking and protection efforts: A person-oriented analysis. *Journal of Interpersonal Violence, 26*, 539-566.

Olsen, L. (2008). Shelter rules: The good the bad and the ugly. *Washington State Coalition Against Domestic Violence.*

Olsen, L. (2007). Battered women's shelters: Reflections. *Washington State Coalition Against Domestic Violence.*

Osthoff, S. (2001). When battered women become defendants: Battered women charged with crimes. In C. Renzetti & L. Goodstein (Eds.), *Women crime and criminal justice,* pp. 232-242. Los Angeles: Roxbury.

Patterson, L. (2003). Model protocol on working with battered women and their teenage boys in shelter. *Washington State Coalition Against Domestic Violence.*

Potter, H. (2008). *Battle cries: Black women and intimate partner violence.* New York: New York University Press.

Rhodes, K., Dichter, M., Kothari, C., Marcus, S., & Cerulli, C. (2011). The impact of children on the legal actions taken by women victims of intimate partner violence. *Journal of Family Violence, 26* 355-364.

Richie, B. E. (2000). A black feminist reflection on the antiviolence movement. *Signs, 25,* 1133-1137.

Richie, B.E. (2005). A Black feminist reflection on the anti-violence movement. In N. Sokoloff (Ed.), *Domestic Violence at the Margins,* pp. 50-55. New Brunswick, New Jersey, and London: Rutgers University Press.

Risman, B. (2004). Gender as social structure: Theory wrestling with activism. *Gender and Society, 18,* 429-450.

Rodriguez, N. (1988). Transcending bureaucracy: Feminist politics at a shelter for battered women. *Gender and Society, 2,* 214-227.

Römkens, Renée. (2006). Protecting prosecution exploring the powers of law in an intervention program for domestic violence. *Violence Against Women, 12,* 160-186.

Rowe-Finkbeiner, K. (2004). *The f-word: Feminism in jeopardy. Women, politics, and the future.* Emeryville: Seal Press.

Rutkow, L., Vernick, J., Webster, D., & Lennig, D. (2009). Violence against women and the U.S. Supreme Court: Recent challenges and opportunities for advocates and practitioners. *Violence Against Women, 15,* 1248-1258.

Bibliography

Saathoff, A., & Stoffel, E. (1999). Community based domestic violence services. *Domestic Violence and Children, 9*, 97-110.

Schechter, S. (1982). *Women and male violence: The visions and struggles of the battered women's movement.* Boston: South End.

Schmidt, J. D., & Sherman, L. (1996). Does arrest deter domestic violence? In C. Buzawa & E. Buzawa (Eds.), *Do arrest and restraining orders work?* Thousand Oaks: Sage.

Shepard, M., & Pence, E. (1999). *Coordinating community responses to domestic violence: Lessons from Duluth and beyond.* Sage Publications.

Sherman, L., & Berk, R. (1983). The specific deterrent effects of arrest for domestic assault. *American Sociological Review, 39*, 261-272.

Sherman, L., & Smith, D. (1992). Crime, punishment and stake in conformity: Legal and informal control of domestic violence. *American Sociological Review, 57*, 680-690.

Smith, A., Richie, B., Sudbury, J., White, J., & the INCITE! Anthology Co-editors. (2006). The color of violence: Introduction. In IN CITE! Women of Color Against Violence (Eds.), *Color of violence: The INCITE! Anthology,* pp. 1-10. Cambridge, MA: South End Press.

Sokoloff, N. (2005). *Domestic Violence at the Margins*, New Brunswick, New Jersey, and London: Rutgers University Press.

Sorenson, S., and H. Shen. (2005). Restraining orders in California: A look at statewide data. *Violence Against Women, 11*, 912.

Spitzberg, B. (2002). The tactical topography of stalking victimization and management. *Trauma, Violence, and Abuse, 3*, 261-288.

Spradley, J. (1980). *Participant observation.* Fort Worth: Harcourt Brace.

Srinivasan, M., & Davis, L. (1991). A shelter: An organization like any other? *Affilia, 6*, 38-57.

Strauss, M. A., & Gelles, R. J. (1986). Societal change and family violence from 1975-1985 as revealed by two national surveys. *Journal of Marriage and the Family, 48*, 465-479.

Sullivan, C. M., & D. I. Bybee. (1999). Reducing violence using community-based advocacy for women with abusive partners. *Journal of Consulting and Clinical Psychology, 67*, 43-53.

Tautfest, K. (2008). How we gave up curfew (and a lot of other rules, too). *Washington State Coalition Against Domestic Violence.*

Bibliography

Tierney, K. (1982). The battered women's movement and creation of the wife beating problem. *Social Problems,* 29, 207-220.

Tong, R. (1998). *Feminist thought.* Westview Press.

U.S. Census. (2010). Retrieved from http://2010.census.gov/2010census/.

Washington State Coalition Against Domestic Violence. (2011). Retrieved from http://www.wscadv.org/.

Wathen, C. N., & MacMillan, H. (2003). Interventions for violence against women. *Scientific Review,* 289, 589-600.

Webber, G., & Williams, C. (2008). Part-time work and the gender division of labor. *Qualitative Sociology,* 31, 15-36.

Websdale, N., & Johnson, B. (1997). Reducing women battering: The role of structural approaches. *Social Justice,* 24, 54-81.

Websdale, N. (1998). *Rural Woman Battering.* Thousand Oaks: Sage.

Weisz, A. N. (1999). Legal advocacy for domestic violence survivors: The power of an informative relationship. *Families in Society,* 80, 138-147.

Weisz, A. N., Tolman, R. M., & Saunders, D. G. (2000). Assessing the risk of severe domestic violence: The importance of survivors' predictions. *Journal of Interpersonal Violence,* 15, 75-90.

West, C., Kantor, G., & Jasinski, J. (1998). Socio-demographic predictors and cultural barriers to help seeking behavior of Latinas and Anglo-American battered women. *Violence and Victims,* 13, 361-375.

Whitcomb, D. (2002). Prosecutors, kids and domestic violence cases. *National Institute for Justice Journal* 248: 1-8.

Williams, C., Giuffre, P., & Dellinger, K. (1999). Sexuality in the workplace: Organizational control, sexual harassment, and the pursuit of pleasure. *Annual Review of Sociology,* 25, 73-93.

Williams, C. & Connell, C. (2010). Looking good and sounding right: Aesthetic labor and social inequality in the retail industry. *Work and Occupations,* 37, 349-77.

Williams, C., (2006). *Toyland: Working, shopping, and social inequality.* University of California Press.

Wright, R., Decker, S., Redfern, A., & Smith, D. (1992). A snowball's chance in Hell: Doing fieldwork with active residential burglars. *Journal of Research in Crime and Delinquency,* 29, 148-161.

Zweig, J., & Burt, M. (2006). Predicting case outcomes and women's perceptions of the legal system's response to domestic violence and sexual assault: Does interaction between community agencies matter? *Criminal Justice Policy Review,* 17, 202-233.

Zweig, J., & Burt, M. (2007). Predicting women's perceptions of domestic violence and sexual assault agency helpfulness: What matters to program clients? *Violence Against Women,* 13, 1149-1178.

Index

Index